STEAM INTO
WILDERNESS

To all those crews who manned the
early trains through the long
stillness of the northern nights.

STEAM INTO WILDERNESS

ONTARIO NORTHLAND RAILWAY
1902-1962

Albert Tucker

Fitzhenry & Whiteside
Toronto   Montreal   Winnipeg   Vancouver

The publisher gratefully acknowledges the assistance
of the Ontario Arts Council.

Fitzhenry & Whiteside Limited
150 Lesmill Road,
Don Mills, Ontario M3B 2T5

Canadian Cataloguing in Publication Data

Tucker, Albert, 1923–
    Steam into Wilderness

Includes index.
ISBN 0-88902-444-8 bd. ISBN 0-88902-558-4 pa.

1. Ontario Northland Railway – History.   2. Ontario
– History – 20th century.* I. Title.

HE2810.05T83   385'.06'5713   C78-001471-5

Printed and bound in Canada

Contents

Preface

The myth of the northern wilderness has been a strong historical force in moulding the awareness which Canadians have of themselves as a nation. A hundred years ago nationalist writers and orators could refer to Canada as a country whose destiny it was to be "northern," populated by sturdy, frugal, and industrious races. These new people and their descendants would not only survive but actually prosper in the snow, the ice, and the bitter winds of the long Canadian winters. "We are the Northmen of the new world," said Charles Denison in 1904.

Behind the myth were the facts of sparse northern settlement compared with the lucrative exploitation of the wilderness. While immigrant settlers were turning the western prairies into productive farms for large exports of wheat, in Ontario the timber, the pulpwood, and the minerals of the North were becoming the new staples, succeeding to the historic role of fish and furs. For Canadians in the centre and east of the country at the end of the nineteenth century, the North meant northern Ontario and northern Québec. It was largely Ontario which attracted American and British capital to finance extraction of the new staple resources.

This book tells the story of the railway which encouraged development of those resources. In 1902 the legislative assembly of Ontario passed an act creating a board or commission which would first construct and then direct the operation of the *Temiskaming and Northern Ontario Railway** on behalf of the people of Ontario. It was the province's first publicly owned utility.

Founded as a railway that would reach and expand settled areas of the northeast, the T&NO very soon became a community railway, serving basic social and economic needs of the towns and farms which grew like limbs from the main trunk of its north-south line. Few railroads in Canada have aroused such implicit approval or so little criticism among local people, most of whom have viewed the government-owned Commission as an integral part of their own history. This attachment to regional interest and feeling induced a tension between North and South, between a sense of regional autonomy in the North and the control which reached out from the offices of the premier and the cabinet at Queen's Park in Toronto.

For the politicians in the provincial capital, over half a century, the T&NO/ONR fulfilled a further promise. It aided with remarkable efficiency the mine owners, the timber merchants, and the pulp and paper companies, enabling them to realize profits that were nothing short of spectacular. Some of this money ended amid the expansive, affluent suburbs of Toronto,

---

*The government of George Drew changed the name to Ontario Northland Transportation Commission in 1946.

the political and financial hub of the province, where brokers and agents of American capital treated the North as little more than a lucrative hinterland. As a result, much of the revenue directly augmented the profits of American corporations. The railway was thus a vital instrument, not only in the regional development of urban communities and farms, but above all of corporate fortunes controlled by men in distant offices who appreciated and used to the full this vehicle which the state had made available to them.

In time, the railway became a transportation system, adapting under public ownership to the acquisition of buses and trucks, of boats and aircraft, even of telecommunications. The combination of assets has led to a complex network of facilities, much like a medium-sized corporation, which must be managed by well-trained personnel, always with a view to sustaining solvency in the public interest. The history of the Commission is therefore closely involved with the issue of corporatism in contemporary society.

Readers of this book should know the debt which I owe to a large number of people. For permission to consult restricted papers in the Archives of Ontario I am indebted to Dr. Edward Stewart, Deputy Minister to Premier William Davis. Ralph Carr, one of my former students and now a lawyer in Timmins, gave me invaluable assistance by interviewing people who either had worked for the Commission or whose lives were directly affected by it. William Michie did the initial research as a student in Toronto.

My own research and writing were generously helped by certain people whose working lives are completely engaged in the successful operation of the ONTC in North Bay. Without the initiative and the quiet tact of Helen Boody, the book might not have come to completion in its present form. In addition, I have enjoyed the congenial counsel of the General Manager, F.S. Clifford; the late T.G. Farmer in his capacity as Director of Corporate Services; the present Director of Financial Services, D.E. McDougall; and Wayne Antler, Director of Tourism Development and Public Affairs. L.K. Smiley described for me the system of telecommunications within the franchise area of the ONTC. Len Dobberman and Hector Duquette talked to me at length on the transition to diesels, and Alvin Telford gave me the benefit of an evening's conversation about Moosonee.

Among former personnel with the Commission, two interviews with Arthur Cavanagh were invaluable for giving me information on the 1930s and 1940s that was not available in documents. Stanley Gowan, a former Secretary to the Commission, answered my many questions about his long years of employment, from the years of depression to the 1960s. W. Roy Thompson, former Industrial Commissioner, Calvin Taylor and Wesley Quirt also responded warmly to my telephone queries.

Of those outside the Commission, I must thank first the Honourable Roland Michener for an interview about his brief time as provincial secretary in the cabinet of George Drew. Donald MacDonald, former leader of the Ontario New Democratic party, confirmed for me the continuing power of the cabinet and the premier, as distinct from the legislative assembly, over the affairs of the Commission.

The late Harry J. Reynolds of North Bay, a former federal judge, reminisced one wintry afternoon on the Conservative party in the North, and enlightened me on the resignation of Arthur Cavanagh and the appointment by Premier Drew of Colonel C.E. Reynolds as chairman. Mr. H.A. Wills, who published and edited the Cochrane *Northland Post* from 1940 to 1970, gave me a long interview on the attitude of people in small northern towns toward the Commission and its affairs. Charles Hyson of Etobicoke, a retired engineer who worked for many years with H.F. McLean Construction, generously showed me papers and photographs which he has collected on Harry McLean. In the Archives of Ontario I am indebted to a most courteous staff, who helped me through the papers of every premier of Ontario since 1900.

Professor Morris Zaslow of the University of Western Ontario made detailed comments for improving an earlier version of the manuscript. The final draft benefited from the professional editorial work of Margaret McKelvey, with her expert eye for clarity of meaning. Norman Williams went far beyond the call of assistance in advising and encouraging as well as typing, selecting the photographs, and compiling the index. It is a pleasure also to record my gratitude to Rollins Burrell, whose many invitations and gourmet meals succeeded in their purpose of relieving the tensions which often accompany research and writing.

Printed and written sources are only a part of the evidence for this book. It derives much of its local colour from the lively recollections of the following people, to all of whom I extend the thanks both of myself and of Ralph Carr, with whom they so willingly talked: William Baily, Earlton; Clinton Bainbridge, North Bay; Homer Blain, North Bay; Mrs. George Booth, Matheson; Arthur Brightwell, Skillington; Samuel Caldbick, Timmins; Mr. and Mrs. Robert Cameron, Cobalt; John Campsell, Porcupine; A.H. Cavanagh, North Bay; Mrs. Eva DeRosa, South Porcupine; Ben Farmer, North Bay; Jim Fletcher, North Bay; A. James Foster, Mimico; Mr. and Mrs. Will Gard, North Bay; Mr. and Mrs. Frank Herron, New Liskeard; Mr. Donald McKelvie, New Liskeard; Mr. William Potter, Matheson; Mr. James Robb, Haileybury; Mr. Bill Ross, Jr., North Bay; Mr. and Mrs. Joe Sullivan, Timmins; Mr. Tom Sykes, North Bay.

Finally, although this book was commissioned as an official history, I wish to record that I have enjoyed that condition so essential to the function of the historian – the freedom to search out documents and to write my own interpretation – without any interference, indeed, with the positive encouragement of all members of the Ontario Northland Transportation Commission.

Albert Tucker, Toronto, June, 1978

CHAPTER 1

The Idea of a Railway

Timiskaming District

Standing at the northern end of the ONR tracks, two hundred miles beyond the fringe of urban settlement, looking out upon the sandy shore and the shallow water of the Moose River winding its way into James Bay, the traveller must ponder a number of questions. Why a railway at all to this remote Indian village called Moosonee? How did such a northern railway come to be built by the government of Ontario? Why has the provincial government retained successful management of a transportation system which operates on north-south, instead of the east-west lines that constitute the traditional transportation corridors of Canada?

The answers to these questions are rooted in the recent history of Ontario. They require some understanding not simply of northern settlement, but of the politics and financial conditions of the province as a whole at the end of the nineteenth century.

To begin, one must imagine a rural, forested, and sparsely settled environment before the automobile or the aircraft existed. For the people of Canada in the 1880s and 1890s – for men clearing a homestead or harvesting a crop, for women tending to washtubs or kneading dough, for children wondering what lay beyond the forbidding forest – the railways meant contact, the communication of people and goods with the world beyond. The sound of the steam locomotive was like a shout into the future; the track itself the straightest path to the stores, the streets, and the community of town life.

In northern Ontario few towns existed at the end of the nineteenth century. The climate and the rugged rock formations of the Precambrian Shield were formidable barriers to settlement. Human habitation consisted largely of scattered bands of Indians around fur-trading posts of the Hudson's Bay Company.

Two events stimulated the growth of small towns, as well as the breaking of land for farms. With completion of the CPR in the 1880s, North Bay, Sudbury, Fort William and Port Arthur developed along its main line. Sudbury soon became a centre for the mining and smelting of nickel, and farther west Sault

Ste. Marie benefited from its location on the American border, at the junction of three of the Great Lakes, to become an industrial town for the processing of lumber into pulp and of iron ore into steel. As late as 1891, when North Bay was incorporated, such towns could still be counted on the fingers of one hand; but their growth encouraged the idea of a "New Ontario," with abundant resources of forest and of mineral deposits.[1]

The second event which introduced change into the North was the definition of the Québec-Ontario boundary in 1884.[2] That decision by the Judicial Committee of the Privy Council extended the northern limits of Ontario to James and Hudson Bays, giving to the provincial government of Oliver Mowat jurisdiction over a territory as large as the State of Texas. The north of Ontario could now be seen as a hinterland, not of Montréal or of Ottawa, but of Toronto, the political capital of Ontario and increasingly a centre of financial power.

To Toronto at the end of the 1890s came the representatives of a small group of settlers at the northern end of Lake Timiskaming, where farms and villages were beginning to appear in the wilderness. The founder of this Timiskaming settlement was Charles Cobbald Farr, an Englishman who had joined the Hudson's Bay Company at Fort Timiskaming in 1873 as a young man of twenty-two. He developed a deep sense of belonging to this part of the country, identifying his life with its future.

Educated at Haileybury in England, a public school oriented to the training of boys for service in the British Empire, Farr saw the west side of Lake Timiskaming as a potential "Little England." This notion was reinforced in his mind by the expanding settlement of French-Canadians at Ville Marie on the east side of the lake, where the Roman Catholic Church directly involved itself in promoting the settlement of Québecois farmers. Farr left the Hudson's Bay Company in 1889, having already bought up lots on the northwest shore. In 1893 he persuaded A.S. Hardy, the Commissioner of Crown Lands in the provincial government, to produce a pamphlet that would attract settlers into the Timiskaming country. Two years later, he travelled to England on a personal campaign for the purpose of stimulating a wider interest in his scheme for development.[3]

Settlers drifted gradually into the area. Some French-Canadians did indeed cross over from the Québec side, but the majority were English and Scots immigrants, encouraged by Farr's propaganda. He divided his own land into lots which he sold as the nucleus for the village which he called "Haileybury," after his old school. Five miles to the north, at the northern tip of Lake Timiskaming, British and Dutch settlers established another village, where George Paget from Cornwall in England promoted the name "Liskeard" (subsequently changed to "New Liskeard"), after the town of his birth.

The provincial government surveyed the region in 1887, dividing it into townships, and in 1891 these crown lands were put on the market for fifty cents an acre. A Crown Lands Agent was then appointed to guide and direct families into the clearings along the primitive paths north of Liskeard.[4] The trees were cut into lumber for building at the sawmill of Angus McKelvie and Tom McCamus at the mouth of the Wabi River.

2

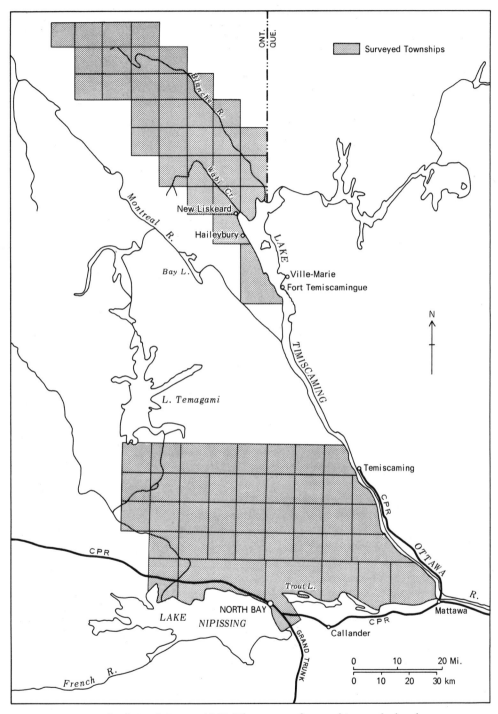

North of North Bay, c. 1900. The surveyed townships at the head of Lake Timiskaming were the "Little England" of C.C. Farr.

Each year new settlers arrived, coming by the CPR to Mattawa and transferring to boats which transported them farther north. Their numbers were few compared to the thousands of immigrants who continued westward to the prairies. Yet by 1887 enough settlers were moving north to warrant construction of the short Timiskaming Colonization Railway (now part of the CPR), which ran from a point opposite Mattawa to the southern end of Lake Timiskaming. From there, newcomers could travel to various points on the lake aboard the steamer *Meteor*, which was owned by the Lumsden Boat Lines of Ottawa.

In winter the lake could be traversed only by horse and sleigh. During the early spring and late fall, with the ice breaking, it was a dangerous route. From December to May every year the settlers were isolated, leading them to petition for a railway that would give them year-round transportation between north and south. Their persistent requests were carried to Toronto by the little delegations which came every year to Queen's Park at the end of the 1890s.[5]

Among the politicians of the cabinet and the businessmen in the Toronto Board of Trade, these small petitions coincided with larger questions. What were the possibilities of diverting immigrant traffic northward into the Clay Belt, an area comprising more than 12,000,000 acres of potential farm land on the same latitude as the prairies? Could Ontario take steps to counter the northwestward expansion of Québec farmers and Roman Catholic priests? Was it possible to build a port on James Bay which would give to Ontario and Toronto an ocean outlet to rival that of Montréal? "It seems to me a strange condition of things," said one MPP in 1898, "that a people so progressive as we are in Ontario, having for a portion of our northern boundary one of the greatest inland seas in the world...should be lacking any means of communication between our commercial centres and this great field of wealth."[6]

Given this variety of questions and circumstances, it is not surprising that a number of schemes were proposed for the building of railways into northern Ontario. Six private companies were projected, and four of them were chartered between 1881 and 1900.[7] The promoters of these lines all hoped to obtain a share of the railway subsidies and the land grants being distributed by the federal and provincial governments. Two of the schemes were visionary, one of them bearing the grandiose title, "The Great Northern Ontario and Northwestern Canada Transit Route." Its description illustrated the disparity in the minds of some of these promoters between the vision and the harsh realities of constructing railways in the North.

Only one of these schemes proved to be practicable, because its purpose was limited to connecting a specific resource with an industrial plant. The Algoma Central and Hudson Bay Railway was chartered in 1899 to haul iron ore from the Helen Mine at Michipicoten, near Lake Superior, to the smelter of Algoma Steel at Sault Ste. Marie. Plans in 1901 forecast expansion of the Algoma Central north and east, with maps placing its northern terminus at the mouth of the Moose River on James Bay. Later, tracks were laid as far north as Hearst to join the National Transcontinental Railway, but the Algoma Central continued essentially as a carrier of ore and pulpwood to Sault Ste. Marie. No influx of settlers or clearing of land into farms ever developed along its route, despite

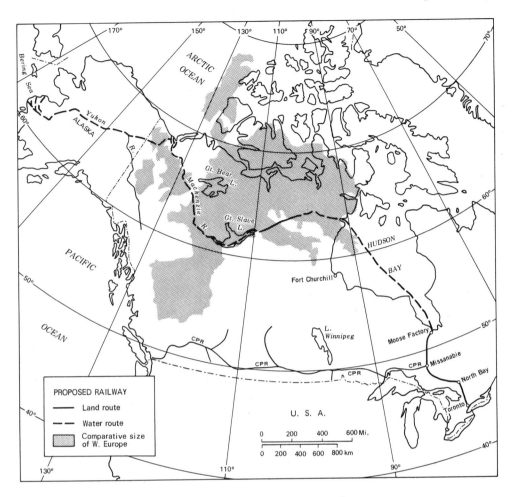

The Great Northern Ontario and
Northwestern Canada Transit Route, 1898

One of the visionary schemes for combining railway and steamship transportation from
James Bay to the Pacific. Caught up in the magnitude of the project, its promoters
superimposed a map of Western Europe onto a part of the Canadian Northwest.

land grants of 7,400 acres to the mile. Nor did its tracks ever reach the vicinity
of Hudson Bay.[8]

By the turn of the century it was evident that chartered railway companies
would not build into northeastern Ontario. Yet the pressures and influences
continued. Beneath the surface, apprehension simmered because of expansion
from Québec. Farr and his friends regarded their "Little England" as a significant barrier to the spread of French-speaking Roman Catholics. British and
Dutch settlers at Liskeard and Thornloe held firmly Protestant convictions.

Prejudice and belief, based on religion and language, reinforced the association between provincial loyalty and resource development. For some people, attitudes toward development served to rationalize these prejudices. For others, the exploitation of provincial resources seemed to be an end in itself. A pamphlet of 1902, published by the Bruce Mines and Algoma Railway Company, asked the provocative question: "Is Toronto and Western Ontario to be side-tracked and New Ontario made a greater Québec or is Old Ontario going to have equal rights within her own province and in the future development of the Greater Ontario?" The main purpose of the essay was to encourage public support and the granting of public money for such "colonization railways" as the Bruce Mines and Algoma.[9]

But its words pointed to a further cross current of influence and pressure. Behind the tensions between the governments and people of the two provinces, rivalries continued between the businessmen of Toronto and Montréal. Northern Ontario could be seen as a colonial frontier for the financiers of Toronto, enabling them to challenge the predominance of the Bank of Montréal and the CPR. The North, said Premier Ross in 1900, must be developed, "because it was only through the medium of New Ontario that the Province could maintain its present foremost position in the Dominion."[10]

At the same time, fused with this battle of railway and business interests, with conflicts over language and religion, the genuine local need of the Timiskaming Settlement could not be denied. But in the decade after 1890 the financial élite of Toronto was not prepared to invest the amounts required to build a railway into the northeast. The money of these men was going into east-west transcontinental lines, such as the Canadian Northern Railway of William Mackenzie and Donald Mann; or it was being invested in the new and profitable street railway companies of Canadian, Caribbean, and South American cities.[11] This scarcity of private capital drew in the provincial government, just as northern development was emerging as a platform in the changing political fortunes of the provincial Liberal party which had held office for almost thirty years.

Enter the Government

Sir Oliver Mowat resigned as premier in 1896, after twenty-four years in office. The choice of his successor remained unresolved until 1899, when the inner circles of the Liberal party persuaded George W. Ross to become leader and the new premier. Ross was a firm Presbyterian, a temperance supporter, and a man seriously committed to politics as a form of public service. He had served for ten years as Education Minister, sitting for the traditional Grit constituency of Middlesex West.

Because of the long tenure of the Liberal party, doubts existed in 1900 that their hold on government could last much longer. Recent elections had given them declining majorities. The electorate seemed sympathetic to change, and Ross decided that he must make the Liberal party more aware of this mood. He had no doubts about the cohesion of the party, or the talents of his cabinet. But the cabinet must find an answer to his question: "Where can we find spheres of operation that will satisfy the public that we have the courage and initiative to maintain the records of our predecessors?"[12]

Implicit in the question, and in the minds of those asked to respond, was the opening of New Ontario. The proposals of previous years, the public pressure, the connection of the Liberal party with railway promoters, all contributed to the answer. Within the first year of his administration, Ross directed ten survey parties to be organized by the Commissioner of Crown Lands, each party to examine a parcel of land which stretched from the CPR north to the salt water of James Bay. A geologist, a surveyor, and soil expert travelled with each survey party. The expeditions returned in the fall of 1900 reporting that they had found in the north "a veritable storehouse of wealth."[13]

The ten surveys cost the government $40,000. Their conclusions had to be taken seriously. "It has been established beyond controversy," said their formal report of 1901, "that in the eastern part of the territory north of the Height of Land there is an immense area of excellent agricultural land...equal in fertility to any in older Ontario..." The forests, they continued, would enable Ontario "to take a leading position in the...pulp and paper-making industry." The surveyors had not discovered new mineral finds, but they were confident that rock formations showed enough promise to justify closer examination.[14]

Armed with this report, and with information that the Crown Lands Department had sold 80,000 acres in the Timiskaming District during the past four years, Ross made up his mind in the spring of 1901 that the government should proceed further with its plans "to open up New Ontario by trunk colonization roads and railways in order to make homes for the sons of Ontario, who otherwise might seek a home in another Province or under a foreign flag."[15] In May of 1901 he approved the appointment of a chief engineer for the project and consulted closely with his Minister of Public Works, F.R. Latchford. Latchford selected the engineer, appointed him temporarily to his own ministry, and proceeded during the fall of 1901 to draft the legislation for a publicly owned railway.

A lawyer by training, Latchford played a crucial role in these early stages. He drafted a bill to meet both the immediate demands from the Timiskaming District, and the longer term expectations of businessmen in the Toronto Board of Trade. The preamble dwelled on "large areas of arable land," on "valuable timber," and on "deposits of ores and minerals...in that district of Ontario which lies between Lake Nipissing and Lake Abitibi." It was "in the public interest" to construct and operate a railway "under the direction and control of the Province," which meant that every detail from location of the line to actual charging of fares and rates must be "subject to the approval of the Lieutenant Governor in Council."[16]

Latchford drew up the bill, but it was Ross who had to persuade the cabinet. Because he combined the position of premier with the office of treasurer, he then presented the bill as part of his budget speech to the legislative assembly in February, 1902. The project, he announced, would be called the *Temiskaming and Northern Ontario Railway*. It would be built and operated under the supervision of a commission, the members of which were to be appointed by the government. Initially, the railway would be just over a hundred miles in length.

Before reaching his decision, said Ross, he had faced three options: offer a large subsidy for construction; build the line and lease it to the Grand Trunk; or go into the construction business. The first two options involved expense and delay. Unless action were taken immediately to connect the North with the rest of Ontario, the trade of that whole region might soon be diverted to Montréal via the CPR. If the government built the line now, future extension to James Bay was possible. "We would then," declared Ross, "have a highway to a northern seaport the advantages of which we are yet unable to realize." As though anticipating the construction of the National Transcontinental Railway by the federal government, Ross added that Ontario industry might well find the T&NO part of a network "into the Saskatchewan valley and the great prairies."[17]

The Conservative leader in the legislative assembly, James Whitney, argued that construction and operation of the railway should be turned over to private interests, such as the Canadian Northern railway of Mackenzie and Mann, who would then be given generous and preferably federal subsidies.[18] That was the way Canadian railways had been built in the past, including the CPR. But Toronto financiers were clearly reluctant in 1900 to venture upon railway construction into the northeast of Ontario. They knew that building the CPR through the rock and forest of the Canadian Shield had been an agonizing and costly project, impossible without lavish financial subsidies and extensive western land grants from the federal government. Mackenzie and Mann, in the course of amalgamating small railways and building others to form their Canadian Northern Railway, were not drawn to a north-south line with prospects of so little profit.

In the absence of proposals from capitalist entrepreneurs, the provincial cabinet made its decision for a government railway, with North Bay as its probable southern terminus. The town was a logical choice, since it had come into being with the CPR and was by now a junction with the Grand Trunk line south to Toronto. North Bay was also the closest major rail point to Lake Timiskaming and therefore a favourable point of departure for the first major enterprise of government into the North.

The timing of the decision and the beginning of construction could not be separated from provincial politics. Ross made his budget speech in February, 1902. Within a month the Act authorizing the T&NO received royal assent – on March 17, 1902.[19] Two months later during the provincial election campaign, the Minister of Public Works, the Hon. F. R. Latchford, turned the first ceremonial sod.[20] That he performed the ceremony as a provincial Liberal became very clear when the Tory mayor of North Bay refused to attend. In his address, Latchford, acknowledging the existence of sceptics and opponents, added "when we have built and built successfully, as I know we shall, there will be a demand that the government will continue the work…after we get access to the million acres of agricultural land to the north and northwest…"[21] On May 29 the people of Ontario voted to re-elect the Liberal government with a slight majority of four seats. Ross had been given a modest mandate to continue.

During the campaign of 1902 speculation arose that the proposed provincial railway represented merely an election project to inject new life into an old government. After the election, rumour had it, further progress could well disappear into the northern stillness like the sunset cry of a loon on a wilderness lake. Railways and commercial development, however, were part of the politics of the time, not only in Ottawa and Montréal but in Toronto as well.[22] Evidence of the intertwining connections could be seen in the appointments made to boards and commissions. During the summer of 1902 the Ontario Legislature approved the composition of the new Commission for the T&NO, granting it authority to build a railway of standard gauge for 113 miles, from North Bay to New Liskeard.

Ross selected A.E. Ames, the young head of a growing brokerage company in Toronto, as chairman of the Commission. Ames had been in finance and banking all his life, starting out in Owen Sound and moving to Toronto in the 1880s. He founded the firm of A.E. Ames & Company in 1889, eventually becoming a director of several large Canadian companies. He was serving as president of the Toronto Board of Trade in 1902, at the remarkably young age of 36, when George Ross asked him to head the first Commission of the T&NO.

Ames knew little about railways. His talents were honed on the sale of bonds and debentures, but he was also well connected by marriage and finance to the most affluent Liberal Methodist circles of Toronto. A reputation for success among businessmen made him appear especially suitable as the first chairman of the Commission to govern a new development railway with such heavy government responsibility behind it.[23]

In addition, the premier appointed four other members to the Commission. They were F.E. Leonard of London, Ontario; B.W. Folger of Kingston; M.J. O'Brien of Renfrew; and Edward Gurney of Toronto. Leonard was a member of E. Leonard & Sons in London, manufacturers of engines, bearings, and boilers for locomotives. The family was generally Liberal. Folger held a partnership in the firm of Folger Brothers, bankers and proprietors of extensive interests in railways, mining and shipping. He also held investments in mineral sites along the line of the Kingston and Pembroke Railway, which he and his brother managed, and in the Rainy River district of northwestern Ontario. Gurney was president of the Gurney Foundry Company, one of the largest manufacturers of stoves and boilers in Ontario, and had served as president of the Toronto Board of Trade before Ames.

Of the five members of this first Commission, M.J. O'Brien knew most about railways. He had worked on them since the age of fourteen and had moved steadily into the business of contracting supplies and buying adjacent properties, sustaining on the way close ties with the Liberal party at both the provincial and federal levels. His contracts for the National Transcontinental Railway through northern Ontario would eventually total over six hundred miles of grading, worth some $15,000,000. Within a few years he would also own 80 per cent of the lucrative O'Brien silver mine at Cobalt, and a large share of the mining properties of Gowganda, together with 125 square miles of timber just over the Québec border. O'Brien lived in the town of Renfrew. The Liberal MPP for the riding of Renfrew South was the Minister of Public Works, F.R. Latchford, who drew up the T&NO Act, influenced appointments, and took responsibility in cabinet for the early stages of construction.

The original Commission was obviously composed of solid businessmen who understood the relation between entrepreneurial activity and government contracts. They also understood the connection between railways and resource development. With the exception of Folger, they were all clearly loyal to the provincial Liberal party. Their meetings took place every other Saturday in two rooms rented as offices for $30 a month above the former Manning Arcade on King Street East in Toronto.[24]

That fall, in October of 1902, the Commission awarded the first contract for construction of the entire line to New Liskeard. They intended the railway primarily as a small colonization line to the settlers around Lake Timiskaming, but Latchford argued, as the minister responsible in cabinet, that transporting lumber and exploring for minerals could lead to a more lucrative future for the wilderness railway. Within the year, events unfolded which abundantly confirmed this possibility. At Cobalt, rich veins of silver lay directly in the path of the approaching construction crews. The Temiskaming and Northern Ontario Railway was aimed precisely at the heart of Ontario's mineral wealth.

CHAPTER 2

The Miracle of Cobalt

Early Construction

The first task of the new five-man Commission, in the summer of 1902, was to choose the route from North Bay to New Liskeard. Two were possible: one west of a high bluff roughly following the old survey for the Nipissing and James Bay Railway; the other east around Trout Lake and through the valley of the North River. While the western line would be shorter and cheaper it presented disadvantages. The differences between the two were clearly presented to the Commission by their chief engineer, W. B. Russel.[1]

For the first stage out of North Bay, the eastern route would be six miles longer, but it would also pass through heavily timbered country of "green virgin forest throughout almost its entire length." Moreover, the first eighteen miles on the eastern side went through rich agricultural land. By contrast, the stands of forest on the west line were uneven, with agricultural land degenerating to rock and scrub only two or three miles beyond North Bay. Heavy rock cuttings and expensive lake crossings at the northern end would make the average cost per mile more expensive on the west side. Because it was shorter by six miles, the total cost of the west line came to slightly less than the eastern route, but the exact difference in the final estimated figures was only $422. Russel weighed the saving against the advantages of the eastern route, and recommended in his conclusion:

> From the above it will appear that, with its six miles of greater length, the east line is the better line to adopt, being about equal in cost of construction with the west line; it besides has the timber and agricultural lands that the west line has not got, also annual local trade, which will pay interest on a very large sum of money...

The commissioners agreed, but hesitated to give formal approval for so significant a choice before obtaining a second opinion from another engineer whose professional experience would itself constitute a form of guarantee. Probably

11

through O'Brien's connections, they asked George A. Mountain, chief engineer of the Canadian Atlantic Railway, a well-established line in the Ottawa valley, to give them his judgement based on the same evidence. When Mountain also expressed a strong preference for the eastern route, they no longer hesitated. In 1902, the Commission decided in favour of the route around Trout Lake following the valley of the North River. The estimated cost per mile of construction was about $21,500, a figure which would increase to more than $30,000 before completion of the first stage to New Liskeard.[2]

Another decision had to be made before actual construction could begin. Should the Commission decide to proceed by employing a contractor or construct the railway directly under its own management? After considerable discussion of the advantages to be derived from direct management, they decided on the contract system, largely to avoid the expense of purchasing "a complete construction plant, which might have to be disposed of at a loss after the work of construction should have been completed." Tenders were called and in October 1902, the contract was awarded to A.R. Macdonell of Montréal. As well as submitting the lowest bid, Macdonell had the advantage of being well known to M.J. O'Brien as an experienced and established contractor in railway construction.

At the same time, the town council of North Bay, then a community of fewer than 4,000 people, sought assurance from the Commission that North Bay would indeed be selected as the southern terminus of the railway, and its station, yards and roundhouse would be located there. The town had literally begun with the construction of the CPR in the 1880s; its politicians and officials were now ready to welcome the headquarters of a provincial railway. The town offered a bonus of $5,000 to the Commission, together with exclusion from municipal taxes for ten years.

Ames immediately consulted legal counsel. He learned that the terminus in North Bay, or in any town, would be exempt from municipal tax, according to Section 7 of the Assessment Act of the province, since the T&NO Commission was "a body corporate representing the Province," with all its property vested "in trust for the public uses of the Province." The town council was therefore advised that the railway needed no grant of exemption, but the Commission would willingly accept the $5,000 bonus.[3] They acted exactly as businessmen on the boards of private railway companies who had received municipal grants for almost half a century.

Construction out of North Bay began in earnest during the summer of 1903, with grading and laying of track going to the 57th mile by fall, more than half the distance to New Liskeard. Comparable progress was not made in digging up and transporting ballast to stabilize the track once it was laid. Macdonell was asked to double the number of his men and equipment for the following year, which meant two steam-shovels and ballast-ploughs, with eight locomotives and 150 flat cars, all of which suggests the scale of Macdonell's capital investment. The Commission clearly expected him to complete the road to New Liskeard by the end of 1904. Their *Annual Report* for 1902 indicates the direct influence of W.B. Russel, who expressed the standards expected to be fulfilled by the contractor.

12

Every effort has been made in this rough country to bring the ruling gradients down to a minimum, as almost any other error than an excessive ruling gradient can be corrected in time. Curves can be flattened, short grades lifted, wooden structures replaced when the life of the timber is reached, but the grades are the life or death of a road that has...any traffic beyond a meagre minimum. In places wooden structures have been used which will last approximately fifteen years, when they can be replaced by masonary structures if it be then considered desirable to do so.

Even as these problems were being faced, as the roadbed wound its way along the edge of a lake or struck a long and narrow clearing through the forest, well before the first stage had been completed, the prospect emerged of a northern extension beyond New Liskeard. Survey parties continued their annual treks north, reaching as far as the southern lowlands of James Bay through 1902 and 1903. More practical and immediate than their reports, however, was the news coming from Ottawa at the same time. The Laurier government introduced legislation in 1903 to support the building by the federal government of a new National Transcontinental Railway. If built, its route from Québec to Winnipeg would pass through the Great Clay Belt of northern Ontario. Here was a stroke of fortune for the provincial government. Junction of the T&NO with a transcontinental route had become more than a remote possibility. It would now become a tangible reality.

Any final decision to build farther north would have to be made by the provincial government and the legislative assembly. But the commissioners themselves knew that a northern extension, even if limited to the specific object of junction with a transcontinental railway, would increase the earning power of the T&NO. In addition, business would expand in the North. The province as a whole would then benefit by the railway's participation in supplying goods and equipment for the West, including construction of the transcontinental line across the northern edge of the Canadian Shield. It is not surprising that an Order-in-Council of 1903 authorized the Commission to undertake the necessary preliminary surveys.[4]

Discovery of Silver

Meanwhile, events unfolded which would soon excite the entire province and draw the attention of thousands of people elsewhere in Canada and abroad. At Mile 103, the railway passed a body of water called by the common name of Long Lake. Early in the spring of 1903 construction workers noticed traces of cobalt bloom and other minerals in the vicinity. Prospectors did not respond until later that summer when suddenly valuable minerals were discovered in quantity near the rock surface along the shore. Some writers credit Fred La Rose, a blacksmith, with the first discovery. According to the story, La Rose was working at his forge when he noticed a fox nearby and threw his hammer at it. The hammer missed, chipping off a piece of rock which revealed a vein of silver. La Rose promptly filed a claim.

13

The story is picturesque and it received wide publicity then and since. But it is probably untrue. Almost certainly other men made the first discovery. According to the provincial Department of Mines and Northern Affairs, "credit for the discovery belongs to J.H. McKinley and Ernest Darragh who were engaged as contractors to supply ties for the railway." While looking for suitable timber they detected the gleam of metallic flakes at the southeast end of Long Lake, both in the rock and among pebbles on the beach. The metal was so pliable that it could be bent with their teeth. After submitting samples for testing in Montréal, they were told they had found silver assayed at 4,000 ounces to the ton. They immediately filed their claim, leased surrounding land, and in 1904 built their first plant, from which grew the McKinley-Darragh mine. This version is supported both by Thomas W. Gibson, then director of the Bureau of Mines, and by a report from the American Institute of Mining Engineers. They point out that the application for the McKinley-Darragh claim was dated August 14, 1903; that of La Rose September 29, and even then La Rose specified the find as copper, apparently ignorant that the metal was silver.[5]

The true value of the discovery was not immediately known. Thomas Gibson took back to Toronto a specimen of rock which he recognized as niccolite. He sent this sample to the Provincial Geologist, Dr. W.G. Miller, requesting him to visit the spot on the shore of Long Lake. Gibson himself expected that Miller would confirm another nickel find, like the one already being developed at Sudbury. At that time he had not heard of the silver discovered by McKinley and Darragh a few weeks before.

Miller was among the most competent men Gibson could have sent to the site. A few years before he had spoken optimistically of the mineral possibilities in this region to the west of Lake Timiskaming, where he found similar conditions to those of the Sudbury district. He quickly realized that this discovery was not copper or nickel. It indicated a rich vein of silver. Miller was not a man easily given to exaggeration, which lent credence to his report to Gibson in which he confessed that he had hardly expected to find ore of such richness and in such quantity.[6] The specimens which he took to Toronto are still on display in show cases of the Department of Mines. What they revealed, even before more extensive examination in the spring of 1904, was a find of silver of such potential wealth that it would in a matter of months change the commercial prospects of the entire region. Prospectors, miners, and financiers would now supersede for a time the settlements of small farmers, tradesmen and small-scale entrepreneurs who had pressed for building the railway in the first place.

One of the first changes came when Miller, as a geologist, decided to call the place of discovery Cobalt after the rock so common in the area. In the early summer of 1904 he nailed a board to a post beside the railway. Printed on it were the words: "Cobalt Station, T. & N.O. Ry." Before long, prospectors signing in at the Haileybury Hotel gave "Cobalt" as their address. By then, in the summer of 1904, other discoveries had already been made. In October 1903, Tom Hébert, a lumberjack with the J.R. Booth Lumber Company, discovered the first vein of the future Nipissing Mining Company, soon to become the largest mine in the Cobalt field. A few days later he discovered the "Little Silver" vein, from which half a million dollars worth of silver was eventually extracted. That same fall of 1903, a labourer and sometime fire-ranger named Neil King sold a claim to M.J. O'Brien for $4,000. O'Brien kept his silence until the ore had been assayed, then consolidated his holding and eventually realized profits of about $10,000,000 from the O'Brien Mine.[7]

Public interest was slight at first. There had been mining crazes before; perhaps the discoveries of 1903 were only freaks, with little of substance beneath the surface. Sceptics seemed more convincing than optimists, even within the Commission of the T&NO Railway. The *Annual Report* for 1903 makes no mention of the discovery of silver, though its wording may have been influenced by the initial reports of Thomas Gibson, before they had been checked by Dr. Miller. "During the construction of the railway near the 103rd mile," said the report, "mineral deposits were discovered which proved to be nickel ore...There appears to be little doubt that the northern portion of the railway passes through an exceedingly valuable mineral territory." By "valuable" the Commission possibly had iron ore rather than silver in mind, since the original surveys had suggested that one of the justifications for the railway would be the exploitation of iron ore in the region of Lake Temagami.

This scepticism from both the public and the Commission disappeared as further discoveries accumulated in 1904. William Tretheway unearthed veins of silver which enabled him to develop both the Tretheway and the Coniagas mines. Shortly after, a friend of his, Alex Longwell, staked out the claim which led to the formation of the Buffalo Mine. It took another year before the first shipment of ore from the Tretheway mine reached the south. The load consisted of "slabs of native metal stripped off the walls of the vein, like boards from a barn." A wave of excitement stirred through the brokerage houses of Toronto with the news that this one shipment alone returned a clear profit of $34,000.

The Cobalt silver rush was on. Prospectors, financiers, promoters hurried to Coleman Township to stake claims or to establish financial connections with potential mines. In his history of mining in Ontario, Thomas Gibson himself was later to comment that prospecting in Ontario had never been so intensive as at Cobalt in those early years.

> Every crack and cranny in the rock, however small, was examined with the minutest care, for it might contain a king's ransom...Prospectors without money, but with a vein which showed calcite and silver, had no difficulty in selling, or in raising funds for development. Much money came from the United States, and many of the mines were brought into being by American funds, as with the Nipissing, Kerr Lake, Buffalo, Timiskaming, Penn-Canadian, Wettlaufer, and other properties.[8]

An Orderly Development

Available money and the prospect of quick profits, as well as the rapid influx of men with no interest in settlement or farming, predictably created a different kind of town at Cobalt; one that grew without planning. The curved streets and crazy, haphazard construction of buildings testified that the town began and continued as a mining community. Around it, by 1905, sixteen mines were operating, and the amount and value of the silver shipped out increased steadily until 1911. During those seven years, Cobalt was a boisterous boom town with its share of brawls and fights, though violence was generally kept to a minimum. Silver bullion was often stacked unguarded in wagons and on sidewalks like so many sandbags. One incident occurred reminiscent of the silver towns of the American West. According to a story told by A.H. Moss in the ONTC *Quarterly*:

> Only once did a "bad man from the West" try to shoot up the town. He lined the guests of the Cobalt Hotel, opposite the station, against the bar-room wall and with the butt of a large gun sticking from his breast pocket, told them what he was going to do to the town. Sheriff Caldbick just happened to come in and, friendly as always, stepped forward to greet the stranger, who shouted to him to get out fast. "Let's shake hands before I go," said Caldbick, as the gunman lunged at him. Perhaps he squeezed a mite harder than was his wont, but down to his knees went the "bad man," with the gun flying across the room. Joe MacKay, Caldbick's assistant, came in from the street and slipped a pair of handcuffs on the man, as he writhed on the floor.

"Sheriff" Caldbick deserved much of the credit for the comparative order at Cobalt during those potentially tumultuous years. More than a man who could handle an incident, Caldbick also had a policy. He met every trainload of new arrivals and searched them before they could leave the railway platform. He confiscated any guns found, took them home and kept them in a locked trunk in his own attic. As a result, possession of a gun became unusual even among the most boisterous of miners and prospectors.[9]

This relative degree of order is all the more remarkable when one considers that Cobalt was then a "poor man's camp," where deprivation might easily lead to violence. As yet miners did not need costly equipment; the opening of the first silver mines required little more than a pick and shovel, a tent and a small stove. The return on such small investments could be substantial.

Some fortunes were made in a very few years. Noah and Henry Timmins, storekeepers from Mattawa, together with John and Duncan McMartin, tie contractors for the railway, acquired control of the La Rose Mine. As a syndicate they later invested their fortune in gold claims two hundred miles to the north at Porcupine. At the same time, the Cobalt camp produced a generation of trained prospectors and miners who spread out over the entire region, discovering other major deposits at Porcupine Lake, Swastika, Larder Lake, Gowganda, Kirkland Lake, and Rouyn. Cobalt was thus not only a fabulous mining field in itself; it generated the incentives and skills which led to the working of other major mineral sites in northeastern Ontario.[10]

For the railway, the discoveries confirmed the possibility of advancing beyond New Liskeard. As early as 1904 the Ross government and the legislative assembly amended the T&NO Railway Act to provide "for the extension of the said railway to a point on or adjacent to the Abitibi River."[11] As the costs of construction increased, mining and resource development added further justification for the expenditure of public revenue. The discoveries at Cobalt in a very real sense changed the purpose of the railway. When the first stage to New Liskeard opened in January 1905, the T&NO was already more than a colonization road to settlers in the Haileybury district; it constituted a major carrier of supplies and equipment for the mining industry, together with prospectors and their gear, heading north. Trains returning south pulled cars loaded with silver ore. Ten per cent of the freight by 1913 consisted of ore, while cars going north were filled with the coal, food and manufactured goods needed by the mining communities. The bulk of freight and passenger traffic came from agricultural and urban settlement, but revenue after 1905 was augmented decisively by rates on ore shipments and by royalties on leased property in the mining area.

In its early phase, the T&NO made a profit from its right of way. Revenue from these rights over property provided a major portion of the earnings of the railway during the decade after 1905. Royalties from ore under the railbed accounted for more than $80,000 in 1913, out of total earnings of just over $255,000.[12]

The existence of silver veins beneath the tracks of the railway (four miles of them through the Cobalt camp), also led to legal differences with the La Rose Mining Company, which lasted from 1906 to 1909. The company disputed the right of the railway to minerals under a portion of its line. The Commission launched a successful counter-suit, forcing the La Rose Company to pay more than $160,000 to the railway and to the Right-of-Way Mining Company.[13]

By 1905 the T&NO was operating a regular rail service from North Bay to New Liskeard. During the first stage of construction the riches of Cobalt had been discovered, and the mining of silver was now closely linked with the railway. By then, too, plans were being discussed for extension farther north, to a junction with the National Transcontinental, holding out the prospect of further mineral discoveries along the way.

The Commission had reason to be satisfied, and to anticipate that the T&NO in its progress northward would fulfil those expectations for development which had been projected since 1890, when a governmental royal commission had recommended the building of railways into the mining districts. Through such tangible encouragement from the provincial government, the mining industry could be expected to attract foreign capital, stimulate manufacturing, increase consumption of iron and steel, and employ larger numbers of people. "An increased mining industry," said this early report of 1890, "would in fact become the complement of the agricultural, manufacturing and lumbering industries."[14] With completion of the T&NO to New Liskeard and the wealth of Cobalt at mile 104, this prediction seemed to be coming true.

CHAPTER 3

Made in Ontario: Financed in Toronto

Regional Manufactures

Cobalt was the first mining settlement to be established, but not the first town north of North Bay. Well before reaching Cobalt the Commission laid out other town sites, giving them names such as Osborne, Temagami, and Latchford. They prospered briefly. Latchford, at the junction of Bay Lake and the Montreal River, provided a point of departure by canoe and boat into the mining country at Gowganda and Elk Lake. The village became a town in 1907, with three hotels and a bank. But the boom ended about 1910 and Latchford reverted to a small lumbering town, dominated at first by the Empire Lumber Company which had received substantial timber limits from the Liberal government of George Ross.

Between North Bay and Cobalt the forest was thick and beautiful. For 1903 the Commission's *Annual Report* said that:

> the timber along the line of railway from the southern end to the 103rd mile is a heavy green forest composed of white and red pine, spruce, black and yellow birch, cedar, hemlock, balsam and maple, in places all growing together.

Most of this information came to the businessmen in Toronto through the detailed reports of W. B. Russel, the chief engineer. Like a hawk hovering over the trees, his eye always seemed sharply focused on the problems and costs of construction. He carefully supervised building of the long bridge, manufactured by the Dominion Bridge Company in Montréal for $20,000, which took three spans to cross the Montreal River at the outlet of Bay Lake, just outside Latchford. But Russel also recognized that, in the absence of farming settlement, the chief function of the railway must be to open new resources.

All hopes centred on exploitation of the forest. As early as 1905 a contract with the Cleveland-Sarnia Lumber Company required a branch line "to transport from ten to twelve million feet of logs per year." Another contract with the Empire Lumber Company provided transport of logs and lumber for their large sawmill at Latchford.[1] From its very beginning, the railway strongly asso-

18

ciated itself with development of the province's natural resources by serving American and Canadian companies.

At the same time, whenever possible, contractors were expected to use Ontario materials. When they were not dealing with finance, the Commission's regular meetings from 1902 to 1905 concentrated on the discussion and granting of tenders. In October 1902 the chief engineer requested supplies to cover the first sixty miles, taking the railroad to the present small town of Temagami. Requests for competitive bids were sent out for 8,200 tons of eighty-pound rail, 520 tons of angle bars, 88,000 bolts and washers, 18,000 tie plates, and 780,000 six-inch spikes. Contracts for angle bars and tie plates were awarded to the Hamilton Steel and Iron Company; bolts came from the Toronto Bolt and Forging Company; spikes from the Pillow and Hersey Manufacturing Company in Montréal.[2]

Toronto did little of the manufacturing, a fact which became evident as further orders followed over the next two years. Toronto's predominance lay more in finance and politics than in manufacturing. Most of the orders reflected both the industrial economy of a developing province and its regional character. The first fifty box cars were ordered from the Rathbun Company of Deseronto at $950 each; seven passenger coaches came from the Crossen Car Manufacturing Company in Cobourg at an average price of $6,800 each. The first eight locomotives were made by the Canadian Locomotive Company in Kingston, at prices higher than those quoted by the Baldwin Locomotive Company in the United States.

In fact, no orders for material equipment or rolling stock were placed with American companies, partly as a result of pro-Canadian preference and sentiment, partly because of prejudice against the quality of American manufactures. The policy of the Commission at this early stage is revealed in the *Minutes* for 20 January 1904, when a further order called for 15,500 pair of angle bars: "the tender of the Hamilton Steel and Iron Works and that of the Nova Scotia Steel Company being equal and the lowest tenders received, the Commission decided to accept the tender of the Ontario concern." Though relatively small, orders like this formed part of the railway technology of the time, creating such a burgeoning Canadian demand for finished iron and steel that the Hamilton Works became the nucleus for merger into the Steel Company of Canada in 1910.

It was not always possible, however, to reconcile the preference for goods manufactured in Ontario, or at least in Canada, with the competitive practices of a free market economy. The commissioners, it should be stressed, were five successful businessmen whose fortunes had been made in a province governed for over thirty years by a Liberal government which had come to accept the dominance of Ontario in the Canadian economy. Had they been building and managing a privately owned railway they would more likely have opted for the lowest bids regardless of their source. But they were functioning in a country where, for more than two decades, the economy had been shaped by the protection and internal preference of the National Policy, initiated and sustained by the Conservative government of John A. Macdonald.

What this meant in the early history of the publicly owned railway is illustrated by the problem of another major purchase: that of heavy steel rails which had to meet specifications on phosphorus and carbon content. The original order for 8,200 tons, each rail to be eleven yards long and weighing eighty pounds to the yard, was placed with the Algoma Steel Company at Sault Ste. Marie. Though the quoted price was higher than other submissions, Algoma was part of a complex network of industries at Sault Ste. Marie, founded by Francis Clergue as the Consolidated Lake Superior Corporation, which had crumbled into such serious financial trouble from 1902 to 1904 that it had to be rescued by special guarantees from the provincial government. At the very time when the T&NO Commission, founded by the government, made its first purchases of supplies in substantial quantities, Premier Ross was seeking ways to make Algoma Steel a secure and viable producer of Ontario manufactures. The government could hardly permit the commissioners of the new railway to purchase steel rails from outside the province.

Why, then, did they finally do so? With so much equipment being supplied domestically for the new roadbed in the North, why should the rails come, not only from outside Ontario but from beyond the borders of Canada? The answer to that question provides a commentary on the tension at the time between government policy and the stage of industrial development in Ontario. If the economy of Ontario was more advanced than elsewhere in Canada, it was still seriously limited in the production of heavy metallurgical goods. Ross would face that problem when he came to it. In the meantime, he met with the Commission and then sent them his written advice:

> In view of the policy of the Legislature, in favor of the construction and equipment of the T. & N.O. Railway with supplies manufactured in Canada, the Government is of the opinion that the Commission would be justified in awarding the contract to the Algoma Steel Company, even at prices in advance of outside tenders....

The encouragement given to Clergue and his industrial empire at Sault Ste. Marie; the need to keep men employed; the reconstruction of the Lake Superior Corporation destined to take almost a decade – all directly involved the Ross government. Ross presented in precise and committed terms his version of an economic policy that was not simply Canadian but Ontarian, with its goal of domestic manufacturing through positive inducements in the form of subsidies and of favourable treatment in awarding contracts.

He was speaking for the Legislature and for both parties when he said that the government had invested money with the special purpose of developing the mineral resources of Ontario. But mining alone could not produce the employment and the profits that would result from adding the next step – manufacturing the ores for use "in the other industries of the country." Algoma Steel, said Ross, had built a plant that was now capable of producing rails from Canadian ore, and of providing a large number of jobs.

> Both of these objects the Government has endeavoured to advance by legislation, as well as by substantial aid in the form of subsidies,

etc. You may, therefore, assure the Commissioners that in the action they propose taking they will have the most cordial approval of the Government.

Then, after patient negotiation over price and quality, the Commission discovered that Algoma Steel lacked the ore to meet the required phosphorus content in the rails. Despite this determined policy of preference, therefore, the contract had to be cancelled. The first rails between North Bay and New Liskeard were manufactured in Sheffield, England, with shipment to North Bay through a Montréal agent. Beginning in 1905 those rails supported long lines of flat cars loaded with minerals or timber clattering south from the rich forests and mines between North Bay and New Liskeard.[3]

Into the Clay Belt

North of New Liskeard the country changed again. The railbed would be laid over clay and be surrounded by farms with houses and barns where people waited for the train to stop because it was the only means of bringing in or shipping out their supplies, their produce and their mail. In 1903 settlement had already reached twenty-two miles north of New Liskeard, and the town itself had 1,500 inhabitants. There were no land grants here for the railway, since the Crown Lands had already been sold at fifty cents an acre. The homesteaders were not miners or lumbermen working for a wage or speculating on a quick profit. They cleared their own land and worked as settlers. Their independence and sense of community made them a democratic force behind the building of the railway, different from the organized influence of large-scale business enterprise. For them, the railway was simply the only road to the towns and markets of Cobalt, Haileybury, and the south, where they could sell the produce worked with hard labour from the good soil of the Clay Belt.

One of them, Jim Foster, a resident of Thornloe, moved into that area in 1903 when he was only five years old. He and his parents celebrated when they heard the whistle of the first locomotive of the construction crew north of New Liskeard. It was summer, he said:

> I figure that it was 1904. Bill Foster and his boys – two boys – were out cleaning the yard, cleaning up chips and piling them up and burning them. And a sharp blow of a whistle in the distance towards the south we heard. We looked at each other in surprise and there was a look of joy came to our faces. And he said: "That's a train!"

> He shouted to his wife, and she came out, and with a great emotion mingled with tears he shouted: "We heard a train whistle! That's the sign of prosperity." Because they had been living almost starving.

> They formed a ring around the fire, with their hands together, and danced around it, round and around, shouting and singing for all that they were worth.[4]

Many things were compounded into that word "prosperity." It meant hope for families who a few years before had faced a timbered wilderness without roads and only scattered clearings. It meant commitment on the part of government and business; freight no longer slowed by the haulage of horse-teams. It meant riding in coaches for cheap passenger fares; or, if one had to walk, following the cleared line of the tracks. Altogether the railway would be a new physical presence for what had till then been remote and isolated homesteads.

Even so, the building of the line was not easy. In 1904 the roadbed from Cobalt to New Liskeard was still incomplete. The Commission took possession of the line in January 1905, but the contract for the road into New Liskeard had to be extended until August, since Macdonell argued that his men would need another three or four months of "seasonable weather" after a hard winter. At the same time, it was necessary to put out the new contract for tender, calling for construction of the line north from New Liskeard to "a distance of 80 to 100 miles, more or less."

The surveys drawn up in 1903 by W. B. Russel pointed out that most of this territory "lies south of the 49th parallel, the southern boundary of Manitoba, and is free from the sweeping winds of the prairie country." With its "fine clay loam and comparatively flat country" this Timiskaming Clay Belt was already drawing settlers. The northward extension was intended to meet their demands, as well as to encourage the beginning of new businesses along the line. In the future lay the prospect of going farther north when the money was ready and the resources more evident. For now, the new contract would simply extend the railway through the pioneer farm country north of Lake Timiskaming.

Of the bids submitted, A. R. Macdonell from Montréal quoted the lowest price and received the contract for just over $1,500,000. Not only were the other three tenders higher; they contained too many inaccuracies. Despite the delays on the first contract, Macdonell still had the edge on his competitors. His submission was based on experience of the railway construction business in Montréal. Its details of costs were efficiently presented without the inaccuracies which had to be corrected in the competing bids. He also had the advantage of machinery and equipment already purchased and on the site. From Macdonell's point of view, he expected to benefit more from the easier construction of a railbed over the Clay Belt than he had done over the rocks and rivers of the first section from North Bay.

The surveys for this second section had been well done. As a result, crews built up the roadbed and laid tracks at the rate of almost a mile a day for the first 33 miles north of New Liskeard, until they crossed the Blanche River. The next twenty-four miles proved more uneven, following the valley of Boston Creek until the roadbed resumed its course along the banks of the Blanche River just north of Round Lake. The road turned west and north there, going over level country to the 65th mile on the east side of Lake Sesekinika. A few more miles and construction had crossed the Height of Land, with the prospect of fairly light construction north of that again.

In more technical terms the chief engineer reported for 1904 that "the maximum and ruling grade which we endeavoured to hold to and succeeded in getting, [was] ... 26 feet to the mile rising north and 21 feet for the mile rising south," and the maximum curve was four degrees with a radius of 1,432 feet. Just what that meant was expressed in an opinion from the chief engineer of the Grand Trunk Railway, who reported that "upon a number of railways which rank among the best on this Continent there are more objectionable curves than any which it is proposed to use on this line." He also found the gradients to be remarkably good. Altogether, the specifications were sound and it seemed construction could proceed without delay.[5]

Money and Politics in Toronto

Behind the scenes, however, problems loomed in the years 1904 and 1905. They originated first from membership in the Commission itself. The first chairman, A.E. Ames, resigned early in 1904 after serving for only a year and a half. Ames was still a young man, not yet forty, but his developing interests in brokerage and trust companies took priority over the railway. He was persuaded to take the position in the first place, not only because of his financial success and his Liberal connections, but primarily through the influence of his father-in-law, George A. Cox.

Cox had begun his financial career in Peterborough by consolidating a number of small Ontario railroads and selling them to the Grand Trunk. By 1889 when Ames married his daughter and founded his own business, Cox was already president of the Central Canada Loan and Savings Company, which had assets of $7,000,000 by 1902. He headed five similar companies at the same time, including the Canada Life Insurance Company. Since 1890 he had been president of the Canadian Bank of Commerce, a position which he held until 1907.[6] He was closely involved in financing projects of the Liberal provincial government and was appointed a Senator by the Laurier government in 1896.

Though not directly connected with the T&NO Commission, the figure of George Cox was like that of an *éminence grise* in the financial and political world of Toronto at the turn of the century. He represented the kind of power that many Canadian businessmen have preferred – the capacity to influence and even to direct decisions behind the scene, to wield authority by means of discreet and unobtrusive connection with men in the highest political office. His was probably the most decisive voice to influence Premier Ross and the Liberal cabinet in its deliberations on the founding and the early affairs of the T&NO Commission.

Like so many Toronto financiers of this period, Cox's beliefs were those of an evangelical Protestant. He was in fact a Methodist, dedicated to sober conduct and the temperance movement. Both could be associated with the making of money. For Cox and his son-in-law, the new wealth came from railway grants, from interest on loans and mortgages, from commissions on the sale of bonds, debentures, and life insurance. The money raised went into the financing of electrical utility, railway and municipal transportation companies. It was all accomplished through chartered banks, or through trust and brokerage firms.

Whatever its forms, the new wealth could be justified as the tangible, outward sign of being worthy in God's eyes. Success brought not only social recognition but spiritual confidence. The new financier, sitting prominently in the congregation of the Sherbourne Street Methodist Church, saw himself as a vehicle of God's purpose. He should be modest in his habits, reticent about his personal life; he should avoid public display of any kind, give no interviews nor put his private views and emotions onto paper. Out of gratitude and duty, however, he should perform prominent public service when called upon to do so. Cox, Ames and most of the financial men of Toronto who influenced the making of public policy seem to have shared these same convictions.

At a more mundane level, and also a more immediate one, Cox had been one of the chief promoters of the James Bay Railway in 1895, when his good friend Oliver Mowat was premier. He was still on the board of that railway in 1900, when it became clear the company had no intention of fulfilling its charter to build north from Sudbury to James Bay.[7] That negative decision, together with Cox's Liberal interest, may help to explain why his son-in-law was persuaded to accept the chairmanship of the T&NO in 1902. It is important to understand these circumstances, since the entire venture into the T&NO stemmed from the central place of Toronto in the finance and politics of Ontario.

Initially, in 1903, the Liberal government of George Ross agreed to underwrite costs of construction at no more than $25,000 per mile. The figure was raised to $30,000 in 1904 when it became apparent that actual costs were exceeding original estimates. Banks were asked to advance loans to the government for payment to the contractor at a rate of 4 per cent. But banks required collateral of a more specific nature than a blanket guarantee from the provincial government, which was in no position to raise or guarantee large sums of money. Bonds would have to be placed on the financial market, backed by generous land grants to the railway of 20,000 acres to the mile, four times the size of standard railway grants of 5,000 acres. From North Bay to New Liskeard, however, no agricultural land existed; and the Crown Lands north of New Liskeard had already been bought by settlers. Except for the sites of small towns, therefore, the bulk of the 4,000,000 acres granted to the T&NO Railway was not conducive to the generation of railway revenue.[8]

Because so much of that acreage could be expected to remain undeveloped wilderness for some time, land grants offered as collateral had to be supplemented by the value of the right-of-way, by equipment, buildings and rolling stock, though not by bonuses or royalties for timber and mineral rights, which were excluded from the revenue of the railway by a legislated amendment in 1903. Allowing for this condition, the debentures could now be issued as more than mere "Land Grant Bonds." It also was essential to enhance their value because money was tight at the time. In his presidential report to the Central Canada Loan and Savings Company in January 1904, Cox observed that "the shrinkage in the value of all classes of securities has been almost unprecedented ..."[9] His words were borne out by the experience of the T&NO Commission when it offered its first issue of $500 bonds in 1903. Out of an initial offering of 5,500, fewer than 1,500 were bid, and 1,000 of the bids came from the Canadian Bank of Commerce, of which Cox was president.

24

1

The "Meteor" and the wharf at Haileybury, about 1900. Before the building of the T&NO Railway, settlers could only "go in" or "come out" from the head of Lake Timiskaming by boat. The "Meteor" was owned and operated by the Lumsden family of Ottawa, which held extensive interests in the lumbering industry.

2

3

Top: Bridge over the Montreal River, neat Latchford. It was the first major bridge on the way to New Liskeard, and was manufactured in 1903 by the Dominion Bridge Company in Montréal. *Bottom*: The "centennial" steam locomotive emerging from the bridge, 1967.

4

5

6

Top: A standard train at the new Temagami station, 1907. The locomotive is a 4-6-0 wheel arrangement with 62″ drive wheels, made by Montreal Locomotive works in 1906. *Bottom*: The same station about ten years later, showing the mix of businessmen and new settlers travelling into the "New Ontario."

7

8

9

Early silver mining at Cobalt, about 1905-1910. *Top left*: Barrel and pulley which lowered miners into the shaft. *Top*: Rare photo, taken by flashlight, of two miners about 120 feet underground. One man held and turned the drill while the other pounded it with a sledge hammer. *Left*: A larger mine where workers used a pneumatic drill.

Diamond drilling for silver on the Nipissing property, Cobalt, about 1905. A tie contractor named Swan Swanson wrote: "Duncan McMartin told me that LaRose, the man who sharpened the drill steel for the drillers, was one day compelled by nature to go into the bush a little ways by himself, and there, while in a crouching position, gazing at the ground, noticed something shiny. Being of a curious nature, he picked it up and took it to Duncan McMartin. Duncan recognized it at once. *It was silver!* This great find... did not seem to excite anyone at all, as none of us really grasped the magnitude of the discovery. We went about our business as usual. We were railroad builders, and our minds were centred on the work we had trained ourselves to do." (Swan Swanson, typescript autobiography, PAO)

The Cobalt station in 1910. The quiet waiting room presents a striking contrast to the crowds milling about the train, some of them boarding for the newly discovered gold-mining country in the Porcupine.

Cobalt, about 1905. Available money and the prospect of quick profit predictably created a particular type of town at Cobalt; one that grew without planning, with little thought given to the nature of an urban community. The curved streets and crazy, haphazard construction of buildings testified that the town began and continued as a mining community.

A contrast in lifestyles, Cobalt, about 1910. *Top*: The wives and the mothers of the men who managed mines and banks had to create their own kind of entertainment. Every birthday was an occasion for a party, where the strongest drink was tea. *Below*: A "Blind Pig," where illegal beer was sold, and stolen nuggets of silver were sometimes smuggled out to a black market.

Left: A.E. Ames, first chairman of the T&NO Commission, 1902-1904. A financier, president of the Toronto Board of Trade, son-in-law to the president of the Bank of Commerce, and a firm Methodist, Ames represented the imperial thrust of Toronto's financial establishment in its competition with Montréal for control of potential resources and expanding settlement in the North.

16

Right: Jacob L. Englehart, chairman 1906-1920. A Jewish immigrant from the United States who made a fortune in the founding of Imperial Oil, Englehart was chosen to chair the Commission by the Conservative Premier James Whitney. Englehart gradually established himself as a conscientious but eccentric figure, known to the people in the North for his remote and formal manner, his European style of dress, his goatee and his *pince-nez* glasses.

17

Swan Swanson and wife, about 1906. Both were Swedes. He was a tie contractor on the Montreal River, and then a sub-contractor for a section of the
line north of New Liskeard. Notice the Union Jacks, presumably to demonstrate that they had become British subjects. Of one group of his workmen,
Swanson wrote: "I had about fifteen Macedonians in a small camp by themselves. They had some very peculiar musical instruments, brought over from
their homeland. Their dances too were odd. They wore bloomer-like pants,
and picturesque shirts when they danced. Over their shirts they wore fancy
vests. Their apparel and dances were gay and colourful. We often took our
baby girl...down to watch them. They would take the baby in their arms and
dance with her. She loved it, and would laugh and shout with glee. Time
passed on wings, and there was no time for loneliness." (Swan Swanson,
typescript autobiography, PAO)

Swan Swanson had a gang working in soft mud north of New Liskeard. "It was extremely hard to get men to stay at this kind of work... One day a gang of about twenty-five Russian Jews came along. They had been hired out from Montréal and taken to some contractors north of me. They did not understand the work and were fired....

They were stalwart, able-looking men, and one of them could talk pretty good English. He... asked me if I would take them on. He assured me of their willingness to work, but their ignorance was a great drawback.... I readily saw that they were exactly what he said."

Swanson gave them a chance working under a patient foreman, who told him at the end of the first day: "These Jews are useless... they don't even know which end of a shovel to use."

Swanson ordered that the men be kept for at least a week, and at the end of the week his foreman reported: "They're such willing workers that I'd hate to fire them."

By the end of the second week, "they had as many trains out per day as any of the other three gangs could do, and later were the best of the four gangs on the cut."

Packing Over Trail,— S. Lorrain.

POST CARD

CORRESPONDENCE HERE · ADDRESS ONLY

MacLean Photo, Haileybury & Cobalt, Ont.

This is how the Italians pack in our
a white man would use a pack sac,
These dagoes buy everything in sack
and carry it the hardest way possib
you can see the white foreman,
walking ahead. That old fellow behin
on the left hand side, I've seen him
dozens of times They are an awful tribe
and no mistake. C.V.

A snapshot made into a post card, 1909. The writing on the back suggests the shallow prejudice which sometimes existed against European immigrants.

22

Good timber was needed for the construction of trestles, which were not always able to withstand the weight of the locomotive and its cars. Gradually, all trestle bridges were replaced with steel structures.

23

Matabnick Hotel, Haileybury, Ont.

24

25

When non-resident millionaires visited Cobalt, many of them stayed at the Matabanick Hotel in Haileybury, owned and managed by Arthur Ferland. His purpose was to see that men of wealth could eat, drink, and sleep in comfort, as though they were enjoying only a vigorous change of scene from the amenities of the King Edward Hotel in Toronto or the Ritz in Montréal.

27

28

Bullion shipments from Cobalt, 1905 and 1910. It was not at all unusual for large shipments of silver bullion to be piled on wagons which stood unguarded on the railway platform until the train arrived.

Ames was forced to drop the bond issue and turn directly to the banks for a short-term loan of $2,300,000 at an annual interest rate of 4 per cent. At the same time, the chief engineer reported that if a railway was to be built which "would be creditable to the province, and which would conform to the standard of a trunk line," then the estimated cost of the road including rolling stock would be revised upward to just under $30,000 per mile. Russel was basing these estimates on the Macdonell contract at $1,464,000 plus the contracts already let for supplies and rolling stock which so far totalled $500,000. Further contingencies, salaries and claims would be inevitable before the first stage of the railway could become operable.[10]

Russel's figure of $30,000 per mile had to be taken seriously, leading the Commission to conclude by simple arithmetic that a loan of $2,300,000 would finance hardly eighty miles of the road out of North Bay. The surveys of location called for a hundred and thirteen miles to New Liskeard, and north of that was the next stage – perhaps another hundred miles – through new farming country to the Height of Land. Placing these circumstances in context with the scarcity of money for railway bonds, and with probable increasing costs, the task of the chairman must have been frustrating. He resigned in December 1903.[11]

The essential difficulty for the provincial government, now that it had made the commitment to build a publicly owned railway, was how to arrange financing. For the previous thirty years, since Ontario had been established as a province at Confederation in 1867, predominantly Liberal governments headed by Oliver Mowat had combined the assertion of provincial rights with persistent economy in all forms of government expenditure. The province had no debt. It had never called for a public loan. Now that money had to be borrowed, in what was for the time a large amount, George Ross and his cabinet made two assumptions.

Both assumptions must have seemed obvious to politicians and businessmen at the turn of the twentieth century in Canada. First, the loan should be floated in the form of railway bonds, not based on public taxation but on the assets, land sales and anticipated revenue of the T&NO, much like a mortgage, just as the bonds of private railway companies had been sold for over two decades in various parts of the country. Secondly, the raising of money should be accomplished through well-trusted Liberal businessmen who dominated the financial houses of Toronto. These assumptions directly influenced early financing of the railway. Ownership by a government Commission implied no socialist methods or goals. Rather, the public character of the Commission was incidental to the basic ideology of capitalist enterprise.

For three months before his resignation, Ames had seen or written Premier Ross almost weekly on the difficulties of raising money through the issue of railway bonds. As invoices from suppliers and contractors began to arrive for payment, banks insisted on the government maintaining minimum deposits before advancing loans. More seriously, investors refused to purchase railway bonds at interest rates of 3 or 3½ per cent. If such rates were maintained, the bonds would be discounted on the market, bringing the Commission less money than it required.

25

E.R. Wood, a close colleague of Ames in the Toronto business world, was also meeting with Ross. Wood was then about the same age as Ames and close to all the financial interests of the Cox family. He had moved from Peterborough with the Central Canada Loan and Savings Company in the 1880s, and was now its General Manager. He was also heavily involved in the formation of the National Trust Company in 1899 and of Dominion Securities in 1901. Wood functioned also as president of Dominion Securities, rapidly turning it into the largest seller of railway and utility bonds in Canada. He held a strategic financial position from which to advise the premier at a time when Ames was on the verge of resignation.

Writing to Ross in October 1903, Wood placed the problems of marketing T&NO bonds in context with the decline of securities in the western world generally. If British government bonds, or "consols," were being discounted to yield more than the traditional 3 per cent; if even Dominion government bonds could not be sold at current rates, to say nothing of the bonds "of our best cities, counties, towns, and townships," then the government of Ontario could hardly hope to market T&NO bonds at less than 4 per cent interest, and probably higher, since "bonds being issued by a railway commission...are in a class entirely different from straight government securities..." This opinion received further support from P.E. Ryan, secretary-treasurer of the T&NO Commission, who wrote to Ross just after Ames had resigned:

> There is in the public mind an important distinction between bonds of a province and railroad bonds guaranteed by a province...The investing public expects to purchase guaranteed railroad bonds at a price to yield them a considerably higher rate than that of the direct obligation.[12]

Raising the initial capital, it transpired, was both more expensive and more difficult than had been anticipated by the government or by the Commission.

To resolve these intricate financial problems required, so it seemed to Ross, another man with the same patience and acumen, and the same contacts, as A.E. Ames. His choice was Robert Jaffray, listed in biographical notes of the time as a "Toronto capitalist." Jaffray was born in Scotland in 1832, so he was over seventy when he became chairman of the Commission in 1904. But he was a logical choice; a dedicated Liberal and a Presbyterian who had started out in the wholesale grocery business and had expanded from small beginnings to become a highly respected figure in the banking and trust companies of Toronto. He moved in the same financial and social circles as Cox and Ames and Wood. He was in fact a director of the Central Canada Loan and Savings Company and also president of the Globe Printing Company and, therefore, publisher of the Liberal Toronto *Globe* which he purchased from the family of George Brown in 1888. Under his nominal direction, the T&NO Commission achieved new financing arrangements in 1904, though the real work was done by the government of George Ross.[13]

26

The original $2,300,000 arranged by Ames through Toronto banks had to be supplemented by a further $1,500,000 advanced to the Commission from the Consolidated Revenue Fund of the provincial government. To borrow on this scale, Ross decided to explore a more secure source of funds in London, England, the largest centre in the world for railway capital. It was a satisfying achievement for the government and the Commission when a short-term loan was eventually negotiated for six months with two of the most prominent banking houses in London: Glyn, Mills, Currie & Company and Messrs. Coates and Company. Together these two banks supplied £1,200,000 at 4 per cent, which netted the Commission, after exchange and commission, more than $5,700,000. The provincial government and the Canadian banks were then repaid the loans they had advanced; the bonds were cancelled, and a new series of six-month Treasury Notes in the amount of $6,000,000 were sent by the Commission to the London banks as security.

By the beginning of 1905 the T&NO Commission had thus paid out in exchange, commission, and interest an amount in excess of $500,000, but its funding was now stable.[14] When necessary it could be supplemented by advances from the Consolidated Revenue Fund of the government, an advantage not available to private railway companies. But 1905 also brought the Liberal government of George Ross down to defeat. In the party rivalry of the time it followed that not only the chairman but the entire membership of the Commission had to be replaced. Building the railway, financing its construction, even day-to-day management would all be affected.

CHAPTER 4

A Change of Government

For a large part of Canada's history, railways and politics have been interwoven. Whether through land grants, direct subsidies, or bond guarantees, collusion between business and politics provides a major theme of Canadian history. Fortunes were founded on the strength of such relationships. Even when publicly owned, the railway was regarded as an enterprise most effectively managed by businessmen with the proper political loyalties. Thus the Ontario election of January 1905 is an integral part of the story of the T&NO Railway.

The election returned seventy Conservatives and only twenty-eight Liberals. Such a victory was unprecedented in the history of the province. Although Liberal majorities had seriously declined in the elections of 1900 and 1902, the party was conditioned to power, having held office for thirty-three years since Confederation in 1867. This sweeping Conservative success in 1905 could be attributed partly to the general desire for change and the disillusionment among temperance advocates at inadequate regulations by the Liberal government. More particularly, it signalled public reaction against bribery among Liberal organizers. Beneath these immediate issues, Protestants all over small-town Ontario felt an irrational, deep-seated suspicion of the Roman Catholic, French-Canadian leadership of Wilfrid Laurier and his Liberal government in Ottawa. The new premier of Ontario, James P. Whitney, had patiently organized his campaign to emphasize these grievances and fears. His leadership had an immediate impact on the T&NO.[1]

No one questioned that the Liberal Commission would resign. Politicians, businessmen, journalists, all accepted it as a fact of political life. Yet few people viewed the Commission as simply a refuge for loyal members of the party in power. On the resignation of Robert Jaffray as chairman, his own newspaper, the Toronto *Globe*, edited by a Presbyterian minister, published an editorial telling the new Whitney administration that its heaviest responsibility should be the continuing development of the North.

> To anyone who considers the situation it will appear impressively clear that in reorganizing the commission the Government cannot be too careful to have it composed of men of large calibre, good business

capacity, and ability to work with an eye single to the public interest. It would be a fatal mistake to treat such appointments as mere rewards for services rendered to the party by political camp-followers.[2]

Whitney accepted this counsel. He did so within the limitations of a party system and democratic rights. The *Annual Report* of the T&NO baldly stated: "Early in the year the then Commissioners resigned from office and the present Commission was appointed." The new Commission consisted of Cecil B. Smith (chairman), from Toronto; J.L. Englehart from Petrolia; and Denis Murphy from Ottawa. Who were these men? Their names occur nowhere in the three-year history of the Commission. How does one explain their selection?

The answer to both questions must be related first to provincial politics and the working of the party system. Political connection, if not outright political patronage, determined membership of the T&NO Commission from its beginning in 1902. Jaffray and O'Brien had exhibited loyal Liberal partisanship, as had Ames through his father-in-law, George Cox. But they had also served from a sense of service in the public interest. Why, then, should they not have retained their positions?

Whitney could not afford to make an immediate sweep of Liberal office holders. After thirty-three years they were too numerous and too well-entrenched. His political lieutenant in the North, Frank Cochrane, actually kept in office many who had been appointed by the Liberals. The policy was deliberate. Cochrane insisted that men be removed from positions considered to be in government patronage only if deliberately partisan activities could be proved against them.[3]

The Commission of the T&NO, however, ranked too highly in the hierarchy of party politics. Its Liberal members had been too closely involved with the inner direction of the party and with campaign contributions. Whatever may be said in favour of public service, M.J. O'Brien acquired control of a large silver mine in the Cobalt region while a member of the T&NO Commission, and by 1906 the O'Brien mine was valued at $10,000,000. All circumstances considered, it is hardly surprising that the first Commission should resign after the outcome of the election of 1905.

Before making new appointments, Whitney had the option of reconsidering the whole policy of a publicly owned railroad. Why did he not sell or lease the line to a company? He need only revise the charter to conform with all the other charters which sanctioned the construction and operation of railroads by private enterprise. As leader of the opposition in 1902, he himself had suggested that the T&NO be built and managed by Mackenzie and Mann, now the owners and promoters of the Canadian Northern Railway. Did Whitney share with the Liberals some special Canadian characteristic which nourished support for public as distinct from private enterprise? The question is fundamental. It must be asked, because in 1905 Whitney could have decided to renounce public ownership of the railway. The Commission had existed, after all, for only three years and railroads in North America were predominantly owned by private companies.

The answer to the puzzle is threefold. First, in an immediate political context, Mackenzie and Mann were allied with George Cox and the Canadian Bank of Commerce, connections which placed them in the Liberal party camp. The two partners had also given strong indications that they had no interest in promoting a railway to James Bay. No other promoters came forward as substitutes. Secondly, the implicit support of businessmen, newspapers, and politicians had been confirmed by the voters, who had indicated in the elections of both 1902 and 1905 that the public had no objection to active and direct participation by the provincial government in development of the New Ontario. And, finally, this implicit public support was focused and excited by the discovery of silver at Cobalt. Nowhere was Whitney likely to find opposition to his new Conservative government assuming direction and management of the publicly owned T&NO Commission. Begun by a Liberal government as a partisan Commission, it was now imbedded in the politics and government of the province.

Some discussion took place in cabinet on new appointments. No reasons for Whitney's choice of membership are evident in the surviving political papers or in the newspapers of the time. Yet certain explanations can be made, allowing for an element of speculation. First, Whitney was not obligated to appoint the same number of commissioners, nor did members all have to come from the south of the province. In fact, he appointed only three, the minimum allowed by statute. None of the three appointees came from the North.

Whitney had yet to find a northern candidate who possessed the desired qualifications, or the established financial and political connections with the Conservative party, then called the Liberal-Conservative party. This omission aroused populist reaction in the North over the next few years, particularly among newspapers such as the Cobalt *Daily Nugget*, the Porcupine *Advance* and the Cochrane *Northland Post*. Why, the editors asked, should there be no northern representation on the Commission? Whitney did arrange the election of Frank Cochrane in East Nipissing, and appointed him to the cabinet as head of a new Ministry of Lands and Mines. Perhaps this was all that was possible for Whitney in 1905. Cochrane remained the central, directing hand of Conservative politics in the New Ontario for a number of years, even after his appointment to the federal cabinet of Robert Borden in 1911.

With a political manager of Cochrane's abilities in the North, Whitney could concentrate on men of proven financial experience, social connection, and party loyalty in the South to direct the T&NO Commission. He chose Cecil Smith of Toronto as chairman, because of his qualifications as an engineer, but his position was considered temporary from the beginning. In fact, Smith resigned in October 1906, to become consulting engineer for the Commission.

Jacob Englehart

Jacob L. Englehart assumed the position of chairman on November 1 of that year. The appointments of Englehart from Petrolia and Denis Murphy from Ottawa were based on reasons similar to those for Liberal members of the first Commission. Both were businessmen and entrepreneurs who had amassed their own fortunes, and who had established intimate ties with the Conservative party. Murphy was one of the few Conservative MPPs defeated in the election of 1905. He was president of the Ottawa Board of Trade at the time of his appointment, and had controlling interests in the Ottawa Transportation Company and the Canadian Railway Accident Insurance Company. His name also appeared as director of ten other investment and resource companies, including the lucrative Nipissing Silver Mine at Cobalt.[4]

But it was Jacob Englehart who proved to be the most dynamic and influential appointment. The fact that he came from southwestern Ontario may not have been directly relevant, though Whitney was seeking to build a power base for the Conservative party in that region which had once provided the frontier roots of Grit and Reform associations. In 1905 Conservatives had been elected for the two London constituencies of Middlesex East and Middlesex North. The primary attributes considered in the selection of Englehart undoubtedly were his success as an entrepreneur, his wealthy independence, his loyalty to the party, and his previous experience in dealing with railway companies.

Born in Cleveland in 1847, Englehart had worked briefly for his father's petroleum company in New York, moving to Canada at the end of the Civil War at the age of nineteen, where he settled first in London and then in Petrolia. By the age of thirty he controlled the brokerage of exported oil as well as the largest refinery in Canada, with its resources of crude oil coming from wells which dotted the farming countryside between Chatham and Sarnia. He proved as adept as his American counterparts in depressing prices paid for the crude products from competing local wells, while sustaining high selling prices for the refined oil, then used chiefly for lighting and for lubrication of axles on wagons and trains.

In 1880, at the age of thirty-three, he took a prominent role in the organization of London businessmen who formed the Imperial Oil Company. Englehart emerged from that transaction as the largest shareholder. On an original investment of $60,000 he owned close to 20 per cent of the issued shares, while holding at the same time the combined positions of first vice-president and general manager. He moved the head office to Petrolia in 1884 and Imperial Oil continued to thrive, expanding its markets for refined oil to western Canada with completion of the CPR. By the 1890s, competition with Standard Oil of New York required transfer of the company's plant to Sarnia, but legislation on behalf of more free trade by the Liberal government of Wilfrid Laurier gave distinct advantages to American petroleum imports. In order to survive, the board of Imperial Oil sold its controlling interest to Standard Oil in 1898. Jacob Englehart remained on the new board as a vice-president and a large shareholder.[5]

By the time of the election in 1905 he had become a wealthy man, with a large estate in Petrolia, where he lived with his wife in the style of a benevolent patriarch. Like most men in the oil-refining industry in southwestern Ontario, he supported a policy of tariffs against American oil, which led him to adopt Conservative political affiliations. As president of the regional Liberal-Conservative Association, he helped to elect his friend and colleague, W. J. Hanna, for Lambton West. Whitney appointed Hanna as Provincial Secretary in the new cabinet, giving him a vital place at the outset in discussions about new appointments. At the same time, Hanna continued to be a director of Imperial Oil and maintained his office in the company's building at Toronto. As Whitney pursued his search to replace wealthy and committed Liberals in government appointments, Hanna suggested that Englehart might solve his problem of finding a chairman for the T&NO Commission.[6]

Although a Jew of European background, possessed of little formal schooling, Englehart had converted to the Anglican Church, married a Christian and donated generously to the local parish in Petrolia. As his wealth increased he became directly involved in local banking and finance. He was vice-president of the Crown Savings and Loan Company, based in Petrolia, and a director of the London and Western Trust Company. By the time of the 1905 election he had also become a director of the Bank of Toronto. The sources of his wealth and his financial connections differed from those of the Liberal Methodists and Presbyterians of the Toronto financial establishment, a fact which made him attractive to the new premier.

Whitney was himself an Anglican who respected Englehart's success and his cultivation of Conservative political loyalties. When the provincial premier re-formed the administration of the University of Toronto in 1906, he appointed Englehart to its first Board of Governors.

A self-made entrepreneur, a man of wealth and political influence in southern Ontario, Englehart agreed to become a member of the Commission in 1905. Hanna, Frank Cochrane and Whitney persuaded him to become chairman in 1906. For the next thirteen years, from the age of 58 to 72, while he continued as a vice-president and director of Imperial Oil, Englehart ran the T&NO from its Toronto office. Since the railway lacked a general manager, and would in fact operate without one until the 1930s, Englehart kept in constant touch with the various divisional officers operating out of North Bay. Gradually he established himself as a conscientious but eccentric figure, known to the people in the North for his remote and formal manner, his European style of dress, his goatee and his *pince-nez* glasses. He travelled into the northeast two or three times a year in his private railway car, which might be stationed on a siding anywhere between North Bay and Cochrane. It was said with some truth that he gave away most of his chairman's salary of $5,000 a year.

Behind this image of polished eccentricity, Englehart was pre-eminently a conventional self-made financier from the south of the province, directing the railway from Toronto and corresponding almost daily with the Conservative government at Queen's Park. His letters indicate a detailed attention to every aspect of running the government-owned railway. Officials in the North were carefully instructed to send copies of their reports to the Provincial Secretary, a practice based first on Englehart's friendship with Hanna, but also on his firm and simple conviction that all employees were servants of a particular government agency, the purpose and function of which was to open the northern frontier to capitalists like himself, or to earnest, responsible and industrious farmers and labourers. In time he became a paternal figure with a town named after him, to whom editors of northern newspapers would express their gratitude in front-page headlines.

The Men Who Laboured

With the issue of the chairman resolved, the construction of the T&NO continued to progress, first towards the Height of Land, and then towards the junction with the National Transcontinental at the place eventually to be called Cochrane. On the way, other townsites were founded and named, such names generally replacing older local names with those of Conservative politicians.

The Commission decided on the names, always with approval from the cabinet. Driftwood City became Monteith after the Minister of Agriculture; McDougall's Chute became Matheson after the Provincial Treasurer in the Whitney government; and Mile 138, twenty-five miles north of New Liskeard, developed into the small town of Englehart. From there southward the railway was in full operation by the end of 1906. North of Englehart the Macdonell contract had to be extended to the end of November 1907, partly because of labour problems and partly because of unexpected clay slides and sink holes.

Like most railways in the nineteenth century, the T&NO was built by immigrant and casual labour. The men on construction gangs were generally unskilled European immigrants who arrived in Canada at the port of Montréal. They were induced northward by the agents of railway contractors. The pay was low, about $1.00 a day with deductions for food and accommodation, even though the men often lived in box cars on sidings. Law required the contractor to deduct 50¢ a month from each man to cover the expenses of a doctor and a makeshift hospital. Few men died from accidents, although some workers succumbed each year to diseases such as typhoid fever caused by drinking contaminated water. The men who performed hard physical labour – laying ties and tracks, hauling rocks from dynamite blasts, digging gravel and slag for the ballast or bed of the road – came almost entirely from Scandinavia and southeastern Europe.

Sometimes they drank heavily, often obtaining liquor from illegal pedlars before hotels or bars were built. Englehart complained of the drinking and opposed the granting of licences anywhere near the construction gangs. Writing to Hanna in 1908, he said:

> I come to you, Dear Mr. Secretary, to help me out, want it very badly.
> So much depends upon retaining Finns, Swedes so as to complete
> and lay rails, at least to junction of Transcontinental before snow....
> The illicit liquor business is giving no end of trouble at Matheson....
> Finns and Swedes...get to drinking, throw up contracts, and go out.

A few years later he judged that the problem was worse. Licences for the sale of liquor were granted in every small settlement, largely through personal political appeals to Frank Cochrane. The shipments of whiskey over the railway had increased, said Englehart, "until it almost passeth understanding what becomes of the very large importation of liquors in the lands of the North. The Blind Piggers surely have a harvest."[7]

The nature of the work and a lack of genuine community partly explain this heavy drinking. It stemmed also from a well-founded sense of isolation. Settlers and residents, whether on the farms or in the small close-knit towns, remembered these gangs of construction workers as strange beings from unknown countries. If a settler could earn $1.00 a day cutting wood, or $4.00 with a team; if a fireman on a locomotive could earn $1.55 for a twelve-hour day, then these "dagos" must work for less. And so they did. They were also more compliant and did not make "extreme demands," according to the contractors and construction managers of the T&NO. The *Annual Report* of the Commission for 1908 pointed out that the construction gangs were composed for the most part of men from Italy, Sweden, Finland, Poland and Bulgaria, with some also from Russia, Greece and Turkey. Swarthy skin, rough dress, and a strange variety of languages were not easily assimilated into the northern towns, where most settlers prided themselves on their English or Scottish backgrounds.

Together with the Irish, the English and Scots made up the majority of immigrants coming into Ontario at the time. They had a sense of owning the country, of controlling its development. Even in hiring men for construction, and gradually for operation of the railway, a policy of discrimination recognized this attitude, since it became a rule on the T&NO that "Canadians and natives of the British Isles...occupied clerical and lighter positions on construction work." The term "Canadian" in this context generally referred to people of English and Scottish descent. British connections and the English language were signs of belonging, of having roots that counted, of carrying on traditions inherited from Canada's status within the British Empire.

Before World War I there was little appreciation in the North of Canada's multicultural heritage. The Italians, the Poles, and the Greeks were "foreigners"; the derogatory term "dago" implied that they were of inferior status. Prejudice of this kind was unlikely to create a stable atmosphere among men toiling for low pay in the midst of a mining boom. Englishmen and Scotsmen refused the heavy work of construction. They were not drawn to the dangerous picking, shovelling, chiselling, and dynamiting necessary to a new mine, especially without adequate safety regulations. Little hydraulic equipment was available, either for mining or for railroad construction. Inevitably, the developing mines competed with the railway contractors for non-British immigrant labour.

To entice labouring men from Toronto or Montréal, contractors advanced them their railway fares and deducted the amount from their pay in instalments. But as the railway moved farther north and alternative employment became available, the men remained on construction crews for only a short time, then accepted work in mines, sawmills, or timbering operations before they were out of debt to the contractor. The *Annual Report* of the Commission for 1907 revealed that:

> ...contractors in the North have lost thousands of dollars by their failure to hold men that were brought in....Men were openly hired off railway work to go to the mines. The management of all the mining properties paid more for ordinary labor than any railway contractor could afford. They thus got the pick of all the men brought upon railway work.

In addition, labour became restless when Local 146 of the Western Federation of Miners moved in to organize the Cobalt miners after 1906. Swedes – skilled labourers at blasting and clearing rock cuts – were most in demand. They were also fewer in number than the Italians, who made up the majority of general labourers.[8]

In addition to the problem of acquiring and holding men as steady construction workers, the work itself offered sheer physical challenges in the mounting of steel and wooden trestles, of banking against land slides or draining out sink holes. These were the hazards of the Clay Belt. Two crossings north of New Liskeard, at Miles 25 and 33, required expensive steel viaducts over the Blanche River. Both were made by the Dominion Bridge Company in Montréal. North of these bridges were a number of temporary wooden trestles, timber for which had to be brought in from the south. Obtaining such materials and putting them in place often caused delay. While they waited, construction crews were put to work rebuilding the banks of cuttings where the clay was so loose and wet that it flowed over the ends of culverts, blocking streams or channels and requiring timbered embankment and additional labour. The contractor often faced unexpected extra costs.

Building to Cochrane

Despite all difficulties, the Commission was operating trains from North Bay to Englehart by the end of 1906. While construction continued northward again, two branch lines and a spur line were added: one branch line from Cobalt west into the Kerr Lake mining district, another from Englehart to Charlton. The spur line went to the wharf at Haileybury, enabling the railway to carry logs from Lake Timiskaming to the saw mill of the Empire Lumber Company at Latchford. The total distance of these three lines was just under fifteen miles. As far as possible, the Commission awarded the contracts to local companies.

The spur and branch lines stimulated revenue.[9] By 1906 it was becoming evident after only three years of construction and two years of operations, that the railway was fulfilling its promise as a development road – opening new land to settlement, uncovering mineral resources, transporting timber, and showing a small profit as a sound business enterprise.

Construction delays continued through 1907. As late as May 28, nine inches of snow fell at Englehart, and frost stayed in the ground until June. Through July, August and September rain fell so heavily that streams held their spring levels all summer and swamps sustained high levels of water. Unexpected complications came not from rocks and curves but from masses of mud which slowed construction. Yet in 1907 the first tenders were let for construction of the final forty miles to junction with the National Transcontinental at Cochrane.

For two years, since the summer of 1905, this extension had appealed to the Whitney government as a means of augmenting the business of the T&NO, and of strengthening the premier's arguments for a federal railroad subsidy. The provincial cabinet passed an Order-in-Council on July 10, 1905, stating that the railway from North Bay to junction with the Grand Trunk Pacific would cost a

35

total of $10,000,000, adding that "the whole of this line is a work of national and not merely provincial utility connecting the Grand Trunk Railway and the Canadian Pacific Railway at North Bay with the great Transcontinental Railway now proposed to be built." Efforts to obtain the federal subsidy of $12,000 per mile were continued when the chairman of the T&NO Commission met with his counterpart for the National Transcontinental in January 1906.

Tension between the two officials is evident in their ensuing correspondence. The chairman of the T&NO sought support from his opposite number for a federal subsidy. It was his understanding, he said, "that in carrying out this construction you would be glad to have the hearty co-operation of this Commission, particularly as regards our pushing forward the construction of our road beyond the point to which our present contracts reach." The Secretary of the National Transcontinental rejected the inference placed upon the word "co-operation."

> We did not...request your co-operation particularly as regards your pushing forward the extension of your road....That portion of our railway which is designed to open for settlement a large and fertile section of Ontario will be constructed whether or not you decide in the interests of the Province of Ontario, to extend your road to a junction with ours.

At a higher political level, Premier Whitney continued the efforts of his Liberal predecessor to obtain a subsidy from the federal government. Laurier resisted on two grounds. The T&NO was a completed and revenue-producing railway; it had no need of financial aid for construction. And it was provincially owned, placing its operation in a different category from private railway companies. A subsidy would add unnecessarily to the existing federal grant of $2,500,000 annually, which was given to Ontario on a basis of $1.00 per head of population.

Circumstances changed in Ottawa with the defeat of the Liberal Laurier government in 1911. Conservative Prime Minister Robert Borden appointed Frank Cochrane as the new federal Minister of Railways. From Toronto, Whitney repeatedly pressed Cochrane to arrange a handsome railway subsidy and Cochrane introduced it into his estimates for 1912. The item was debated at some length in the federal parliament, finally passing both House and Senate in 1913. The amount of $2,000,000 was granted that year to the provincial government of Ontario, with payment into the Consolidated Revenue Fund. The subsidy therefore never appeared in the revenue of the T&NO Commission.[10]

Despite political influence, there could be no doubt of the advantage to the builders of the National Transcontinental. Having the T&NO Railway extended to a junction at Cochrane would enable supplies to be brought in directly from centres as far south as Toronto. Nor was there any question that the provincial railway would be completed to that point. The contract was let in February 1907 to McRae, Chandler & McNeil. Work commenced that summer, although it was not until the following spring in 1908 that they knew the townsite of Cochrane would be the specific point of junction.

During this phase of construction, controversy continued in Toronto over the policies and management of the Commission. In the newspapers, editorial opinion differed over the effectiveness of the new Commission to maintain an efficient model for public ownership. The *Globe* frequently expressed the apprehension of Liberals over the future of the railway. In June 1906 its editor stated: "Now is the time to prevent the stigma of failure from being affixed to the Temiskaming Railway by inexpert management, or narrow-minded statesmanship." Englehart found these words "impertinent, an outrage on common decency." They hurt him especially because he had talked with the editor for well over an hour "in the quiet stillness of the night at New Liskeard up and down the platform."

Other papers expressed more sympathy. The Toronto *News* under the editorial direction of John Willison, the most prominent newspaper editor in Canada, expressed satisfaction at the extent to which the Commission was already influencing northern development. Willison moved from a Liberal to an independent editorial position, which enabled him to support the Whitney government more openly, accepting as the cabinet did a ready association with public ownership. Both Liberals and Conservatives were now of the same mind on this question. They differed only over methods, a situation apparent in another *Globe* editorial of November 1907, which criticized Englehart again for the short mileage constructed since the election of 1905:

> The delay and neglect are most unfortunate....Governmental railway construction is on its trial as an experiment, and this failure by the Commission will discourage those who hope slowly to release the railed highways from private control. If the Government cannot appoint a Commission free and able to see that the work is carried out, there will be no likelihood of an extension of publicly-owned railways.[11]

Meanwhile, construction of the additional forty miles to Cochrane ran into difficulties when the small local contractor, McRae, Chandler & McNeil, proved unable to meet deadlines. Shortage of capital made it impossible for them to pay their men. Accordingly, the Commission compensated the contractor for work accomplished, then once again assumed completion of the line, appointing a superintendent of construction and setting up construction headquarters at Mile 218, also called Driftwood City. That meant the railway had reached 218 miles north of North Bay at the beginning of 1908, eighty-two miles north of Englehart. A roundhouse and repair sheds for locomotives were built at both Englehart and North Bay by the Forest City Paving Company of London, Ontario, the town where Jacob Englehart had his strongest political connections.

All through the late winter and spring of 1907-8, supplies were brought forward by teams and sleighs over snow-covered paths. By June 1908, when the tracks had been laid as far as Driftwood River, the Canada Foundry Company began erection of the steel bridge which took a month to complete. Then from July to November of 1908, construction crews worked at a steady pace north from the bridge, arriving at the Cochrane "Y" before the end of the year. The "Y" enabled engines to be turned around for the trip south. Further levels of gravel ballasting had yet to be added before the locomotives could be permitted to travel at more than moderate speeds, but for practical purposes the T&NO was completed for service as far as Cochrane by the spring and summer of 1909.

It was none too soon, since the National Transcontinental urgently required supplies. The contractor building westward had already awarded a contract to John McChesney, the store-keeper at Matheson, to build a road through the bush and to supply rails by wagon and horse-team, rather than haul heavy, bulky supplies from Québec City. The enterprise and profit of McChesney lasted only one season before being displaced by the T&NO, but it illustrated the important and mutually profitable connection which could develop between the T&NO and the National Transcontinental.[12]

With completion of the provincial railway to Cochrane, total mileage had reached 270, including Division 1 from North Bay to Englehart (139 miles), Division 2 from Englehart to Cochrane (113 miles), and the branch lines to Kerr Lake, Charlton, and the Haileybury wharf, plus another seventy miles of sidings. After 1905, the Commission also made annual payments to the Provincial Treasurer as direct returns on the original investment, which stood at more than $15,000,000 by the time the railway and facilities had been completed to Cochrane.

Financing by Conservatives

By then, too, a series of amending acts had been passed to clarify the responsibilities and the means by which the provincial government would fulfill the financing of the new railway system. Some nine months after being elected in 1905, Premier Whitney sent to London his Provincial Treasurer, A. J. Matheson, to renew the Treasury Bills originally negotiated by the Liberal government of George Ross. If possible, Whitney wished to transform these notes into a long-term loan. The partisan character of business in the higher affairs of the T&NO Commission became obvious in Matheson's deliberate slighting of the English banks, Glyn Mills, and Coates and Company, who had arranged the original loan.

Matheson went directly to Lord Strathcona who, as Donald Smith – his untitled name – had accumulated an immense fortune through the CPR and the Bank of Montréal, and who held the post of Canadian High Commissioner in London in 1905. Strathcona, then eighty-five, continued to be alert and active, still able to sustain his financial contacts in the City of London and to command the respect of Matheson, the small-town lawyer who had grown up in eastern Ontario. Matheson clearly preferred the self-made Scot from Canada to the managers of the English commercial banks. He renewed the Treasury Bills through the Bank of Montréal, pleased and confident that the terms were as favourable as those being granted to the Dominion or even to the Imperial governments.[13]

Subsequently the Whitney government removed dependence of the Commission on bank loans and debentures, and made it possible instead for the T&NO to draw on the Consolidated Revenue Fund of the province. In 1907 an Act of consolidation which synthesized and repealed all previous legislation, established a separate account in the Treasury Department, called "The Temiskaming and Northern Ontario Railway Account." All previous loans were now centralized in this one account, to which the Lieutenant Governor in Council – namely the cabinet – could advance money from the Consolidated Revenue Fund. It followed that "all expenditures on account of construction...shall be charged against the said account." The purpose of this legislation was to stabilize and secure the financing of the railway. It committed the Whitney government to a large public liability, more clearly defining responsibility for public ownership. The Act of 1907 also gave the premier flexible powers over the railway system.[14]

Controversy over these powers lay in the future. It seemed more important in those promising years, when Ontario was just embarking on the development of its mineral resources as the industrial heartland of Canada, that the unique venture of a provincial railway to the North had so far proved to be a sound commercial enterprise. The project had taken three years from conception to the letting of the first contract; six years – from 1903 to 1909 – to build; with improvements and extensions still to come in the future.

So far, the richest of the mineral finds were at Cobalt, where mines such as the Nipissing, the McKinley-Darragh, and the La Rose were becoming major producers of silver, shipping ore southward on the cars of the T&NO. Their wealth stimulated the probings of prospectors and the dealings of brokers who backed them or who bought out their claims. From these exciting and continuing explorations came the discovery of gold in the Porcupine, which opened a whole new chapter in the historical development of the T&NO Railway.

CHAPTER 5

The People's Railway

Extremes of Wealth

By 1910 the T&NO employed 1,472 workers on a payroll of almost $630,000. Assuming three to four dependents for each worker, the railway supported close to 6,000 persons, nearly 20 per cent of the population in the entire north-east of the province. In addition, sub-contractors were still working to complete the roadbed to Cochrane. Some of them were young men, eager for work and ready for challenges.

Frank Herron, a resident of New Liskeard, freighted with a team of four horses on construction of the railway in 1903, at the age of 18. The lake boat, the *Meteor*, transported the horses up Lake Timiskaming to Haileybury. Since the town lacked a wharf, the animals were led from the boat and struggled through the water to shore. Herron also recalled two brothers who laboured at building trestles and bridges between New Liskeard and Cochrane. In such ways the railway not only opened the country but provided jobs and opportunities to young men who otherwise would have been confined to the South or induced to go West.

The railway also affected the lives of people in direct and personal ways. Mrs. Herron, for example, remembered her mother's death at New Liskeard in 1905. Hers was the first corpse removed from the North by train, returning southward for burial to her home town of Brantford. And Mrs. George Booth, a pioneer resident at Matheson, could recall how it was in the early days when

> We used to get groceries from Eaton's, even coal oil if we ordered it and big orders from Grills in New Liskeard and it all used to come up on the way freight. We kept the post office at Watabeag for thirty-five years and our mail came in on No. 47 three times a week. It was a catch post service and the mail clerk kicked or threw our bags of mail off. [From the railway siding at Watabeag]. . . the settlers shipped out their baled hay and pulpwood.

Accidents stayed in people's memories. Jim Foster of New Liskeard recalled what could happen to boys anxious to earn money in the building of the railway. A local farmer with a good stand of tamarack could sell the wood for ties once the trees were cut. One of these local farmers was a Mr. Brittain, who,

...wanted to hire some men, to cut the trees down to make ties. Wesley Bass was thirteen years old and his brother was eleven. They were going to start on Monday morning to cut, and when they started to cut – they just cut down one tree – and Wes' axe flew and cut Lew in the throat.

He had to be hauled by Mr. Brittain in three hours to New Liskeard in 40 below zero in the cutter, and five stitches put in there to tie his neck up. And he would ha' been dead if it had been a warm day, but the cold stopped it from bleeding....So they never cut any more timber.

Good timber was also needed for the construction of trestles and bridges, which were not always able to withstand the weight of the locomotive and its cars. A near tragedy occurred, for instance, in 1909, just out of New Liskeard. The boy who watched never forgot the event:

So, they built the bridge and a few years later the train was going over there, and they always went over very slow – just let it glide over.

The bridge collapsed – the half of it, and went down, on the north half. And most of the train fell right in the river and the engine stayed on the end of the broken bridge, swaying there in the wind, and the two men got out and ran along the bridge and got off.

And quite a while later they come up [with another engine] and they had quite a job to get anybody willing enough to go out there and fasten a cable onto the engine, it hanging out there on the bridge. Because it was even off the tracks, just sittin' there on the rails. Finally one man was brave enough to go out and hook it on. And they pulled it slowly and it came crashin' and crunchin' and cutting the ties, and they finally got the engine off the bridge.[1]

Some time passed before the bridge was replaced with a steel structure. Meanwhile, tracks were laid down the banks of the Wabi River, across a culvert and up the other side.

Even on level ground engineers were forbidden to travel at speeds in excess of twenty-four miles per hour. If they travelled faster, demerit marks could be given for speeding, as well as for sideswiping or faulty coupling. A total of sixty demerit marks meant dismissal, but engineers wanted their jobs too badly to pile up such dangerous penalties. For one thing, the pay was good. Enginemen on the T&NO earned $1,050 to $1,100 before World War I, a figure more than double the annual pay of firemen and brakemen who worked on the same locomotives. A Member of Parliament received only $1,000 a year.

Like the railway itself, the engineer merged into the growing northern community. He developed an identity with the steam locomotive. Each had its own number. By 1907, fourteen of them were in operation, most of the 4-6-0 wheel arrangement. Eight were manufactured specifically for the T&NO by the Canadian Locomotive Company in Kingston; four by the Montréal Locomotive Works, and two were bought second-hand from the Pittsburgh and Lake Erie Railway. Between 1907 and 1909 another eighteen engines were added, twelve of them manufactured in Kingston, six in Montréal.[2]

The trip from North Bay to Englehart took at least twelve hours, with a five-hour rest for the engineer before starting back. Stops on the way included individual farms to make deliveries or to pick up children for school, or to fill boilers at sidings from the silo-like water tanks holding 40,000 gallons each, built by O'Boyle Brothers of Sault Ste. Marie.

In addition to the way freight and the cheap coaches, to the cars weighted with ore, to the flat cars piled high with pulpwood and timber, the "Cobalt Special" came into service in March of 1907. It left Toronto each evening at 9:00 p.m. and arrived in Cobalt at 8:45 the next morning. By arrangement between the Grand Trunk Railway and the T&NO, this overnight train constituted a vital link from Toronto to North Bay and then to Cobalt. With its Pullman cars, its library car, and its luxurious dining facilities, the "Cobalt Special" provided comfortable accommodation for the businessmen, the brokers, engineers and entrepreneurs who financed the silver mines from offices in New York, Chicago, Montréal, Buffalo and Toronto. American money flowed in and ore was freighted out to American refineries. But the engines steaming and whistling through the winter nights were Canadian, as was most of the equipment, and a small boy standing near the station at Orillia recorded the scene as part of his growing up in Ontario. Stephen Leacock wrote in his *Sunshine Sketches*:

> On a winter evening...you will see the long row of the Pullmans and diners of the night express going north to the mining country, the windows flashing with brilliant light, and within them a vista of cut glass and snow-white table linen, smiling negroes and millionaires with napkins at their chins whirling past in the driving snowstorm.[3]

Leacock's term "millionaire" was accurate. On April 9, 1909 the Cobalt *Daily Nugget* printed a list of thirty-five millionaires whose fortunes had been made in the silver mines of Cobalt. The names were extracted from a booklet entitled *Facts about Cobalt* published in Boston that same year. Surprisingly few of these men came from Boston or New York. Some were listed from Buffalo and Rochester. Others resided in Montréal, Cornwall and St. Catharines. From Toronto appeared the names of mining engineers, geologists, lawyers and brokers.

At least twelve of these newly rich men resided in Haileybury or New Liskeard. Included were Angus McKelvie and Thomas McCamus whose partnership had begun in the 1890s with a sawmill at the mouth of the Wabi River. McKelvie had been among the first in the New Liskeard settlement to lobby in Toronto for the building of the railway north of Lake Timiskaming. He and McCamus now owned a silver mine which yielded six million ounces of silver before the end of World War I. W. B. Russel, the first chief engineer of the T&NO, who resigned in May 1905, became one of the early directors of the large and productive Nipissing Mine. The mine, backed initially by a New York investment banker, later came under the control of the International Nickel Company. Russel's good friend, F.R. Latchford, the former Commissioner of Public Works, dabbled in the Hunter-Cobalt Mine, and recalled some years later how he had included in the T&NO Act of 1902 the words: "there are...deposits of ores and minerals which are expected upon development to add greatly to the wealth of the province."[4]

When non-resident millionaires visited Cobalt, many of them stayed at the Matabanick Hotel in Haileybury. Its owner and manager, Arthur Ferland, also part-owner of a silver mine, was listed among the millionaires. His dining room glowed like a warm, expansive dining car with white linen and china, glassware and silverware glittering against the finely sanded floors, walls and ceiling fashioned from the lumber of local sawmills. The Matabanick symbolized the opening of the North. Men of wealth ate, drank, and slept in its comfort, as though they were enjoying only a vigorous change of scene from the amenities of the King Edward in Toronto or the Ritz in Montréal. While the talk of business may have been more concentrated and specialized, it took place over tables well appointed with food and wine.[5] Supplies and clientele both arrived on the T&NO; no other road or vehicle existed. And beyond the hotel, for those wealthy men who lived in the area, new and spacious houses were rising along the shore of Lake Timiskaming, a virtual "millionaire's row" only a few miles distant from the source of all this shining fortune, the "poor man's camp" at Cobalt.

On Cobalt's rocky and barren townsite, the rust-coloured tin and wooden sheds and the ugly boilers and pipes at the pit-heads added to the shabbiness of the dirt paths which served as streets. Rows of little box-like stores and cheap frame houses spread out from the solid stone railway station. With its long platform and gabled roof the station seemed to be the real centre of the town. Among the shacks and houses were the "blind pigs" or illegal bars, and the "cathouses," the town's brothels. Because so little room was available for building on a site hemmed in by the lake on one side and projections of rock on the other, many mine-workers and their families lived in Latchford to the south or in Haileybury or New Liskeard to the east and north. According to law, liquor sales were forbidden within five miles of a mining camp, so that miners were also induced to the thriving bars and smaller hotels of Haileybury. In all that concerned the work and leisure of its people, Cobalt depended upon transportation provided by the T&NO, a fact that became the substance of reporting and editorials in the Cobalt *Daily Nugget* through the summer of 1909.

Newspaper Criticism

The editor of the newspaper assumed the role of spokesman for the interests of the people, whether they resided in Cobalt itself or in the tri-town area of Cobalt, Haileybury, and New Liskeard. He concentrated on two grievances. The first concerned the unilateral control of the T&NO Commission over the sale of town lots. As early as 1904 the rights of the Commission to grant town sites needed clarification. The legislative amendments of that year included the statement that the Lieutenant-Governor may:

from time to time...transfer to the Commission for town sites portions of the ungranted lands of Ontario along the line of railway
adjacent to stations...and the Commission may for the same purpose
acquire other lands so situate by the same means as it is authorized to
acquire lands for right of way...which lands acquired for town sites
shall not, however, exceed one thousand acres for any one site.[6]

Payment for these lands was deemed to be "payment for works necessary to
the preservation, improvement and maintenance of the said railway..." Four
years later the amount of land held by the Commission, and the policy of holding land near expanding towns until its value increased, required the functions
of a Land Agent to negotiate land sales. Whitney, Cochrane, and Englehart considered this function significant enough to be handled by a member of the
Commission, rather than by a member of the staff. Frederick Dane, appointed
to the Commission in 1906, became the first Land Agent in 1908.[7] In the view
of the *Daily Nugget*, his work seemed to be carried out more in collusion with
the mining companies than in the interests of the miners and residents.

The second grievance, closely related to the first, involved the revenue of the
railway and the annual payments being made to the Treasurer of Ontario. This
financial success was contrasted with the necessity for mine-workers to settle
outside of Cobalt, because of the railway's control over the land. For many, it
then became impossible to walk from their home to their work. According to
the *Daily Nugget*, the railway had been built by the government as a utility, it
was protected as a monopoly, it was helping to acquire fortunes for businessmen from the South. It should therefore be required to meet the needs of local
people for efficient and cheap transportation. Yet the passenger cars were so
congested that conductors could not push through to collect tickets; service
was not integrated with hours of work; and stations and platforms were badly
overcrowded.

A series of critical editorials appeared in the *Daily Nugget* on June 23, 24 and
25, 1909, all under the title "The People's Railway not for the People." They
complained of the overcrowding, and argued the need for better service. The
editor concluded that "the people of this part of the country are being bled for
the sake of financial statements at the end of the year." While the railroad
helped make new fortunes for businessmen and remitted substantial payments
to the Treasurer of Ontario:

> The transportation facilities are so limited that the first-class coaches
> in which women and children are accustomed to ride are made worse
> than the lawless bar-rooms through their herding of...drunken per-
> sonages in these coaches. If the T.& N.O. desire to be called "the
> people's railway" they should put on more local trains, and at least
> treat the silver belt as well as a private corporation would.

The charges were elaborated in following editorials. In an open letter to Premier Whitney on September 3, 1909, the *Daily Nugget* stated that the T&NO

was charging "the highest freight rates on the continent," and on behalf of the average resident the paper claimed that "every 20,000 people in New Ontario means added prosperity to the Dominion because practically everything we need is manufactured in Old Ontario or in other provinces." The editor went on to ask:

> Man to man, is it square dealing to bring these new settlers into this new country and then rob them of a few cents on every barrel of flour, every article of furniture, every piece of clothing they or their families need by means of surcharges on freight or express parcels?

> We are just as good Canadians as the people of the eastern section of the Dominion, and are just as entitled to your protection. If it was a private railroad corporation that was overcharging, we would have redress before the tribunal appointed for that purpose. But in the case of your railroad we have no redress except to your sense of justice.

> We call it "your railroad" and advisedly so. We once had the delusion when we were bringing settlers into this new country that it was a people's railroad, but we have gotten bravely over this misapprehension.

A Canadian populist tone emerged in editorials and open letters of this kind. They were not written, as American editorials might have been, to advocate turning the railway over to private interests. The writer did not imply that the T&NO could be managed more economically and more in accord with the interests of the people if it became a private company. As a provincial government railway its freight rates could not be appealed to the Board of Railway Commissioners in Ottawa, as could those of federally chartered lines. But the writer expressed a widespread, underlying confidence that the premier and the government would listen sympathetically to complaints and dissatisfactions expressed through the columns of the small-town newspapers.

Workers and their families felt these criticisms to be fundamental. Grievances were shared by the large community from Latchford in the south, through Cobalt, Haileybury, and New Liskeard. Populist in the sense of opposition to the apparent élitist leadership and exploitation by the South, the editor borrowed some of the terminology of western progressive newspapers when he referred to the protected privileges of "the eastern section of the Dominion." But behind the borrowed phrases lay a sincere and deeply felt resentment in the North against the financial control of the South.

Some eighteen months before these editorials, a protest meeting at Cobalt, reported as "the largest public meeting" ever held there, endorsed a motion that Northern Ontario become a separate province of the Dominion. Held in the "Opera House," the meeting was chaired by Mayor Lang. One of the most forceful speakers was the president of the Cobalt Miners' Union, a man convinced of the exploitation of New Ontario by businessmen to the south. Others questioned expenditures and direction by the remote commissioners of the T&NO while workers at Cobalt were forced to pile carloads of freight in the snow and rain at the side of the tracks because no freight sheds had been built. The railway provided a focal point for grievances against the hold of the impersonal financial tentacles of imperial Toronto into the northern economy.[8]

Nipissing Central Railway

This concern with monopoly, with inadequate response to real and evident needs of local people, found further expression when a delegation from Haileybury waited on Premier Whitney and some members of his cabinet in October 1909. They advanced the interests of a proposed electric railway to compete for traffic along the northwest shore of Lake Timiskaming. The company, named the Nipissing Central Railway, held a charter granted in 1907 by the federal government of Sir Wilfrid Laurier. J. L. Englehart, chairman of the T&NO Commission, attended the cabinet meeting and opposed the deputation. The Nipissing Central Railway, he said, "is intended for a great deal more than railway accommodation for Haileybury, Liskeard, and Cobalt. It is simply the entering of the wedge. We are entitled to the trade of the north country."[9] His emphatic rejection was based on the conviction that the provincial government, having spent millions of dollars on the T&NO steam railway over the previous five years, had opened up and transformed the north country. Competition now could only hurt the return on its investment.

Whatever the roots of criticism in the North, Englehart had substantial grounds for the position he adopted. In 1906 the Whitney government had arranged a forty-year loan of $6,000,000 with the Bank of Montréal to redeem the Treasury Bills that came due that year. In 1907 the same government had eliminated the land grant of 20,000 acres to the mile, since it had itself assumed the obligation of paying the costs of the line. The Whitney government was therefore even more directly involved in underwriting and managing the T&NO than the Liberal government of George Ross.[10]

The attitude of the provincial government toward public ownership of the northern railway pointed to later assumptions behind the development of the Ontario Hydro-Electric Power Commission. Large outlays of public money can contribute to greater efficiency and maintain political loyalties, but the monopoly has to be protected. Monopoly and service to thriving business interests lie at the heart of public ownership.

Most historians of Canada and particularly of Ontario agree that the Conservative government of James Whitney from 1905 to 1914 was "progressive" in its concern with the growing urban population of the province. From this focus grew a willingness to develop utilities and resources under public ownership, even when that policy met opposition from some of the wealthiest men in the financial community of Toronto.[11]

In order to avoid accusations of debt-ridden socialist policies, the government had to reconcile financial solvency with its obligation to serve the growing urban centres of the North. At the same time, it had to persuade men in commerce and industry that government participation in resource development would ad-

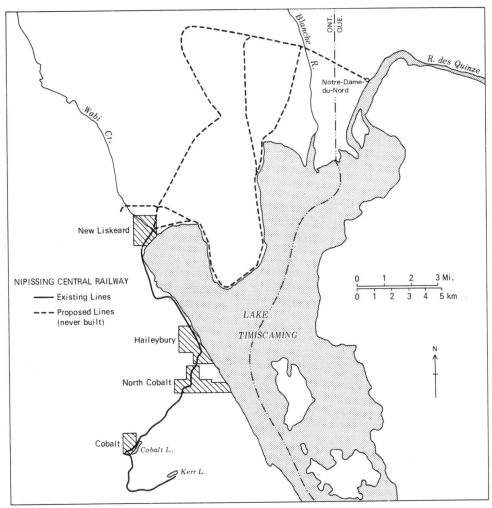

Nipissing Central Railway

Chartered originally to haul resources as well as people, using the hydro-electricity of northern rivers, the NCR was in fact confined to passenger traffic between Kerr Lake and the tri-town area of Cobalt, Haileybury, and New Liskeard.

vance their personal financial interests. The tensions involved in maintaining this balance were illustrated by relations between the T&NO and the Nipissing Central Railway through 1908 to 1911.

The original federal charter incorporating the Nipissing Central had been granted in 1907 to a group of private businessmen, including F.R. Latchford, former Minister of Public Works in the Liberal government of George Ross. The foremost promoter behind the charter was M.J. O'Brien, another Liberal supporter whose timber and mineral interests in the North were making him one of the very wealthy men in the country.

The plans of this original board of directors were ambitious. They intended to draw upon two seemingly unique opportunities – the expansion of radial electric lines in most North American cities, and the potential for cheap electric power from the rapids and falls of northern rivers. A series of interconnecting rail lines beginning at the town of Latchford would extend north through New Liskeard, eastward into Québec around the northern shores of Lake Timiskaming, then north again to the National Transcontinental Railway, with other similar lines on the Ontario side of the provincial boundary. When completed, its promoters expected that the system would provide cheaper, more regular, and more lucrative transportation throughout the entire frontier region in northeastern Ontario and northwestern Québec. With these grandiose aims in mind, the original company was capitalized at $3,000,000.

Local criticism of the provincial steam railway prompted municipal officials in Haileybury and Cobalt to sell a franchise for an electric line to the Nipissing Central Railway in 1909. Construction began that year, with the five-mile line from Cobalt to Haileybury completed in the spring of 1910. Partly responsible for this local support of the radial electric line was the anticipation of cheap power from the High Falls Power Company; another was the opportunity in the new company for local representation, an opportunity still denied by the Commission of the T&NO.

The company provided a thirty-minute service between Cobalt and Haileybury from six in the morning to eleven at night. Miners crowded its trolley-cars for the morning and evening shifts. At other times during the day, the cars carried only shoppers, visitors, and those bound for drinks at one of the four hotels in Haileybury.

The company could not succeed with such limited revenue. Fares were only ten cents and passengers did not provide sufficient revenue for solvency or expansion. The original scheme proved overly ambitious. Minerals and timber were there, but neither the investment nor the population could support an extensive network of communication; certainly not in competition with the T&NO and its various spur lines. Faced with these financial difficulties, its board sold out to a Toronto group led by lawyer Alex Fasken. In June 1911, J.L. Englehart purchased the line from this group for the T&NO at a price of $250,000.

Absorption of the Nipissing Central Railway with no change in the management or composition of the T&NO Commission spelled defeat for northern populist arguments. Monopoly and Toronto control had been sustained. The Cobalt *Daily Nugget* fruitlessly continued its campaign for northern representation and cheaper freight rates. But the merger of the two lines did make possible more regular passenger traffic at nominal fares, and after extension of the radial line to New Liskeard in 1912 the tri-town area was serviced as a community. By 1913 six double-end radial cars were carrying over 1,000,000 passengers a year. The Commission then electrified the branch line from Cobalt west to Kerr Lake in 1914, combining passenger traffic with freight on a van and two flat cars.[12]

The extensive plans of the Nipissing Central Railway ended there. Nothing came of the proposal to expand across the Québec border, although the T&NO

later used the interprovincial charter of the NCR to extend its tracks from Swastika through Kirkland Lake to Rouyn and the mines of Noranda. In 1917 the car-barns burned at North Cobalt, and while the equipment was partially replaced, the decline in silver mining and the advent of the automobile prevented any return to the profitable peaks of 1915 and 1916.

Cars continued to run along the tracks from the foot of Argentite Street in Cobalt to King Street, Lakeview Avenue and Main Street in North Cobalt; then to Georgina Avenue in Haileybury, eastward on Blackwell Avenue, up Ferguson to Browning Avenue and finally north on Armstrong Street to the terminal on the Wabi River. But the steady loss of passenger traffic after World War I resulted in a series of annual deficits, increasing with the depression of the 1930s, until the service had to be terminated in 1935. Removal of the tracks ended a quarter century of radial railway service in the tri-town area at the head of Lake Timiskaming.

CHAPTER 6

Gold and Fire

Gold in the Porcupine

Gold in the Porcupine area had been suspected for some years. Reports from the Ontario Bureau of Mines in 1896 and in 1899 had indicated that the region was a promising one for the prospector. Between 1905 and 1909 numbers of claims were staked on the islands and shores of Night Hawk Lake. While they never developed into productive mines, more prospectors arrived as word spread southward that gold in profitable quantity might be found in the vicinity.

In 1909 the Chicago promoter, W.S. Edwards, sent a small party of eight men north on the T&NO. They left the train at the present site of Monteith and headed westward with equipment and food to last several months, exploring in the region of Porcupine Lake. At that point they divided into smaller groups. On one of these lighter expeditions a man named Harry Preston slipped down a slight incline and dug in his heels, stripping the moss covering from a vein showing flecks of gold. Preston traced the vein to a large mound. Scratching the moss away, he discovered a dome "all covered with gold." Leading up and over it seemed to be a "golden stairway," a sample from which, taken for assay, may be seen today in the main corridor of the legislative building at Toronto. This claim resulted in the establishment of the Dome Gold Mine, the first of the three major gold mines in the Porcupine.

Benny Hollinger and Aleck Gillies prospected in the same general area three months later. On Preston's advice, they explored farther north where they found old pits and trenches abandoned by another prospector named Reuben D'Aigle some three years before. Aleck Gillies told the story of their discovery in his own words:

> I was cutting a discovery post, and Benny was pulling the moss off the rocks a few feet away, when suddenly he let a roar out of him, and threw his hat at me. At first I thought he was crazy, but when I came over to where he was it was not hard to find the reason. The quartz where he had taken off the moss looked as though someone had dripped a candle along it, but instead of wax it was gold. The

quartz stood up about three feet out of the ground and was about six feet wide with gold all splattered over it for about sixty feet along the vein.

Benny Hollinger and Aleck Gillies staked six claims each. They had discovered the future Hollinger Mine. While returning to Haileybury to record their claim they met Sandy McIntyre, whose real name was Alexander Oliphant. An iron moulder, who liked his freedom and his drink, he had fled from his wife in Scotland and taken the alias McIntyre. After talking to Hollinger and Gillies and examining their samples, he hurried in and staked claims adjacent to theirs. Though its gold lay deeper beneath the surface, the McIntyre Mine soon became the third largest gold producer in the Porcupine.[1]

The prospectors did not make fortunes from these mines. W.S. Edwards, the promoter from Chicago, made a handsome profit selling his claims in the Dome Mine to Ambrose Monell and a New York banker named DeLamar, who at the time were the President and Vice-President of International Nickel Company. Sandy McIntyre sold his Porcupine claims to two other New York financiers for a reputed $15,000. Benny Hollinger probably made the best bargain, selling his claims for $300,000 to the Timmins-Martin-Dunlap syndicate which already controlled the La Rose Silver Mine at Cobalt, although Benny had to pay half to an uncle and a friend who had grub-staked him for $150.

Aleck Gillies was less fortunate, and so was his backer, M.J. O'Brien, the self-made mining and lumber baron. The samples brought out by Gillies gave little indication of the true worth of his claims and O'Brien did not take possession of them. They were absorbed by the Hollinger Mine, controlled by the Timmins family.[2] But there was nothing unusual in this outcome; the claims of prospectors generally ended in the hands of investors. Of paramount importance to the North was the long-term investment of new capital; the availability of work and good pay for miners, engineers, and technicians; and erection of new buildings as centres of new communities. Inevitably, demands would be raised for extension of the T&NO Railway.

The gold discoveries had an immediate effect on the nomadic population of prospectors who congregated in the boarding houses and hotels of Haileybury – waiting, resting, drinking and telling their stories. As word of new finds in the Porcupine spread through the town, men gathered together their equipment – canoes, toboggans, tents, utensils and food; they took money on deposit for staking claims in the names of speculators, and headed north on the coaches of the T&NO.

At Mile 222 they stopped at a siding where an old day-coach served as the station-house. The place was called Kelso and there the prospectors unloaded their equipment from the baggage car. Then by canoe and portage in the summer, by toboggan in winter, they moved lightly and easily along the twenty-five or thirty miles of river and lake which took them to the region bounded on the north by Frederick House Lake with Night Hawk Lake to the south and the upper reaches of the Mattagami River to the west. The Porcupine River and Porcupine Lake lay roughly at the centre.

Those who wanted transport could use the stage service described in the *Northland Post* of Cochrane. From Kelso the regular stage, pulled by horse-teams, left for Frederick House River at 7:00 a.m. In the winter some sleighs were equipped with foot-warmers; in summer and fall the wagons creaked over a natural road with a clay bottom, bordered by poplar and birch, spruce, balsam, fir and jack-pine, some of which had already been cut for use as railbed ties. Shrubs and blueberry bushes grew everywhere on the ledges of rock. After two hours, passengers arrived at Crawford's Landing where they transferred to gasoline launches which took them upstream to the northwest side of Night Hawk Lake. From there the boats ascended the Porcupine River to a place called Hill's Landing – the half-way point – about five or six hours travel from Kelso.

On the way, stops were made at "half-way houses." These were log shacks where, for fifty cents, a traveller could use "the soft side of three feet of plank and a pair of blankets." Heated constantly by wood-burning stoves, they were rough but comfortable in winter. For another half dollar a meal could be bought with "plenty of pork, potatoes, black tea that would float an iron-wedged tin cow, and that inevitable pie to be found all up and down the line of the T&NO Railway – pumpkin." After that, if you were tired you might sleep, "but otherwise the constant coming and going of teamsters and others, the snoring of tired travellers and the indescribable odour of drying garments [were] not conducive to slumber."[3]

Passenger fare from Kelso to Porcupine was $3.50 per person; freight was charged at $2.75 per cwt and the eighteen-foot canoes could carry 1,100 pounds. Flat-bottomed pointers had greater capacity but they could only be used on the calmest water. The stage service provided a slow and cumbersome but colourful means of transporting people and commodities for that short distance of thirty miles. As mining in the region developed, horse teams, wagons, sleds, canoes, and gasoline launches proved inadequate. Improved transportation methods were of natural interest to the Commission of the T&NO. Englehart ordered preliminary surveys early in 1910 and the mining engineer, Arthur A. Cole, noted in the *Annual Report* for that year:

> Since the discovery of these new gold fields in the autumn of 1909 interest has gradually increased until now it is widespread. The companies now in control of the leading properties are not only strong financially, but are composed mostly of experienced mining men, so that progressive and, at the same time, rational development is expected.

Cole's optimistic report went directly to the chairman, who in turn forwarded it with his approval to Sir James Whitney. After study by Frank Cochrane, Minister of Lands, Forests and Mines, the report formed the basis of an Order-In-Council made public in late November 1910. Cochrane purposely delayed release of both the report and the cabinet's decision to discourage speculators and "wild-catting" operations. But by the end of 1910 no doubt remained that

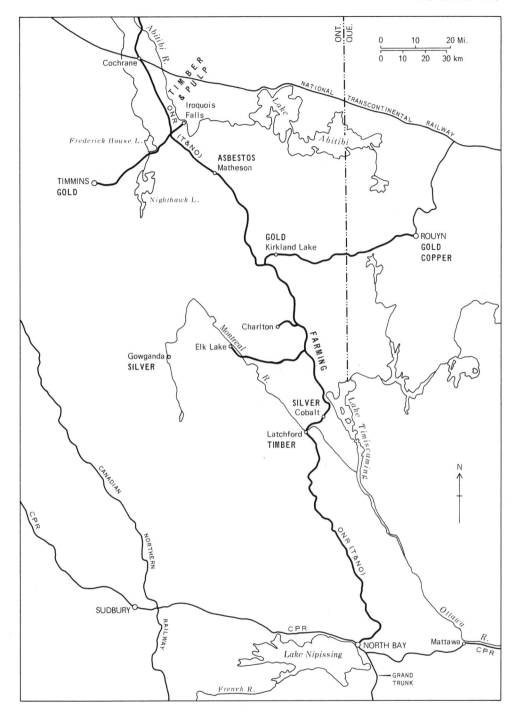

Resources, North Bay to Cochrane. The railway opened unexpected
reserves of lumber, pulp, and minerals in northeastern Ontario.

the railway would be extended westward a distance of thirty miles from a point on the main line between Matheson in the south and Nellie Lake.[4]

Though the people of Matheson argued that their town should be the point of junction, it was considered too distant. Instead, the Commission selected Iroquois Falls, a point farther north near Mile 225. When the Abitibi Paper Company appropriated the name "Iroquois Falls" for its company town farther east, a new name had to be found, and the junction was renamed Porquis, a combination of Porcupine and Iroquois Falls.

In December 1910, the Commission determined to build the new line itself, rather than contract it out, using cheap day labour under the direction of the chief engineer. The high estimated cost of $450,000 was explained by the necessity of laying the railbed during the winter for completion by July 1, 1911. Almost 52 inches of snow fell in the Porcupine district that winter. It had to be laboriously shovelled out by hand and excavation proceeded over a lightly graded surface which had frozen solid. Construction crews, some of them prisoners from town jails as far south as North Bay, worked in the deep snow clearing the right of way; then removed the snow for the grading of the railbed.[5]

In spite of these problems, the clearing had progressed so well by February 1911 that laying of the tracks could begin, and by spring the railway had established a freight and passenger service from Kelso to the Frederick House River which superseded the horse-drawn stage service to that point. By the middle of June 1911, the laying of steel reached the concentration of mines then called Golden City, and by the end of the month service was opened to South Porcupine, with freight sidings and a passenger station ready for inauguration day on July 1st.

The selection of South Porcupine had taken time and study. It was difficult at first to determine the exact direction of the line as it approached its western terminus, since the community as yet lacked either plans or shape. Given the expectation of rapid population growth stimulated by the Hollinger and Dome discoveries, the line was built that summer along the southeastern side of Porcupine Lake. Then, anticipating further mining development in the district of Pearl Lake, the Commission ordered another four-mile extension through heavy rock cuttings to the townsite of Timmins in May 1911. This final project was completed early in 1912.

By then the entire extension from Porquis to Timmins through South Porcupine covered a total distance of thirty-one miles. A whole new area had been opened to mining and settlement. As they developed, the towns of Timmins and Schumacher were linked with Englehart, New Liskeard, Haileybury, and Cobalt to the south, with Cochrane to the north, and all by means of the coaches and freight cars of the T&NO Railway.[6]

Fire in 1911

Freight cars always stood on the siding, most of them filled with supplies and equipment for the mining companies. Beside the tracks stood the storage sheds and just beyond, the rough-timbered buildings of the town that was beginning to take shape. Dirt roads served as streets and wooden planks for sidewalks. Surrounding the town stood the forest, its poplar and birch trees dominating the land, with the scrub of grass and juniper covering the ground. South Porcupine was still no more than a small and isolated settlement on the edge of the lake. Settlers made their own clearings and burned the brush.

Some of these small fires were burning on the morning of a hot July day in 1911, when a strong and unexpected wind swept them together into a conflagration. Flames engulfed the town, destroying the pit-heads of the mines and rushing down on the railway cars at the siding. One of these cars contained 350 cases of dynamite.

Forest fires were an ever present danger for people living in frame buildings on the edge of a wilderness. John Campsell, born at Mile 104 near Cobalt in 1902, arrived in Porcupine by horse-drawn stage with his parents on Christmas Day of 1910. He lived through three bush fires between 1910 and 1916. In fact, he said in an interview, "I was beginning to accept bush fires as a way of life." He remembered especially the fire of 1911; the dry hot days preceding it and "the neighbour women with tears running down their cheeks standing near their homes with arms upraised praying for rain, a rain that never came in time..." On the morning of July 11 the stifling air, laden with smoke, turned grey and ominous. Ashes swirled in the wind caused by the approaching fire as it sucked in great gusts of oxygen. The wind increased throughout the morning until "it was blowing with almost hurricane force."

> The fire jumped Porcupine Lake and as Porcupine started burning we lost all hope of saving our home. I remember looking down our street and watching the houses catch fire one at a time as the fire came up the street. There was a well near our home that had gone dry, so we dumped our bedding and blankets in the well. Some of our blankets had holes burned in them when the fire followed the wooden cribbing down the well. We had a bag of flour which we put in a ditch in front of our house and covered with clay. The flour was okay. A roast of meat was put in the oven and was nicely done when the house burned down.

The people rushed to the lake, brushing sparks from their clothing, trying to protect their eyes from the smoke and ash, yet watching at the same time for the whirling fireballs which had been the roofs of homes and stores only a few minutes before. Everyone waded into the lake and stood out as far from shore as they dared, for the wind churned the water into furious waves and canoes were launched only to capsize. Men and women drowned in attempts to keep afloat on upturned boats, heavy planks or logs. Horses, crazed by showering sparks, broke from harness and ran into the converging flames where they were burned alive. Then, early in the afternoon, the car of dynamite exploded. Fortunately, it blew vertically rather than horizontally; otherwise the people in the lake would have been decapitated. The explosion tore a hole twenty feet deep into the ground; shock waves lashed the water to a higher fury, hurled rocks and

55

rails upward and outward from the siding, and terrorized those who could find no shelter from the falling debris.

More than seventy people were drowned or burned; many others were listed as missing. John Campsell recalled for some time after the fire seeing "stretcher-cases carried to the Porcupine station...probably bodies being shipped home for burial...also people with their eyes bandaged who had become smoke-blinded..." Mrs. Eva DeRosa then living at Englehart received a message asking her to come by train to identify the body of a female relative:

> The only way I could recognize her...she had in the palm of her hand the skin like of a pig – that rough hair like a pig's got? Otherwise I could not have recognized her. All of a sudden I thought of that birth-mark. And when I took the hand to turn it over to see that, the whole arm stayed in my hand – she was so badly burned.

Mrs. DeRosa also told of the young woman who gave birth to a baby in the lake, even as the fire raged:

> There were eight men who held the blanket, and the doctor worked, and eight other men held the blanket on top of her. And they kept throwing water on the blankets, so it wouldn't be too hot. And when it got too hot for the men they'd change and some others went in. And that's the way the doctor delivered the baby...And the mother was fine, so was the daughter.

The courage of these people in the Porcupine enabled them to recover from a disaster which had wiped out everything except the core of Golden City. The essentials remained – the gold in the mines, the railway, the stubborn will of people determined to rebuild their way of life. The railway played a crucial role in this work of recovery. The buildings of every mine in the district had been destroyed. At the West Dome Lake Mine fifteen people had perished when they followed the mine's captain into the shaft, believing it to be safe from the flames, but dying of asphyxiation as the fire sucked out all the oxygen. The four construction camps of the T&NO were also burned together with supplies, plant, and rolling stock, though no railway employees were killed or injured and the station and freight shed at Golden City remained standing. Telegraph lines were burned out but service was restored the next day together with regular trains.[7]

For some time after the fire the construction department of the T&NO concentrated on restoring freight and passenger traffic. Victims were taken out and relief supplies were brought in from Toronto, including not only food and clothing, but bell-tents for housing and stoves for cooking. Cables could be sent free of charge over the telegraph wires of the T&NO. In ways like these the railway demonstrated its integral role in both the daily routine and in the exceptional tragedy of life in the North.

Before long, new equipment at the pit-heads restored work and pay; new stores were built and goods were brought in to fill their shelves. Interspersed among shops and homes the "blind pigs" again emerged, selling illicit liquor, together with "cat-houses" such as the *White Rat*. And in the hole created by the dynamite blast a spring of clear water flowed, pumped into a water-wagon and sold about the town for 5¢ a pail.

The railway played an even more crucial role for the town of Cochrane which succumbed to a worse devastation on this same day in 1911. There, townspeople went about their tasks unaware of the fire raging through the Porcupine camps. They smelled the familiar smoke of small brush fires burning beyond the town – controlled fires which smouldered or burned almost daily as farmers and settlers cleared their land for planting or building. Such harmless fires were a routine part of life in the North during the summer months. But as the Cochrane *Northland Post* pointed out later, on July 11 strong winds fanned a number of smaller fires into a converging mass of flame which sent a pall of smoke over the town, darkening the sun and raising fears which reached a state of panic about noon.

By then the wind had increased to gale force, with the hot flames creating a horrifying roar, and smothering smoke descending everywhere, seeping through every crack and opening of the vulnerable frame buildings. The wind could change direction at any moment, threatening or sparing the town; fear and hope fluctuated from minute to minute. Was it still worth while to fight the flames? By early afternoon the answer became evident. One building after another burned in the searing whirlwind. In a moment of panic the fire-fighters dropped pails and shovels, shouted warnings to others, and fled to join the women and children huddled together in the railway yard.

There, the T&NO agent – W.H. Maund – had ordered engine No. 126 in from the roundhouse. All available freight cars were attached and people were packed into them with whatever belongings they could carry. Then the train moved east out of the town to the "Y" at the junction with the Transcontinental Railway. The refugees scrambled out and the train returned, making several such rescue trips during the early afternoon. Two construction trains were also engaged in similar missions on the Transcontinental line to the east and west of Cochrane. From the west steamed the engine and a string of flat cars belonging to a contractor named Fauquier. From the east came the engine and cars of Messrs. Foley, Welch & Stewart, together with the private car of M.J. O'Brien, the "Calabogie," which was quickly filled with women and children. These trains evacuated some two thousand people or more, leaving behind only a determined few to fight the flames and to save whatever property they could. The courage and accomplishments of these remaining few were described by the *Northland Post* in words which highlight some of the physical details of the early town:

> The result of their untiring efforts was the saving of the T. &. N.O. station and the new Union Station, which saved the part of the town to the south of the track, the corner on Railway Street, including the T. & N.O. building, the T.C.R. office, and two other buildings, and finally the corner of Fourth Avenue, between Railroad Street and

Third Street, which includes the Imperial Bank, Geller and Kertzer's store, and the Assembly Hall. It was terrible work, and none of those who went through it will ever forget the strain under which they laboured.

As the fire roared and the flames leapt from building to building, a wireless operator named Taylor stubbornly tapped out bulletins to North Bay over the telegraph lines of the T&NO. His determination to maintain contact with the outside world remained firm. Whenever the line burned out, he moved to the "Y" by train. As soon as crews restored the line and the station seemed safe, he moved back again.

The fire had done its destructive worst by six p.m. Except for a few buildings Cochrane survived as little more than a number of smouldering piles of rubble. The town had been destroyed in a matter of hours, leaving three thousand people homeless. Instead of clamouring to leave, the refugees returned on trains which backed into the devastated town from the "Y." Immediately they formed a relief committee. Foley, Welch & Stewart, the contractors of the National Transcontinental on the east side of the town, arranged supper for them that evening and food for the following day. The T&NO's station and railway cars provided sleeping accommodation. Together with the Union Station and the Assembly Hall, shelter and food were assured for almost three thousand refugees during the next twenty-four hours.

Practical and humane aid of this kind helped to ensure that the town would not be abandoned. About a thousand persons did leave on trains during the following two days and all were given free transportation on the T&NO. But most people remained, forming themselves into groups through a central relief committee. Its members organized the supply of tents, poles, water, food and cooking facilities; a further breakdown into sub-committees distributed this relief and maintained order in the four wards of the town. Converted into a kitchen, the Union Station fed a thousand people the day after the fire. Utensils and dishes came in from the construction camps; food, blankets, tents, stoves and medical aid arrived on the trains of the T&NO, just as they did at South Porcupine. They were donated by many centres; some from the northern towns of Englehart, New Liskeard, Haileybury, Cobalt and North Bay; some from the Toronto Board of Trade; and some from individual firms such as Eaton's Department Store in Toronto.[8]

The fires at Porcupine and Cochrane in July 1911 destroyed property and life on a tragic scale. But they also increased the sense of community in the North as people recognized their vulnerability and their dependence on one another; as they acknowledged, too, their reliance on the trains and telegraph lines of the T&NO in maintaining contact from town to town, and from the North to southern Ontario.

CHAPTER 7

Toward a Northern Community

Trains in an Empty Landscape

At the beginning of World War I in August, 1914, the British Foreign Secretary remarked that the lamps had gone out all over Europe. For the next four years a momentous conflict would disrupt the lives of millions of people. Its social and economic repercussions influenced every industrial society of the western world, stimulating production of commodities, expanding the manufacture of munitions, enlarging the bureaucracy of governments, employing larger numbers of women, and taking thousands of men from peacetime vocations to the monotony and dampness of the primitive network of trenches which stretched through northwestern France. Canadian troops were recruited from across the country, at first voluntarily and then by conscription. Men and women invested their savings in victory bonds and contributed their services to the Red Cross.

Northern Ontario was no exception to this patriotic effort. Men enlisted in the new Algonquin Regiment, formed in 1903 with depots in Sault Ste.Marie, Sudbury, Thessalon, and Sturgeon Falls. Mining companies invested millions of dollars in government bonds. By 1917 more than twelve per cent of the employees of the T&NO – about 180 men – had joined the armed services. Some members of construction crews and section gangs returned to Europe to enlist in the armies of their native countries, such as Italy or Russia. For those who joined Canadian regiments, the Algonquin (97th) or the Northern Pioneers (23rd), the T&NO Commission established a fund of nearly $14,000 to provide grants to those who enlisted.

Employees who did not enlist made their own contribution. They formed a Patriotic Association in 1916 which collected more than $32,000 in that single year, and gave all of it to the Canadian Red Cross Society and the Canadian Patriotic Fund. Before the end of the war the Patriotic Association had collected and donated nearly $96,000, and employees had invested almost $240,000 in victory bonds. Behind this generosity was a work force hauling heavy loads of ore, pulp and timber south on the T&NO cars, passing through towns that steadily increased in population as demands for goods stimulated jobs and income.[1]

The consequences of the war were, in these ways, similar to its impact in other parts of the country. Yet it was also very far away. Most people were still basically concerned with pay and work and raising a family. In the mind of a man aged twenty-five, with a wife and two small children, just beginning his first job with the T&NO, the war seemed to be a long distance away. Its effect was minimal on his daily life.

William Gard came to the North for his first job there in 1914, as a watchman or "hostler" with the T&NO at Elk Lake, the end of the branch line which ran west from Earlton. He was called Bill or Will, later Pop or Father by his family and intimate friends; he always hated to be called "Mister." Born in England in 1889, he came to London, Ontario, about 1910 with his wife. Through the depression of 1912-1914, he worked at odd jobs for the Grand Theatre, drove a horse for a bakery, ran a street-car, and walked the streets looking for work. At the urging of his wife he replied to an advertisement for workers in the North. When word came of a possible job at Elk Lake, his wife pawned her wedding and engagement rings for twenty dollars, and paid his fare to North Bay where he signed on for the T&NO at sixty dollars a month. His wife and two children joined him shortly after. For the next seven years they lived and worked at Elk Lake.

There, the winters were extreme. For days the temperature dropped to -50° Fahrenheit and the sandwiches and eggs in his lunchpail froze. He and his wife later remembered and wondered at the hardships they endured. They looked forward especially to the arrival of the train which brought his monthly pay.

> The snow plough used to be in front of the coaches in those days; there wasn't snow ploughs like they have today. They were just in front of the engine...And if the other trains couldn't get in, well, we'd have to wait 'til the snow plough come in to plough before we'd get the pay car, and the pay car would be on the back of the train. Well of course that was a big event; everybody had to go and meet the pay car. And all we got was sixty dollars; and by the time we'd bought a bag of flour and all that kind of thing, there wasn't much left of your sixty dollars.[2]

The Elk Lake Branch had only just been completed, in February 1913. For two years previously the Commission had discussed the route the tracks should follow. Good agricultural land lay westward from the main line between Earlton and Englehart; timber was there to be hauled out; prospectors working at Gowganda, west from Elk Lake, were making strikes that indicated silver deposits. A survey had been done on a line northward from Sudbury to Gowganda; another from Porcupine south and west; and still a third on extending the Englehart-Charlton branch line another seventeen miles westward. But all three surveys were abandoned in favour of a twenty-eight mile line west and slightly south from Earlton, where more level land and railway access would develop the agricultural potential of the region. If it proved necessary in the future, a further extension could be made to Gowganda, though in fact the silver mines in that area never did prove lucrative enough to justify a railway; instead they continued to rely on teams of horses and winter sleds.[3]

At Elk Lake the train came in from Earlton at 2 p.m. and left the next morning at 8 a.m. Through the long winter nights Will Gard had to watch the engine and the cars. Like so many workmen on the T&NO, he had a wife who understood and accepted the demands made upon them both. It was she who broke the ice on the pail of water in the morning before she could cook breakfast; it was she who brought the water from the neighbour's pump; it was she who dug out the wood from the frozen wood-pile. But she also recalled the humorous incidents that sometimes broke the routine, such as one Christmas-time when Will arrived home in an unusual state.

> There was a Polack family, lived in a shack near the station. Piney, they used to call her – her and her brother Pete and her husband – and they used to make this home-made wine.
>
> Well, Will and the other man went in and the other man could take it and Father couldn't, and he still can't take it to this day. He wouldn't take a drink of brandy if you paid him. And he come home, this was about nine o'clock for his supper. And talk? He talked like a streak. And I couldn't get him out the door to go back to work.
>
> But I was ignorant of all this drink. I didn't know anything about it. I'd never been used to it so I didn't know. Come to find out, he'd been in to Piney's and had some of this home-made drink and o'course it just knocked him out, but all it done for 'im was make him talk – and he talked like a gramophone.

Mrs. Gard recalled another incident, fifty years after it happened, one which demonstrated that for all the release from labour provided by drink in the hotels, the bars, and the blind pigs, the men who worked in the North and especially on the T&NO, were generally steady and sober men rooted in the affection of their families, for whom strong drink was exceptional and memorable.

> And Will would be working from about two o'clock [in the afternoon] when the train come in if it was on time until about eight o'clock the next morning before the train went out. And that's the hours he'd have to put in. He'd come home at supper time and just get his supper and then go back again. And then every second or third Sunday they'd have to go to Englehart for a washout [of the engine].
>
> Well, this day he went out there. He was out Saturday and he should ha' been back Sunday afternoon. And I thought now what's happened now; and I could see the train from my back door, down by the "Y" where they had to turn to back into the station; and I thought, dear, there's something wrong. And it was so long before he come home and I couldn't think what happened. Finally, Mr. Lacey

that looked after the coaches, he said: "Bill won't be home tonight Missis." And I said: "Why, what's the matter with him?"

Evidently some of the section men – it was so cold – had given the engineer a drink, and he had the top of the bottle. Well o'course he was young then and that was the end of it. So I think they put him to sleep up in the engine and covered him up, and there he stayed until Monday mornin'. Well, I don't think I spoke to him for a week when he come home.

Both in their labour and in their recreation, men who worked on the steam locomotives were aware of the need for steadiness, for endurance, and for an intelligent grasp of the mechanics of their engines. Bill Ross Jr. started firing with the T&NO in 1924. His father was already an engineer, having moved to the T&NO from the Grand Trunk in 1907, and he had two uncles working on the railway between North Bay and Cochrane. Bill Jr. never wanted to work at anything else; even as a boy he was determined to become a locomotive engineer. And that was what he became. The fact was, he said:

> ...that with the steam locomotive there were certain things that you did yourself – manually... when you opened the firebox door or you looked over at the firebox door, there was something alive in there – the flames flickering...and for that reason a lot of us...steam men loved the steam, and we still do.

> And we suffered in the early days on the steam, don't ever kid yourself. We'd leave here in the winter time, thirty-five to forty below zero with a snow plough tacked on the head end. And you had canvas side curtains...and they'd be flapping in the wind until we pulled them in and piled a little coal on them to keep the snow from comin' up underneath. And by the time we'd been thirty-five miles on the road the fireman would be soakin' wet.

Sometimes he fired the locomotive with Jim Fletcher as the engineer. Jim had signed on as a fireman in 1918, and he never forgot those cold winter runs when the snow would pile up in the cabs, "and you'd throw it out the side curtains and half of that would come back in your face, and one leg would be all wringin' wet with snow and the other one you'd open the furnace door and it'd be burnin' pretty near."

Besides the cold and the wet, there were the long hours. In those early days, said Jim Fletcher:

> We had the old 106 and the 123, and them other smaller engines that was hand-fired. We had an old chain door; we had to catch the chain, open the door, throw in the coal, shut the door. And it would take us about twelve or thirteen hours going from North Bay to Englehart. We'd have a five-hour rest and then come back another twelve to

thirteen hours, go to bed again and start up in five or six days for another trip. And things were pretty tough them days.

When the engine stopped to take on water and the fireman stepped down from the cab, his wet clothes would freeze in the biting cold. Yet he thought it a good life, one in which he shared a run with a crew, with the brakeman and the engineer, the men on the tail end, the baggage-men, and the conductor who was responsible for making reports. "The most amazing thing of the whole operation," said Bill Ross Jr., "you'd be dead tired...fourteen or fifteen hours maybe going up and soakin' wet; and you would have by this time cursed every operational manager...not from any personal enmity, just because you were tired and angry. And the minute you entered the yard at Englehart you were hollerin' when are we goin' to turn back, let's get home."

For these train crews in an empty landscape, the work held a fascination that drew them together into willing co-operation. In the early history of the railway they generally stayed aloof from radical politics and militant trade unions. Basic in their consciousness was the local, even isolated character of the work. They knew it was essential. They operated trains carrying not only timber, pulpwood, and ore for corporations, but the grain and the livestock and the necessary supplies for farmers and townspeople who had no other road for their livelihood but that of the railway.[4] Social life, too, depended on the railway coaches which took citizens to local hockey and baseball games, or to fairs and dances. An excursion ticket from South Porcupine to the fall fair at New Liskeard cost only a cent a mile. Coaches on these occasions tended to be crowded and convivial.

The leisure and the work of men on the train crews were closely interwoven into the life of the stretched-out community in the northeast. Most men took pride in their skills and belonged to the craft unions of the international brotherhoods. But they carried with their membership a degree of diffidence, since they knew that the T&NO was a small railway by comparison with the CPR and the Grand Trunk (later the CNR). Workmen on these major national lines carried greater weight in the international railway unions. Employees of the T&NO were also aware that they worked for a Commission or agency of the provincial government, which did not operate entirely free of partisan politics. Any expression of radical views, of overt sympathy with an opposition party, or an aggressive stand on trade-union membership, could meet with the suspicion of businessmen appointed to the Commission by the provincial government.

Rules of operation dwelt at length on the need for safety. "Safety First," said the *Annual Report* of 1913, "has been the shibboleth of the T&NO. More than 4,180,462 passengers have been carried over the T&NO and not one passenger has been killed." Again, much of the reason for this record lay in the discipline and abilities of the engineers. In the early twenties the speed limit was still twenty-four miles an hour, said Jim Fletcher, "and the conductor had to mark down the time we passed every station and every siding, and one trip I was on, the engineer exceeded the speed limit by two minutes between these sidings, and he got a letter about it from the Superintendent, Mr. Griffin."

As Superintendent of Traffic, W. A. Griffin, one of the chief executive officers of the Commission, mailed monthly reports to J. L. Englehart in Toronto. Griffin had started out as traffic accountant in 1908, achieving promotion in 1911 to Superintendent with jurisdiction over enginemen, despatchers, trainmen, operators, station agents, "and other matters pertaining to transportation." Most engineers knew him as a fair, church-going man whose letters of criticism or commendation were much respected because of his authority to hand out the sixty demerit points which could lead to dismissal.

Griffin was not the only presence of authority. By 1914 the annual reports of the Commission listed twenty-one chief officers with functions that ranged from development of mines and towns through every aspect of operating trains pulled by steam-powered locomotives, from the General Roadmaster and Master Mechanic to the Air Brake Inspector and the Chief Engineer.

With the exception of the Secretary-Treasurer and the Chief Accountant, who still maintained their functions close to the chairman in the executive office at Toronto, all the chief officers were now based in North Bay.[5] In 1908, a solid limestone building with Gothic peaks was built in the southern part of the town, housing the operational headquarters of the Commission. As the railway expanded and northern towns developed, this centre enabled the T&NO to become less dominated by Toronto. Gradually the Commission established itself as the single most important vehicle for the settlement and development of northeastern Ontario. The railway not only hauled ore and pulpwood and timber southward, and carried supplies and passengers between towns and farms; it developed its own deliberate policy of inducing men and women to move into the North.

Encouraging Settlement

The Commission opened a Land Department in 1908 to implement this policy of settlement. Its direction lay with Frederick Dane, who had joined the Commission two years previously as a member who would spend more of his time in the North, in contrast to Murphy in Ottawa or Englehart in Toronto. His assistant as Land Commissioner was George W. Lee, then just beginning his career with the T&NO as General Agent in North Bay. Over the next two decades Lee became the most powerful man on the Commission, succeeding Englehart as chairman in 1921. At this early stage, however, he was merely a young man starting out under the political patronage of Frank Cochrane. Neither Lee nor Dane brought any particular expertise to their new responsibilities.

Even so, over the next five years, the two men administered a programme which sought to fulfill one of the original aims of the Commission – to attract and settle people in the North. Efforts at settlement in northeastern Ontario hardly compared in scale with the ships and the agents of the CPR, recruiting immigrants by the thousands through the ports of Europe to settle on lavish land grants in the Canadian West. But the goal itself was similar. The new Land Department surveyed lots which became sites for stores, offices, and houses in the small towns. Newly-drawn maps divided land into concessions and farms of 150 to 160 acres. Confined within a limited budget, Dane and Lee then directed publicity campaigns designed to entice settlers northward, whether from older Ontario communities or from the port of Montréal where they landed as immigrants from Europe.

Within the Commission this striving for development led to the nucleus of a public relations department. The T&NO distributed pamphlets and set up booths at local fairs to publicize the extent and quality of the land. Advertising stressed that the new mining towns must inevitably develop into burgeoning markets for farm produce. Fitted out with illustrations and exhibits, a special rail car began the first of many journeys through southern Ontario in 1911. Supported by the Ontario Department of Agriculture, the Land Department elicited letters and newspaper reports supporting indications of a growing interest in the North.[6]

Despite rural discontent across the Dominion generally, leading to the actual abandonment of farms in parts of Ontario and the West; despite protests of farmers at the high costs of maintaining their farms, interest in northern agriculture seemed to flourish during the years just before World War I. Even as the Canadian Council of Agriculture petitioned the federal government to take action encouraging people to stay on the land, the Commission of the T&NO continued to tour its demonstration car. Over five hundred letters were received in 1913 from prospective settlers and 938 new farms began operation in the district north of New Liskeard. At an average farm size of 160 acres, land settlement totalled 150,000 acres in that year alone. Recruiting campaigns continued, with the demonstration car making annual trips until 1915, when most of the desirable land along the railway had been taken. By then, new problems were emerging.[7]

The short summer season made it difficult to break the land and produce a cash crop from mixed farming on wooded land. The first few years could leave the farmer settler desperately short of cash. While the mines and lumber mills provided alternative winter employment, they also competed with the established farmer for labour during the months when hay, potatoes, and grain had to be cultivated. The thin layer of arable soil and the harsh climate, together with the high cost of labour and implements, were problems especially serious for the farmer whose land did not border the tracks of the T&NO Railway. He then faced the difficulty of transporting to market not only his produce and livestock, but the wood which the Commission purchased for ties. All these factors inhibited the anticipated development of agricultural land in the Clay Belt.

The Whitney government established a Northern Development Branch in 1912, authorizing expenditure of $5,000,000 to build access roads for the transport of timber, ore, and farm produce. But the real wealth in New Ontario still came from the mining of precious metals at Cobalt, Porcupine, and Kerr Lake. Expectations were high for new gold discoveries around Larder and Kirkland Lakes. The value of silver alone for the years 1904-1915, from ore shipped by T&NO cars out of Cobalt, totalled more than $122,750,000.[8] Moreover, in the years before the internal combustion engine had introduced alternative locomotion, railways received the largest percentage of government transportation subsidies. The T&NO also benefitted from legislation which gave it virtual control throughout northeastern Ontario over the granting of sites for towns and farms.

For these reasons, the Commission could be held responsible for limitations and failures in settling the North. As Englehart said, commissioners were the trustees for much more than a provincial railway.[9] He became involved in correspondence with a serious critic during the early months of 1916, amid the crisis over food production for the war. A former provincial civil servant, Dr. C.C. James publicly questioned whether settlement was developing to improve national agricultural production. Writing directly to Englehart, rather than to a government department, he cited complaints in northern newspapers, and commented on his observation of settlers across Canada, "that they need [financial] assistance from the time they go on the land."[10] Englehart responded with a banal eloquence, refuting the argument that settlers required a policy of financial subsidy for the first few years of settlement. "We repeat and emphasize," he said, "there are thousands of acres...that would furnish a...homestead, a heritage, to the settler who is willing to do an honest day's work."[11]

Englehart prefaced this reply with figures indicating that the railway had settled more than 1,500 farmers on 247,000 acres since 1914. Another critic considered the average farm too large for the initial stage of agricultural development by small farmers. Writing to the premier, Commissioner J.F. Whitson of the Northern Development Branch stated in explicit terms that farms of 160 acres were unsuitably large given the isolated conditions of the new settlers. His memorandum said in part that "the area now being located is far in excess of what the average settler will ever clear and put under proper cultivation during his lifetime..." The grants of land, he said, should have been limited to half the average size of farms – say seventy to eighty acres.

Both these criticisms carried far more weight than Dane or Lee in the North, or Englehart in Toronto were prepared to acknowledge. As T&NO Commissioners, they interpreted their policy of supporting settlement as little more than a guarantee to purchase logs for railway ties. Northern farmland, said Englehart, could be purchased from the Commission at fifty cents an acre, compared to $15 in the West. In addition, the settler had the opportunity to sell logs at the side of the tracks at $4 a cord if quality met the standards of the tie inspectors. Each acre could produce from eight to twenty cords, giving the settler a minimum of $32 an acre for the purchase of implements. The Commission willingly accepted this obligation to buy logs at the side of the tracks, leading the Roadmaster in the North to comment that "the general inclination of the producers is to assume that they have more or less claim on the Government Railway..."[12]

Whitson held the view that this policy diverted energy from working and improving the soil. If the size of farms had been reduced, then "we would have had better schools and roads and churches...and we would have had a class of settlers devoting their energies more to the cultivation of the soil than the farming of the timber."[13] He argued that the absence of roads meant a lonely existence for families, in which mothers often bore the responsibility for educating the small children at home, since schools existed only in the towns. In addition, little was known about the quality of soil in the North, at least until the opening of experimental farms, such as the one begun in 1915 by the Department of Agriculture at Monteith.

Despite these difficulties, farming which bordered on the railway attained some success before and during the years of World War I. Early in 1916, for example, some 704 tons of hay, 125 tons of potatoes, and 52 tons of grain were shipped out from Haileybury by freight car.[14] Close to three thousand settlers had purchased over 400,000 acres through the Commission since 1913, at a cost of approximately $200,000. Results could be seen in the increased acreage under cultivation from New Liskeard north to Cochrane, an area which now had the benefit of regular freight service at a time of rising demand for agricultural produce. The ready cash offered for timber supplemented this farming income in the early stages of settlement, while the mines and mills provided opportunities for winter employment.

For these reasons, criticism of the T&NO failed to reach strident proportions. Grievances were muted by comparison with the discontent expressed over the privileges, the profits, and the freight rates of larger privately-owned railways, such as the Canadian Pacific, the Grand Trunk, or the Canadian Northern. Critical articles which had appeared in the Cobalt *Daily Nugget* frequently in 1909 appeared less and less often by the 1920s. The criticism of C.C. James and J.F. Whitson failed in general to inflame northern sentiment. Probably the majority of people in the North had come to associate the T&NO with the genuine development of their communities. Their feelings of association were tragically focused by the terrible Matheson fire of 1916.

The Matheson Fire of 1916

During the warm dry weather of June and July, 1916, settlers in the area between Matheson and Cochrane casually burned the brush around their clearings and along the railway tracks. Burning piles of branches and twigs was customary practice for farmers clearing new land. No laws yet existed to regulate or prevent such fires. Numbers of them were burning when a strong wind rose on the morning of July 29. At first only a few of the fires were united, but then in little more than an hour the wind in a sudden spreading gust gathered them all together, driving huge balls of flame at a speed of twenty-five to forty miles an hour from Ramore to Nellie Lake.[14] By noon the front of the fire had become almost eight miles long at Cochrane. In the next few hours, the flames once again destroyed most of the town, five years after the previous disaster. To the south, the villages of Matheson, Nushka, Kelso, and Porquis Junction remained as little more than skeletal ruins of frame.

Though portions of the residential and business districts of Cochrane were burned out, only one loss of life occurred. A small baby left by its mother in a store while she rushed to see if her house had caught fire, perished in a wall of flame and smoke which prevented the mother's return. But to the south, all along the tracks of the T&NO, the inferno so engulfed the streets and buildings that few escaped who were caught directly in its path. Estimates of the dead on farms, in lumber camps, and in the small towns varied from three hundred to four hundred and fifty.

Some sought escape in root-houses or wells, only to suffocate. More than fifty people at Nushka just north of Matheson refused an invitation from an engineman to board an empty southbound freight train. Their children left but they hoped to save their homes by staying. Almost all were French Canadians who had recently migrated from the Québec side of the provincial boundary. Their names varied from Perrault, Duchésne, and Guinard, to Séguin, Labarge, and Houle. When the roar of the wind and the heat of the flames made destruction inevitable, they hurried into a rock-cut with a priest named Gagné; all of them prayed and perished as the fire sucked the oxygen out like a monster vacuum. The town was later renamed Val Gagné after the young priest who had stayed with the victims.[15]

A fire resulting in tragedy on this scale affected the whole province. Death and destruction had struck at home. Its impact was immediate, crowding out war news from France on the front pages of provincial newspapers. For the people of the North the common bonds of danger and tragedy brought them together, often in the box-cars and the coaches of the T&NO Railway. Trains rushed refugees out of Cochrane, or waited at Elk Lake for 450 residents to hurry in from surrounding farms and saw-mills. The railway provided these people with their only means of escape to Earlton, Thornloe, and New Liskeard. Every southbound train stopped for those willing to leave their homes and belongings behind. Engineers took hazardous chances over twisted tracks and burning ties; one train arrived at Swastika with flames licking the sides of a box-car filled with children. They scrambled to safety and the car was shunted away for a heavy spray of water.

Others stayed in the fire zone and lived to relate its terrors. Mrs. Bob Cameron was sixteen at the time; she lived with her parents and two sisters just north of Matheson. Her father looked after a pump-house which drew water from a creek to a nearby water-tank for the steam locomotives. On that Saturday morning of July 29, 1916, she and her sisters went berry-picking. On the way up, she said,

> ...we noticed a lot of the farmers were burning their brush. We just went ahead to the berry patch, and after I'd been picking for a while I noticed the smoke was getting worse and worse, and it looked like there was a fire way north of us. So we thought we'd better head for home. So the three of us...we come back down, headed for home, and we would see the fire coming behind us faster than we could go. And by the time we got home – we lived beside a small creek – the smoke was just terrific, and we could see the flames right behind us, only it was on the other side of the creek.

> The wind got up then, and there was big limbs of trees on fire blowing over the creek, to where we lived in this little – And only for the tin roof that my dad had on the house that we lived in – we could never

have saved that house. But it was a tin roof and my dad had a little bit of hose, and he went out and started puttin' the water up on the roof. And you could hear it sizzlin' – the tin was so hot.

Well, it just got worse and worse, and every one of us crept under the bed, on the floor, to get breath. But my dad kept goin' out, and he got all of his hair burned off his head, and all his moustache – he just had a moustache, he didn't have a beard…And the top of his head got all burned. But he stayed out and he kept puttin' the water on the tin…And finally the fire burned over us, but the tank didn't get burned. The tank never burned…nor our house didn't get burned.[16]

Mrs. Cameron remembered the astonishment of the survivors in Matheson that she and her family, and even their home, were safe. For the rest of her life she also remembered the pitiful sight of the trains bringing in rough boxes and coffins for the dead who were burned in Matheson and the surrounding countryside.

With the grim freight of empty coffins and boxes, the trains also transported the food, the clothing, and the bedding which would enable the living to survive. From Eaton's in Winnipeg came a carload of dry goods together with another car of groceries and provisions ordered by Frank Cochrane, the Federal Minister of Railways. They were carried on the "National" coming east on the National Transcontinental to Cochrane before it turned south on the T&NO to North Bay. By the time the "National" arrived, the stations of the T&NO which still stood had become headquarters for aid and refuge among those left homeless by the fire. At Cochrane the station once again became a relief kitchen, receiving emergency supplies from every northern town as far south as Cobalt. When the "National" arrived from Winnipeg on Monday it dropped off supplies and took on three hundred people who departed for the safer and more stable work of munitions factories in southern Ontario cities.

To cope with the required scale of relief, not only immediately but for the near future, the provincial government established the Northern Ontario Fire Relief Committee. It was dominated by representatives of the Toronto Board of Trade and the Canadian Manufacturers' Association, with responsibility to report to the provincial Minister of Lands, Forests, and Mines. Possibly because of these auspicious connections, the committee raised over $200,000 in addition to donations of foodstuffs, clothing, and medical supplies. The response was remarkable, considering it was wartime. In its report to the Minister, G. Howard Ferguson, the committee paid tribute to the work of George Lee who had been charged by the provincial government to organize the first stage of relief.[17]

He and his officials together with special committees of citizens at Cobalt, Haileybury, New Liskeard, Englehart, etc., at once organized very complete staffs of doctors, nurses and undertakers and dispatched foodstuffs and other necessaries to the stricken people farther north by special trains in charge of representatives of these committees.

The Fire Relief Committee arranged first for the transportation of women and children out of the fire zone. The T&NO sped engines and cars to wherever they could be of help. All railways operating in the North granted free transportation to the south of the province. The Canadian Pacific Railway and the Grand Trunk Railway extended free passage to any point in Ontario or Québec. Some families packed their few belongings and never returned. Individuals and families who decided to return and rebuild took advantage of free return fares, paid for by the Fire Relief Committee as far as North Bay, where the T&NO Commission issued free passes northward.[18]

Subsequently, a group of settlers in the Matheson region filed damage claims against the T&NO Commission. They charged that a fire tended by a T&NO employee in the Matheson railway yards had caused the devastation in that area. Rumours also circulated that the fire had originated from sparks flying from the stack of a locomotive. Most people did not believe the rumours. Mrs. Bob Cameron remained convinced that the flames that followed her had come in a massive sweep from the north. But grief-stricken settlers who had seen their property destroyed, or who felt deeply the loss of life among relatives, persisted in their charges through the legal firm of Slaght and Slaght in Haileybury. Arthur Slaght, a rising member of the Liberal party, proved eventually successful. Despite strong objections written at length by George Lee, who refused to accept any guilt on the part of the T&NO Commission, the Matheson fire claims of 1916 were eventually arbitrated in favour of a cash compensation to the settlers.[19] The claims were not acknowledged, however, until after the third major fire in the North. But this disaster, the Haileybury fire of 1922, together with other changes in the T&NO, must be placed in context with the new provincial government of E.C. Drury and the United Farmers of Ontario.

CHAPTER 8

Private Decisions and Public Policy

The flux and pressure of politics were bound to affect a government-owned railway in a democratic parliamentary system. Party patronage and personal business connections have traditionally played an integral role in the history of Ontario government commissions. That fact does not make Ontario unusual, or its politics necessarily corrupt. Similar influences have prevailed in other provinces and in the federal government; they are a legacy from the British parliamentary system.

Parliamentary politics are distinguished not only by the contest between parties. Once elected, the majority leader has at his command the executive power of the cabinet, with its profound authority over government departments. The Ontario cabinet possessed considerable power, but until after World War II it lacked the comprehensive bureaucratic structure capable of articulating a clear public policy for the management and direction of government commissions. Under these circumstances, the T&NO Commission functioned much as a privately owned railway, managed by businessmen. The problem had been defined as early as 1905 by that intrepid proponent of a "people's railway," Charles C. Farr. In his northern newspaper *The Haileyburian*, he argued that, before joining the Commission its members had always "worked for themselves, not for the State." An efficient manager should be appointed, he continued "and leave with the Government the final...power of veto or endorsation."[1]

The provincial government paid scant heed to this advice, continuing to treat the Commission as an arm of the cabinet, directed by businessmen who had demonstrated both financial skills and loyalty to the party in power. With those requirements and an acceptable degree of efficiency, the Commission could be assured of financial support from the government for capital costs, so long as it showed a modest return on investment and promoted northern development.

The cabinet also maintained the right to select executive personnel. In practice, this executive power originated in the office of the premier. Lacking a framework of policy, his delegation of authority tended to be pragmatic and he was often swayed by individuals who had gained his confidence. For example,

71

George Ross delegated the drafting of the original statute of the T&NO in 1901 to his Minister of Public Works, F.R. Latchford, a lawyer who consulted informally with the railway contractor, M.J.O'Brien. To finance the railway, Ross arranged through the brokers A.E. Ames and E.R. Wood to borrow from an English bank historically associated with Canadian Liberal governments. Under J.P. Whitney, financing was rearranged with partisan intent at the Bank of Montréal in London. Since 1906 the day-to-day running of the Commission had been left to J.L. Englehart, who had no general manager in the North. He in turn corresponded regularly, not with any assigned government department, but with his friend and business associate, W.J. Hanna, who held the post of Provincial Secretary.

After two decades, the T&NO Railway still operated without a definite policy. That fact grows in significance from 1917 to 1923; years which witnessed an interruption of continuous Conservative government, the retirement of Jacob Englehart, another destructive fire in the North, and a major extension eastward to the great iron mines of Rouyn-Noranda.

These events must be considered in the light of the provincial election of 1919, which terminated fourteen years of Conservative government. William Hearst had succeeded Whitney as premier five years before. Hearst's leadership coincided with the declining fortunes of the Conservative party. The discontent of farmers at the manner in which the Union government in Ottawa had handled conscription presented the Hearst government with a complicated issue. Ontario farmers equated the federal Conservative government of Borden in Ottawa with the provincial Conservative government in Toronto, and blamed the latter for the national conscription policies which took their sons from the land. The end of the war in 1918 did not alter the grievances of farmers and workers against privileged manufacturers, mine owners, timber merchants and railway directors, who used their influence over government to exploit high tariffs, fixed freight rates, and inflated prices. Farmers found themselves unable to match sales with costs. A pervasive fear arose that their historic way of life held no future. Voters in rural districts and small towns were also discontented at what they considered to be weaknesses in the Ontario Temperance Act.[2]

Based on these potent reasons to oppose the government, a loose political group organized themselves as the United Farmers of Ontario in 1918. Suddenly – as much to their surprise as anyone else's – they were called upon to form a government after the 1919 election. With the support of a small Labour party and a few Independents, the United Farmers held a bare majority over both the Liberals and the Conservatives. Overnight, they had become the governing party.[3]

The prospect of governing the province challenged but also intimidated the new farmer-members. It took time even to agree on a leader. When they finally selected E.C. Drury, a farmer from the Barrie region, he accepted less from ambition than from a conviction that the farmers' movement would be defeated if he did not assume the responsibility of forming a government.[4]

Nevertheless, during his brief four years as premier, Drury illustrated an astute capacity to select men, and to reconcile goals with political reality, despite the objections of his more doctrinaire colleagues. He reacted with responsible, efficient action when faced with perplexing issues. Three particular issues on the T&NO required decisive action during his tenure as premier. The first concerned the chairmanship of the Commission; the second involved the extensive Haileybury fire of 1922; the third a proposed further extension of the railway eastward beyond the new gold mines of Kirkland Lake.

The Appointment of George Lee

By 1919, J.L. Englehart had been chairman of the T&NO for thirteen years. He maintained his dominance over the railway in spite of age and ill health, and remained a patriarchal figure, respected even while considered eccentric by those who dealt with him. His strong loyalty to the province and the railway was vividly demonstrated in March of 1919 when the newly formed Canadian National Railway attempted to remove its "National" train from the T&NO tracks.

The "National" ran three times a week from Toronto over the Grand Trunk line to North Bay; from there to Cochrane it steamed its way over the tracks of the T&NO; and from Cochrane to Winnipeg it carried a large passenger traffic on the east-west line of the National Transcontinental Railway. The "National" constituted a vital connecting link between Toronto and western Canada. Its use of the T&NO tracks had been one of the reasons for extending the provincial line north to the junction at Cochrane. Lease of the right of way had been negotiated by Englehart with the Grand Trunk in 1911. After 1915, the agreement brought a rent of $300,000 per annum plus yearly maintenance charges of $250,000, money which helped to maintain jobs in northern railway towns.[5] The train passed through fourteen towns between Toronto and Cochrane, expanding the dimensions of the T&NO beyond those of a local railway. For good reason, therefore, Englehart determined that the arrangement should continue.

The traffic manager of the newly-formed CNR, however, now had to sustain traffic on the old Canadian Northern Railway running from Parry Sound north to Sudbury and then northwestward to Fort William. He wanted to divert the "National" to that line, enabling it to travel from Toronto to Parry Sound and Sudbury, then to Fort William and from there to Winnipeg. George Lee heard rumours of this proposal and, obtaining permission from Englehart, went first to Ottawa and then to Montréal to intervene with C.A. Hayes, vice-president of the Canadian National Railway. Lee reported to Englehart that Hayes did indeed intend to divert the "National" and bypass the T&NO. "We want," said Hayes, "100 per cent business to go over CNR, Toronto to Winnipeg."

Lee replied "that we had helped to build up the business of the 'National' and made it the most paying train in the country and had developed the most popular route to the West." He pointed out that the train served close to 75,000 people between Toronto and Cochrane – about 30,000 of them in small towns from Aurora to Huntsville and over 40,000 in the six northern towns of North Bay, Cobalt, Haileybury, New Liskeard, Timmins and Cochrane. By then the population of North Bay had grown to about 10,000; the tri-town area contained over 12,000; and the Porcupine mining towns added another 15,000 persons.[6]

Lee may have exaggerated in describing the "National" as the "most popular route to the West." But no doubt existed of its value to the T&NO. Apart from rental income, it earned over $182,000 annually for the T&NO in 1919. This represented 30 per cent of the railway's total passenger earnings. Englehart immediately wrote to G. Howard Ferguson, provincial Minister of Lands, Forests and Mines. His letter was typically direct and clipped in style, as though dictated by a telegrapher with no concern for the trivia of expression. For Englehart, prose simply served as a means of stating the essential points of an issue. One wrote as one spoke, without verbiage or ornament. What difference was there between a letter and a telegram? After all, he had been sending telegrams for most of his working life. To Ferguson he wrote:

> What is the underlying menace – is it endeavor additional knockout for G.T.R. [Grand Trunk Railway], your Province and Western Provinces, and for the G.T.P. [Grand Trunk Pacific] west of Winnipeg... Personally, have for many weeks, months anticipated just about – may possibly go as far as to say, exactly what they propose to do, aggregation C.N. Railway, but from Chairman's point view it is not a knockout...

> Further, matter of five, at outside limit, ten years, our connecting railways will be bidding for the tonnage and local passenger traffic within confines of T.N.O.R....But have the faith, my dear Mr. Minister, that you propose to call upon Dr. Reid [Minister of Railways in Ottawa] and advise – inform him, in unmistakable terms that Province of Ontario will not stand for any such highway robbery...

Ferguson instantly brought this correspondence to Premier Hearst's attention. Within the day, Hearst directed two telegrams to Ottawa. One went to W.T. White, Minister of Finance and Acting Prime Minister; the other to J.D. Reid successor to the ailing Frank Cochrane as Minister of Railways and Canals. Both White and Reid represented Ontario constituencies; both had close ties with the Ontario Conservative party. Hearst sent identical messages to each, saying in part: "any action such as suggested would be strongly condemned by a very large portion of the people of the province."[7]

Reid also replied by telegram. Sensing a serious political rift, he stated bluntly that any attempt to remove the "National" must first have his approval. He added that he had no intention of granting it, assuring Hearst that the premier was unnecessarily alarmed. But the CNR was determined. Hayes came to see Hearst and stated the proposal in person. He only retreated when Hearst vigorously confirmed the opposition of the Ontario government.

For the time being no further attempt was made to remove the "National" from its T&NO run. That the matter had been settled in just over a week's time confirmed the unique place the T&NO held by contrast with other railways across the Dominion.

The Canadian Northern had been nationalized by an Order-in-Council of the Union Government in Ottawa in 1917. After that it was inevitable that the

National Transcontinental, the Grand Trunk Pacific, and the Grand Trunk itself would all be absorbed by the new, government-controlled Canadian National Railways.

The T&NO remained independent of the new system; the provincial government made no suggestion that it should be sold or included in the federal network. Reasons for this continuing autonomy were obvious. The provincial railway had a close association with the development of the North's social and economic community; it was dependably solvent, remitting cheques almost annually to the Ontario Treasurer in amounts which may have been at a low rate of return on the full capital investment, but which were deposited with silent appreciation in the government's Consolidated Revenue Fund.[8]

The railway's management also demonstrated a detailed eye for efficiency. Englehart and Lee developed a working relationship from 1914 to 1919; with Englehart as the dignified remote chairman, supervising affairs in Toronto, and Lee as the conscientious, affable administrator, scrutinizing the day-to-day affairs of the railway from his office in North Bay. Lee provided the detailed information and the management, supported by W.H. Maund as Secretary-Treasurer. Englehart expressed the interest and the loyalty of the T&NO, with a flair for his own kind of rhetoric.

Taking dictation from him must have resembled listening to Mr. Jingle in Dickens' *Pickwick Papers*, though Englehart's style of expression was decidedly more American than English. Writing to Premier Hearst on March 11, 1919, he said:

> The old Texan, David Crockett, looking up the tree, found the Coon – the Coon saw David, and without hesitation, said: "Do not shoot. I'll come down." Appears to me, your prompt following-up our good friends of C.N.R., they found that they were not the only people on earth. Will do them good, and largely satisfying to our good people.

The next day he added that the chairman of the CNR, D.B. Hanna, to whom he referred as the Commander-in-Chief, "was the Coon who came down."

Englehart's health was deteriorating, however, and this contributed to a worrying frame of mind. He wrote to the premier on March 13:

> Unfortunately my disposition is so serious that I lack confidence, the C-in-C of the Canadian National Railways, and with these thoughts, conference, my rooms, Queens, last night, Comm'r Lee – Chief Engineer Clement, and Sup't Traffic Griffin – review of situation, and with the solemn instruction that the one above all others at this hour is the possibility of Diversion, i.e. diverting the traffic, freight particularly, which has heretofore come over your Railway...

In Hearst's mind the issue had been settled. Reid had assured him from Ottawa that the CNR would take no action which would threaten the revenue of the T&NO. Of concern now was the health of Englehart and arrangements for his eventual retirement, "relieving him of his heavy burdens." Early in July of 1919 Englehart travelled to the Algonquin Hotel at St. Andrews-by-the-Sea in New

Brunswick. Hearst wrote to him in terms which indicated that both men knew his services were drawing to a close.

> Your work, not only in the management of the railway, but in making known the great wealth of our North and in helping its development, will stand as a monument for all time, and few public men can look back on fifteen years of such devoted, unselfish and successful work in the interests of his country.[9]

When Englehart returned in September, Hearst wrote an even more flattering letter of recognition, which Englehart said left him speechless. But he could no longer serve as chairman. Then, within a month, the election of October replaced Hearst with Drury as premier.

Understandably, when Drury took office in November 1919, certain apprehensions arose throughout the T&NO. To some degree, unease existed in the North generally, stirred by a number of questions. The chairman was more than a nominal figure; he gave active, executive direction to the management of the railway. Who, then, would succeed Englehart? Should the new chairman be a political appointment, as Ames, Jaffray, and Englehart had all been? Should the new head of the Commission come from the North? Should he be experienced in running a railroad? Behind these immediate questions an even more fundamental one surfaced. With the untried United Farmers in office would the T&NO be sold to the federal government and merged with the new Canadian National Railways?

Swiftly and decisively, the question of sale met vehement opposition in the North. In November 1919, only a month after the election and before Drury could even form his cabinet, the Board of Trade in Cobalt sent him a telegram urgently asking that he delay any appointment to the Commission until he visited the North. The businessmen of Cobalt had their own recommendations and they were certain other towns shared their opinions. The qualifications of each northern candidate, they said, should be fully weighed. Three weeks later letters followed, from both Matheson and Cobalt. Again, they pressed for continued control by the provincial government, and also that men from northern Ontario be appointed to the Commission. While Drury carefully considered these requests, he took his time reaching a decision. He sympathized with opinion in the North for provincial government control of the railway, but he adhered also to the platform of the UFO in its opposition to political patronage, whether from the North or elsewhere in the province.[10]

In the meantime, Drury appointed George Lee as acting chairman. Lee had joined the T&NO in 1907 as General Agent at North Bay, doing the real work of surveying and administering the sale of land for the Land Commissioner, Frederick Dane. When Dane retired in 1914, Premier Hearst appointed Lee to the Commission. His administrative powers expanded, placing him in a position to run the railroad as Englehart's age and illness gradually prevented his leaving Toronto and living in his private car in the North, as he had done during the first decade of his chairmanship. Lee was managing the railroad for $4,500 a year – $2,500 as General Agent and $2,000 as one of the three members of the

Commission. He continued at this salary as acting chairman even after Engle-hart's honorarium of $7,500 had been cancelled in January 1920.[11]

Drury made his choice in the early summer of that year. Lacking a partisan choice of his own, he put aside his objections to Lee as originally a Conservative political appointment. Lee had become the most experienced man on the Com-mission, an affable administrator and a resident of North Bay, with acquaint-ances and connections from there to Cochrane. In many ways he was the high-est ranking civil servant on the railway. His appointment marked a departure from the past, one which pleased both Drury and the businessmen who had pleaded for a northern chairman. George Lee remained chairman for the next fourteen years, until 1934. He maintained an unprecedented executive power by combining his new post with his position as general manager.

The Third and Last Great Fire

An urgent telephone call from Lee to Drury on the evening of October 4, 1922 informed the premier of another calamitous fire in the North. The country from Haileybury to Englehart and beyond had been laid waste. New Liskeard escaped the worst of the flames, but most villages together with outlying farms, lumber camps, and pit-heads had been burned out. The number of dead was not yet known. Lee asked the premier to come North personally and in his *Memoirs* Drury later described the arrangements he made to hold the 8:45 train for him that night at Toronto's St. Clair Station. Before arriving in North Bay the next morning, he stopped at Aurora, Allandale, and Bracebridge, at each stop mak-ing a long-distance telephone call to organize a relief train which would leave Toronto before noon the following day. The cars were loaded with supplies from the military stores of the federal government, with food and blankets from provincial institutions, and with thirty provincial policemen to supervise and guard the distribution of goods.

Without the railway, and the adjacent telegraph and telephone lines, relief could not have been provided for 6,000 people left suddenly homeless. The following night a train pulled out of North Bay, consisting of five baggage cars loaded with supplies, a passenger car with policemen and Red Cross nurses, and a private car for Drury and Lee. It made stops at every siding where people gathered, waiting for food, blankets, and tents.

Drury saw nothing remarkable in the fact that he was first informed of the fire by the chairman of the T&NO Commission; that George Lee should be the first person to meet him at North Bay; or that Lee had become so vital in the affairs of the north country. The office of chairman gave Lee an importance as easily accepted by the premier as that of any elected representative or official of a government department. Together the two men travelled in the private coach called the "Temagami," stopping to talk with survivors, learning details of the disaster, and giving encouragement and sympathy. The train moved slowly through the night from Cobalt to Englehart, pausing at mounds of smouldering debris which had once been station-houses or stores, or homes, or barns and stables, but whose red embers now provided the only light and warmth in a charred and desolate countryside.

At Englehart the train stopped. The bridge to the North had burned. Drury remained until afternoon, observing the devastation of the surrounding country and the burned corpses lying on the earthen floor of the Agricultural Fair Building. As the train returned south he stared out on a scene which he recalled vividly when writing about it more than forty years later:

> We left for home in the middle of the afternoon. The sky had cleared, with a brisk north wind and a promise of a heavy frost that night. Across the blackened country we could see the white tents we had borrowed from the military set up here and there, and we knew that the most pressing needs had been taken care of. None would perish of cold or hunger. And none did.[12]

From the tranquillity of hindsight, Drury could express satisfaction at his efforts. He did not describe the immediate grief and despair of survivors, or their state of shock at the ghastly scenes they had witnessed. They had heard the wind become a sudden roar, had seen the invisible force become a mass of flame, hurling burning logs to the roofs of buildings, lifting roofs into the air to land on other structures, the whole fearsome turmoil creating an inferno of smoke and flame wherever buildings stood close together. Only grotesque empty walls remained of churches, schools, and public buildings, giving the appearance of those grey, ghost-like French towns which had been heavily bombarded during World War I. "Scenes at Haileybury," said the Toronto *Mail and Empire*, "were beyond description, so suddenly and almost without warning did the holocaust descend. Men who went unmoved through the worst battles in France, broke into sobs."[13]

Grief mingled with the need to blame. People wondered about the cause. As at Matheson in 1916, suspicion arose in some minds that sparks from a steam locomotive had started a small fire by the tracks and no one had put it out. Others claimed that the worst of the flames at Haileybury originated at the frame railway station.

In truth, the fire had started some distance away, from the burning of brush by saw-mill workers near Elk Lake to the west. Vagaries of the wind had spread the fire to the region of New Liskeard where, ironically, fire rangers had recently been dismissed because municipal authorities considered them unnecessary and expensive. The wind changed direction again on the morning of October 4, by-passing New Liskeard and sweeping down on Haileybury without warning. Embers, lifted on the crest of the swirling flames dropped onto the roof of the railway station, which burned to the ground, while the wind swept the roof to another structure and set it ablaze. For survivors lacking accurate information, these events were proof enough of the railway's guilt. Why wasn't the station renovated months before with roofing materials able to withstand northern fires?[14]

Criticism lingered in varying degrees, to fade gradually as the trains once again played a special role in the work of recovery. Stories circulated about the stolid service and sometimes the bravery of engine crews. One story told of the action of Jim McKerrow, an engineman on a locomotive journeying south:

> He was a tall skinny guy. And when they were comin' down on the last relief train from the north, down through...Thornloe...up on the hill there was a sod shack and logs...Everything else was burning. And there was a red flag up in front of this house.
>
> Now in those days a red flag meant typhoid. And there was somebody in there – typhoid – which was contagious. So, the train stopped and all the people are getting on, and Jim gets off and sees this woman out in front, and she's screaming and waving her arms. Big Jim runs across over there, says what's the matter; she says my twelve-year-old daughter's in there's got typhoid. I can't leave 'er, I won't leave 'er – what're we goin' to do? Jim just rushed in, grabbed the kid up in his arms with a blanket around 'er and run down and put 'er on the train, got on the locomotive and they went on down ...And he never got typhoid or anythin' like it.[15]

Immediately after the fire, flat cars of the T&NO transported eighty-five discarded street cars from Toronto, to serve as temporary shelters for homeless families between Cobalt and Englehart. Some of these, boarded over and crudely insulated, had to last through the long winter. Supplying these cars could be considered a small gesture, but it symbolized the widespread concern over a major disaster in the north of the province. Forty-three people had burned to death or suffocated, as compared with seventy-three in the fire of 1911, and 223 in 1916, but at Haileybury and the surrounding area, six thousand people were homeless. The damage to property and buildings was placed at $6,000,000.[16]

Such immense losses required revival of the Northern Ontario Fire Relief Committee. It assembled immediately, sitting through the night of October 4, giving the benefit of its previous experience to officials acting directly on orders from Premier Drury. Its members had no hesitation in taking some of the credit for the train which left Toronto late on the morning of Thursday, October 5 containing "10,400 blankets, 510 tents, 2,100 ground sheets, a supply of lanterns, camp kettles and pots, and 12½ tons of foodstuffs." The Committee represented the Toronto Board of Trade, the Associated Boards of Trade for the province, and the mayor of Toronto. Its members were generally Conservative. They resented Drury's direct interference, believing he should have assigned the organization of relief entirely to them.

In a sense, the North was still a colony of Toronto. Riches from the mines and forests of the northeast all flowed into or through the provincial capital. Relief for victims and recovery of property at a time of emergency were responsibilities which these businessmen could readily associate with their profitable financial interests in the North.

But Drury was right to give the orders he did, and to become directly involved. The office of premier held the ultimate responsibility for organizing

79

relief and for the conduct of the T&NO. His action tapped an intuitive response of sympathy and service that went far beyond the offices of businessmen and officials. During the following six weeks, donations were generously given by individuals, by groups, institutions, and by town councils all over the province. Villages the size of Beamsville and Waterford, or small towns such as Aylmer and Keewatin, contributed $100 each. Peterborough and Fort William each sent $500, as did Regina in Saskatchewan. The Danforth Business Men's Association in Toronto and the town of Guelph each raised $1,000. The Belleville Cheese Board sent $500, and the Christian Scientists of Toronto $700.[17]

Altogether the Committee received $272,600 by mid-November, and they could boast that total receipts since formation of the original Fire Relief Committee in 1916 were over $600,000. The Drury government then established a new, more representative Committee, which assumed responsibility for distributing an unspent balance of $247,000. Its chairman was George Lee.

Meanwhile, at Haileybury, an abandoned house served as the centre for assessing need and doling out relief. Refugees lined up for supplies which arrived daily on freight cars of the T&NO. A tent now stood in place of the burned-out railway station, with only a red house, a hen coop and a small garage around it. The railway was an integral part of the devastation, as it would be of the rebuilding and recovery of the next few years.

Indeed, at every level of its operation the T&NO had proved itself to be an essential link in providing relief through the three major fires of 1911, 1916, and 1922. In the future, the Department of Lands, Forests and Mines would insist on imposing more efficient regulations. Fire rangers would be appointed and paid, with the requisite skills and authority to control the burning of brush. Disastrous fires on the scale of these three would never again sweep through northern towns.

Eastward to Rouyn-Noranda

The tragedy of fire, the destruction of homes and farms, did not halt the discovery, extraction and transporting of resources. Forest fires left underground ore unaffected. Mining continued to be the most lucrative industry in the northeast. Royalties to the provincial government and dividends to shareholders did not bring a new technology to the North, with numerous jobs or a larger urban environment. But the wealth from silver and gold, and eventually from copper, zinc and iron, lent a glamorous if superficial justification for provincial investment in the T&NO as a railway promoting the original goal of colonization and development.

Where new resources appeared, neither the Commission nor the government could ignore the need for expanded service if the railway was to compete as a sound business enterprise. Shortly after the fire of 1922, Lee received a report from the Commission's Mining Engineer, Arthur Cole, recommending the building of a branch line eastward from Swastika. The Mining Association of Canada presented a similar request some months later. Lee approved the proposal and building began for twenty-three miles beyond Kirkland Lake to Larder Lake, while surveys were carried out in anticipation of further extension to Rouyn, Québec. This extension, said the *Annual Report* of 1924, would "open up a territory which is daily increasing in importance, and second only to the Porcupine district in its potential mineral wealth."

Where were these places? Why were they selected? These questions can only be answered by an account of mining in the Kirkland Lake area, where prospecting for gold had begun in the late nineteenth century.

Swastika is thirty miles north of Englehart, on the main line of the T&NO. Rumours circulated at the turn of the century that gold was certain to be found in the area between Swastika and Kirkland Lake, six miles to the east. At that time the Cobalt discoveries of 1904 and those at Porcupine in 1909 dominated the potential of other regions. Not until 1911 was gold found for certain at Kirkland Lake, but prospectors realized that the metal lay deeper in the ground, and claims were therefore staked at greater risk than at Porcupine. Veins would not be found easily and accidentally by stripping off a thin covering of moss.

Harry Oakes made the difference at Kirkland Lake. He arrived with a knowledge, a persistence and a stubborn independence of mind which enabled him to amalgamate a group of claims into his Lake Shore Mines Limited. An American from the state of Maine, Oakes rebelled at the idea of settling into a conventional middle-class business with a college degree. Oakes had youth and a venturesome nature. He wanted his own wealth, and he wanted it from the most elementary and trustworthy source; from gold which came directly from the rocks and streams of the earth. Attracted to the gold rush in the Klondike and later in Alaska, he confidently set out for both of them, coming back an ambitious and self-centred young man with a determination to outwit others and establish independent control when and where he found his own gold mine.

From Alaska he journeyed to the Kalgoorlie mines in Australia, where he learned that gold might be found with tellurium in the form of tellurides, from which gold could be heated out and distinguished by its different colour. Here was a new complexity in gold mining which Oakes had never seen in Alaska or the Yukon. When he returned to America, he tried prospecting in California and Cripple Creek, Colorado. Here again he observed tellurides taken out of porphyry. He also learned to distinguish between porphyry and granite. From Colorado he came to Canada, having heard of the riches of Cobalt and the Porcupine. In 1911 he went to the Department of Mines in Toronto to enquire about the latest information on rock formation and the likelihood of minerals in the Timiskaming district. He learned there of the possible existence of porphyry east of Swastika. In June he arrived in the region when the T&NO was nearing completion of its new line into Porcupine. The rock formation was indeed porphyry as he had seen it in Colorado. But Oakes kept his silence, waiting and watching for claims which he might acquire.

He learned in Toronto that a claim central to the staking then being made in the region would be coming up for renewal or sale. Oakes paid a local "bushwhacker" to stake the claim and transfer it to him. He then staked two claims

81

of his own during the next winter. At the time the Mining Act allowed only three claims to be staked in any one year on an individual licence. That deterrent, together with his lack of money, induced Oakes to play a waiting game in the hope of steadily assembling a concentrated holding which would give him control over a "one-man" mine. His methods worked. Through the winter of 1911-12 he persuaded the four Tough brothers, then working on a road from Larder Lake to Swastika, to take up a claim at the eastern end of Teck Township, a partnership which led to the Tough-Oakes mine with Oakes himself largely in control.

About the same time, W.H. Wright appeared in the area. An Englishman and a former cavalryman with little knowledge of mining but ambitious to find gold among Kirkland Lake claims, he staked three claims during the early summer of 1911 and found free gold on one of them. Over the next few months he acquired additional property, putting some of it in the name of his sister's husband, Ed Hargreaves, then living in Cobalt. Again, one of these claims contained a vein of free gold and by September 1911, he had assembled the property which became the Wright-Hargreaves Mine. Wright then negotiated with Harry Oakes on yet another claim, enabling Oakes to complete the grouping of claims which he called the Lake Shore Mining Company, chartered in 1914.

Oakes developed his property over the next few years to a depth of 8,000 feet, making it the deepest gold mine in North America. It was also among the richest; certainly the richest ever controlled by one man, yielding more than $265,000,000 in gold before ceasing production in 1968. This figure exceeded the combined total of the Wright-Hargreaves and the Teck-Hughes mines, the next two largest mines in the Kirkland Lake region. The Ontario Department of Mines calculated in 1970, after the area had generally ceased to be a major producer of gold, that in the previous half century more than $700,000,000 had been mined, with at least a third of the value coming from Oakes' Lake Shore Mine.[18]

Harry Oakes and William Wright, like the Timmins brothers when they ventured into silver at Cobalt and gold at Porcupine, were examples of the fabulous success made possible by a combination of shrewd, determined bargaining, of knowledge and experience, but above all of persistence and sheer luck in turning very small amounts of risk capital into millions of dollars by the extraction of minerals imbedded in the rock of northern Ontario. Wright received 200,000 shares in Oakes' Lake Shore Mine for transferring one claim, and those shares alone sustained a market value of $10,000,000 on the Toronto Stock Exchange through the depression of the 1930s, quite apart from the greater wealth which he derived from control of the Wright-Hargreaves Mine.

Leaving the management of the mine to others, Wright took his shares and moved south to Barrie. Near the small town he bought some fine farm land on which he erected an elaborate racing stable. In 1936 his flow of easy money from the North enabled Wright to provide the capital by which the Toronto *Globe* became a Conservative newspaper, absorbing also the *Mail and Empire* which had been controlled until then by I.W. Killam of Montréal. As for Harry Oakes, he displayed his wealth more flamboyantly, acquiring an estate and a town house in England, his Oak Hall estate at Niagara Falls, a chateau at Kirkland Lake, and extensive property in the Bahamas, where he was mysteriously murdered in 1943. Wright and Oakes both remained foreigners in the North. Neither gave a thought to reinvestment of his money as capital for development of industry and technology in the region which had so readily given of its bounty. For them the North began and ended as a hinterland of vast mineral wealth which could be lavishly expended elsewhere.

The ore of Kirkland Lake could be transported without use of a branch line. In 1917 a macadam road sufficed, allowing trucks to haul the ore a short six miles to Swastika, where it could then be loaded onto the main-line cars of the T&NO. This arrangement appeared adequate at the end of the war, but the Commission came under repeated pressure in 1920 to extend its track a distance of twenty-three miles eastward from Swastika to the area around Larder Lake. There, promoters sought to attract the Commission's aid in developing what appeared to be yet another gold field. The response of Lee and his staff, and of the Drury government, demonstrates a fundamental feature in the history of the Commission – its caution and accountability.

It can be argued that since its inception the railway had acted as a vehicle or form of subsidy by which the provincial government provided transportation for entrepreneurs intent upon the exploitation of mineral and timber resources in the North. Politicians, civil servants, and officials of the railway itself agreed on this function. But they were wary of requests for new services and extensions of the line.

In 1910 J.L. Englehart had authorized study of a possible extension westward into the mining fields of Gowganda. The report he received described a new mining frontier containing close to five thousand people, with a crowded and inadequate stage road from Charlton. Freight cars, loaded with supplies, were backed up on the sidings of the T&NO. The writer suggested that the Commission would be compelled to build or face serious competition from the Canadian Northern Railway, which could build to Gowganda from the south and west.[19] But the Mining Engineer of the T&NO insisted that only a limited body of ore existed and that a branch line from Charlton was not justified. The Commission finally provided a short line from Earlton to Elk Lake, thereby reducing its commitment. At Kirkland Lake in 1917 the building of a road for trucks was left to the Northern Development Branch of the government.[20]

Now in 1920, similar problems emerged over the extension of the railway eastward to Larder Lake. The issue began within the cabinet itself. Drury's Minister of Lands, Forests, and Mines wrote to the premier in March 1920, informing him that the Associated Goldfields Company wanted construction of a branch line twenty-six miles eastward from Swastika. The Toronto-based company had so far produced gold in small quantity, but its executives argued that development was being hampered only by lack of adequate transportation. The Minister's letter to Drury said:

> Before the Government gives any attention to the request of the Associated Goldfields Mining Company Limited for assistance in

building a railway into Larder Lake the Company should be made to furnish a report on the properties by a Canadian mining engineer of standing – preferably the mining engineer should be a graduate of one of our Universities – Toronto, Queen's or McGill.[21]

Drury turned the problem over to the T&NO Commission. A month later Lee replied enclosing reports from the chief engineer and the mining engineer of the Commission. Their conclusions stated that the value and extent of the ore bodies would not justify the construction of a branch line. At the present time, said Lee, "there is not enough traffic in sight...to warrant the extending of any railway into Larder Lake."[22]

The pressure persisted, nevertheless, not only from companies in the district, but from hundreds of prospectors. In May of 1920 one petition went to the Lieutenant Governor in Council from the "New Ontario Prospectors' Association." All the members held claims in the Kirkland Lake and Boston Creek areas. An extension into Larder Lake, they said, "would provide cheaper transportation for the prospectors, who have been the pioneers of this country." The 103 names on their petition included the manager of the Wright-Hargreaves Mine. A second petition, also sent to the Lieutenant Governor in Council, and similarly worded, was signed by an additional two hundred persons. Among them was the stamp of the Teck-Hughes Mine with a signature; and towards the end, with no stamp or title, similar to the signature of any other scraping and grubbing prospector, is the scrawled name: Harry Oakes.[23]

At that time, in 1920, the petitions were simply filed and ignored, but more forceful influences were brought to bear on Drury. A.A. Powers, Executive Director of the United Farmers Co-Operative Company, sent him a letter strongly supporting the proposal of Associated Goldfields for the sale of land on a large scale to finance construction of the line. Drury deflected his request by telling Powers that he intended to travel North himself to assess the possibilities.

At the end of July he received another long letter from Lee, giving detailed estimates which indicated that the line would cost $1,000,000 to build and that current anticipated revenues would lead to an annual deficit of over $100,-000. The Chief Inspector of Mines for the province wrote to the premier in August to confirm all the previous negative judgements. Whatever the claims of the companies and the prospectors, the government, on advice from the T&NO Commission, clearly refused to be hurried into spending on resource development unless adequate returns on investment in the railway could be anticipated. Drury had sufficient evidence for withholding his approval.[24]

A slight paradox exists in this correspondence. The reputations of Teck-Hughes, of Wright-Hargreaves, of Harry Oakes and his Lake Shore Mine, were already accomplishing for gold-mining in the Kirkland Lake region what Dome, McIntyre, and Hollinger had achieved for Porcupine only a few years before. At the end of World War I, they were turning Ontario into one of the major sources of gold in the world. In 1920 the true obstacles were the scarcity of capital and the high price of materials. Canadian railways were overbuilt and war had inflated the cost of goods. Any government had cause to be wary of more investment in railway tracks. The Canadian National Railways had only just been formed from the bankrupt Canadian Northern and Grand Trunk systems.

The optimistic prospectors' petitions in 1920, however, indicated the anticipation of finding not only gold but other metals. While activity in the region had led to the conclusion that the mines at Larder Lake might be small, farther east in the Québec region of Rouyn-Noranda were large reserves of copper mixed with gold. Information about this ore came to the fore in the summer of 1922, and led to a recommendation in the report which Arthur Cole submitted to Lee that November:

> Considering the success that has attended the developments of the past summer, I now think the time is opportune for the very careful consideration of a branch extension from Swastika through Kirkland Lake, continuing east to a point on Larder Lake.[25]

The evidence now seemed convincing. Drury gave his approval, as did his Conservative successor in the office of premier, G. Howard Ferguson. Lee announced in April 1923 that the roadbed would be constructed as "the Nipissing Central Railway, under a charter which we hold from the Dominion Government, to enable us to enter the Province of Québec and proceed over to the Rouyn region, if further developments warrant it."[26] Construction began that summer and ended at Larder Lake in the fall of 1924.

In the meantime, the Conservatives had been returned to power under the leadership of Ferguson, with whom George Lee quickly established an amicable relationship. The new premier had no cause to contemplate a change in the chairmanship of the Commission. Instead, he and Lee worked closely together to complete this new eastward extension into Québec, whatever the financial and constitutional problems. During the summer of 1925 construction proceeded to the Québec border, where they were stopped by opposition from the Québec government. The delay lasted for two years while the government of Québec contested the Dominion charter of the Nipissing Central Railway in the courts.

Ferguson determined to press the advantage of the Ontario government railway. As Minister of Lands, Forests, and Mines in the Hearst government from 1914 to 1919, he had acquired a strong interest in northern development. Mineral and forest resources had been a part of the ethos of the Ontario Conservative party since the days of Whitney and Frank Cochrane before World War I. And in 1924, no other railway possessed such close access to the Noranda mines.

But in Québec City and Montréal, in the offices of the Liberal provincial government of Premier Taschereau and in the financial houses of St. James Street, powerful traditional interests were determined to keep the exploitation of the new Rouyn-Noranda mines within the province of Québec. The business created by those mines could go either to Montréal via an extension of the Canadian Pacific Railway from Mattawa north, or to Québec City by means of a new line south from the transcontinental route of the Canadian National Railway. The Ontario weekly, *The Northern Miner*, pointed out in the summer of 1924:

> ...the Canadian Pacific Railway, which has a branch running north within seventy miles of the Rouyn gold field, has under consideration the construction of an extension to the Québec gold district, with a possible branch running into the Northern Ontario gold fields; and it was felt by the Government that in such case, the inevitable result must be that a great deal of the traffic which now passes down the T. & N.O. through North Bay and Toronto would be diverted through Québec to Montréal, and that Toronto would lose much of its business to Québec city.[27]

The Northern Miner, a Toronto publication, referred to Ontario when it used the word "government." That "government" won its case in the Supreme Court of Canada. Québec then appealed the decision to the Judicial Committee of the Privy Council in London, England, the highest court of appeal for all legal disputes in the Dominion of Canada. In 1926 the Ontario government again received a judgement in its favour, giving the Nipissing Central Railway, a subsidiary of the T&NO, the right to build and operate a railroad from the provincial boundary to the Rouyn-Noranda mining field. The victory had cost $65,000 in legal fees and a delay of two years at Cheminis on the Québec border.[28]

With legal obstacles cleared away by 1927, Ferguson as the premier of Ontario authorized extension of the branch line in Québec from Cheminis to Rouyn-Noranda. The *Annual Report* of the T&NO for 1927 stated that the total distance was sixty miles and that the district was fast becoming an important source of gold and copper ores, with some companies already in production while prospecting continued. The next year, in 1928, this branch line finally reached its destination beyond the Québec boundary.

By then the T&NO with its subsidiary the Nipissing Central, provided access to Cobalt, the Porcupine, Kirkland Lake, and Rouyn-Noranda.[29] The railway became identified more strongly than ever with northern development – with the movement of ore, timber, pulp, and paper; with the traffic of people to schools and jobs and stores; with the steady growth of communities such as Cochrane, Timmins, Iroquois Falls, and now Rouyn. The T&NO Commission was also associated with the increase of speculation and wealth in the brokerage offices of Toronto, fast becoming the financial capital for northern investment. Inevitably, all this growth led to thoughts of finally extending the railway to an ocean port on James Bay.

chapter 9

The Illusion of Moosonee

Searching and Surveying

The vision of a northern ocean port had never been far from the surface since the founding of the T&NO in 1902. As early as 1905, the Whitney government had authorized a survey of the country north from the site of the present town of Cochrane. It included a study of conditions adjacent to a possible railway route. A sum of $7,500 had been voted by the Legislature to complete the survey and the figure had been carried on the estimates of the Department of Public Works. This study favoured the region close to Moose Factory over the mouth of the Albany River as a terminus. The study also showed disappointing prospects for mineral development. Only gypsum and lignite appeared in quantity. No signs pointed to reserves of petroleum or natural gas which the government had hoped to find beneath the James Bay Lowlands, though peat seemed to occur "in almost limitless amount."[1]

Exploration remained incomplete until Englehart authorized another probe north from Cochrane in 1911. Conducted by a private firm of consulting engineers, with the appropriate Conservative connections, this expedition undertook "an exploratory survey of the country between Cochrane and James Bay and instrumental surveys of the estuaries of the Moose and Harricanaw Rivers." Again, the reports recommended the mouth of the Moose River as the terminus of any railway at James Bay. The reports of 1911 were called "the first accurate instrumental surveys that have ever been made" of the region, according useful information for the future choice of a terminus and harbour between the Nelson River and the Québec boundary.[2]

The most remarkable implication in these early surveys was the inherent assumption that Ontario could and should develop a northern ocean port. The consulting engineer, J.G.G. Kerry, addressed the Toronto branch of the Canadian Society of Civil Engineers and then published his talk in the *Canadian Engineer* in 1914. Moose Harbour, said Kerry, "provides a magnificent site for the creation of a great port." He had studied silting in the Mississippi River and at Toronto Island. The problems he found there were not repeated at the mouth of the Moose River, "which can be readily converted into a protective harbour of the Montréal type..." Englehart sent all of this favourable material to William Hearst, then Minister of Lands, Forests, and Mines, recommending that "your department quickly reserve the right-of-way from Cochrane to Moose Factory."[3]

Interest in a northern ocean port was not confined to the government or to the T&NO Commission. Oscar Skelton, an influential advisor to Laurier and later to Mackenzie King, wrote an article in the *Queen's Quarterly* for 1909 entitled "A Seaport for Ontario." Though Skelton denied the worth of constructing a railway to any harbour site within Ontario's boundaries, he did suggest that Ontario acquire Port Nelson on Hudson Bay, in the province of Manitoba, and extend a railway line to that point. Then Ontario might develop an outlet to the ocean which would stimulate the whole economy, particularly that of New Ontario.[4]

The proposal aroused a mixture of opposition, doubt and acceptance in northern towns. It was almost completely supported in Cochrane, where the *Northland Post* reported some years later:

> "On to the Bay" was the slogan which as far back as 1911 took hold of our visitors from the southern parts of Ontario and brought forth a resolution passed unanimously at a subsequent meeting of the Ontario Associated Boards of Trade, urging the Provincial Government to extend the T. & N.O. Railway immediately to James Bay. And as our Premier, Sir William Hearst, at that time voiced the feeling of the meeting: "This would be for the benefit, not for the people living in that portion of the Province alone, but for the advantage of the whole of Ontario."[5]

Other towns exhibited less enthusiasm. Some were preoccupied with their own immediate priorities. South Porcupine and Timmins needed development before supporting larger schemes, and T&NO extensions were completed to this new mining area through 1911-1912. At the same time, the Abitibi Pulp and Paper Mills Company was moving in to the east of the main line to harness the water power of Iroquois Falls. A branch line for that purpose was completed in 1913 for a distance of just over six miles eastward from Porquis Junction, with a shorter private spur line operated and maintained by the company itself.[6] In 1913 the branch line from Earlton to Elk Lake was also completed. Understandably, the people in the new towns which depended on the railway were primarily interested in local development. By comparison, extension of a line so far north as James Bay seemed unduly ambitious, even unfair, to small communities concerned with communication among themselves or from the North to the South of the province.

World War I put a stop to all discussion for a route to James Bay. In 1919 the surveys resumed. Then came the election of October 1919, and the victory of the United Farmers with Drury as premier. His government proclaimed its faith in the project but without making any commitment, on the grounds that the cost would be prohibitive in a post-war economy. Drury himself said that the

Top: The "Cobalt Special" entering the town of Englehart, 136 miles north of North Bay. *Bottom*: At Englehart locomotives could be serviced and "turned" for the return trip, and crews could briefly relax in the spacious quarters of the large, frame station.

Prospecting in northeastern Ontario. *Top*: A portage in the search for gold at Larder Lake. *Below*: Repairing a cook stove in a prospector's camp.

"Sandy" McIntyre. His real name was Oliphant, but his alias was assigned to the large gold mine which he discovered in the Porcupine. With the Hollinger and the Dome mines, the McIntyre mine opened a whole new phase in the development of northern resources and the expansion of the T&NO Railway.

Farming and settlement between New Liskeard and Englehart. By the time of World War I, the T&NO Commission was actively promoting the immigration of farmers into the Clay Belt. The migration of people from southern Ontario, from Britain, and from Europe led to the raising of barns, the opening of schools, and the clearing of farms such as these, where oats and peas are being harvested.

The fire of 1911 at Cochrane. The "Union Station" was barely finished in 1910, but its brick structure was so substantial that it provided a refuge for the townspeople, who saw their town decimated to little more than the rubble of amputated tree stumps.

The dock at Porcupine Lake after the last boat had left, July, 1911. The roofs of homes and stores became whirling fireballs. Everyone waded into the lake and stood out as far from shore as they dared, for the wind churned the water into furious waves.

Top: Pottsville, on the stage road from Kelso to Porcupine, 1910. At such half-way houses a traveller could use "the soft side of three feet of plank" for 50 cents. Heated by wood-burning stoves, they were rough but comfortable in winter. *Below*: One of the early stores of Murray Outfitters, where prospectors came for the gear required in their search for silver and gold.

Top: The first run of a car on the electric line of the Nipissing Central Railway, 1910. The company provided a thirty-minute service between Cobalt and Haileybury from six in the morning to eleven at night. Miners crowded its trolley-cars for the morning and evening shifts. *Below*: A car of the NCR on the way from Cobalt to Haileybury, with a passenger train of the T&NO passing under the bridge.

Scenes from the Haileybury Fire of 1922. *Top*: The "doomed home."
Below: Twisted rails at North Cobalt.

8

Only grotesque empty walls remained of churches, hospitals, and public buildings, giving the appearance of those grey, ghost-like French towns which had been heavily bombarded during World War I.

Two "Mikado" locomotives, 2-8-2 wheel arrangement, made by the Canadian Locomotive Company, Kingston, in 1921 and 1924. Some were streamlined in the shops at North Bay, but crews still had to endure the severe conditions of a winter run.

Top: The cutting and floating of logs on the Abitibi River. Below: The Abitibi Pulp and Paper Company at Iroquois Falls, where the T&NO Railway began hauling freight in 1913.

Right: The Honourable G. Howard Ferguson, Minister of Lands, Forests and Mines, 1914-1919. Conservative Premier of Ontario, 1923-1930.

54

Left: George W. Lee, chairman of the T&NO Commission, 1920-1934. An affable administrator and a resident of North Bay, with political connections from there to Cochrane, he maintained an unprecedented executive power by combining his new post with the position of general manager.

Top: The head office of the T&NO Railway, North Bay, as it appeared on its completion in 1908. *Below*: The plant of Noranda Mines Limited, at Rouyn, Québec.

58

One of the annual summer picnics for the staff of the T&NO Railway, held on the beach at New Liskeard, August 19, 1922.

extensions northward could develop further pulp industries and stimulate exploration for minerals, but he continued:

> I believe the time is inopportune for great capital expenditures. I believe the scarcity of money and the high price of labor and materials render it impossible to build this railway at the present time. While it is not advisable at the present time, however, it is exceedingly important that we should serve notice on all and sundry that it is our intention to go to the Bay.[7]

Such indefinite postponement gave little satisfaction to the town of Cochrane, whose Board of Trade looked upon commercial access to James Bay as tantamount to manifest destiny for the entire province. They passed and sent a resolution to Premier Drury:

> BE IT THEREFORE RESOLVED that the Cochrane Board of Trade re-affirm the utmost urgency of the building of the James Bay extension of the Temiskaming and Northern Ontario Railway as being of immeasurable importance to the progress of the province as a whole and view with dismay the practical shelving of the project through the omission of the clause recommending immediate legislation to this effect.[8]

Noting the resolution, Drury's government placed it in context with other information. All studies showed only a remote possibility that adequate income could be generated by building the new line. The scarcity of labour and materials presented a prospect of such high costs that economic arguments in favour of construction were hard to justify. In addition, geography and terrain presented further costly problems. The distance from Cochrane to Moosonee was nearly 200 miles, and any railway route decided upon would have to go through two different regions. The Canadian Shield continued north of Cochrane, with vast forest resources covering its rock surface, and major potential hydro-electric power sites wherever rivers plunged down to the Hudson Bay Lowlands. But the region of the Lowlands themselves, apart from deposits of gypsum and beds of peat, with pottery clay and some thin forest along the banks of rivers, consisted almost entirely of muskeg. Few opportunities existed there for economic exploitation.

Lignite was seen as the most potentially important mineral in the Lowland region between the Shield and James Bay. An Ontario Department of Mines report in 1911 defined lignite as a fuel "about half way in the state of carbonization between peat on the one hand and bituminous coal on the other." The quality of these particular deposits could not easily be determined. Irregular in thickness, they lacked coninuity, tended to disintegrate when exposed to air, and were covered with a surface difficult and expensive to remove. The costs of extraction had to be compared with potential use. Not only was lignite dirty to burn, it yielded a low heat. Altogether, said the report of 1911, "it does not seem that the lignite of the Moose Basin has an economic value."[9]

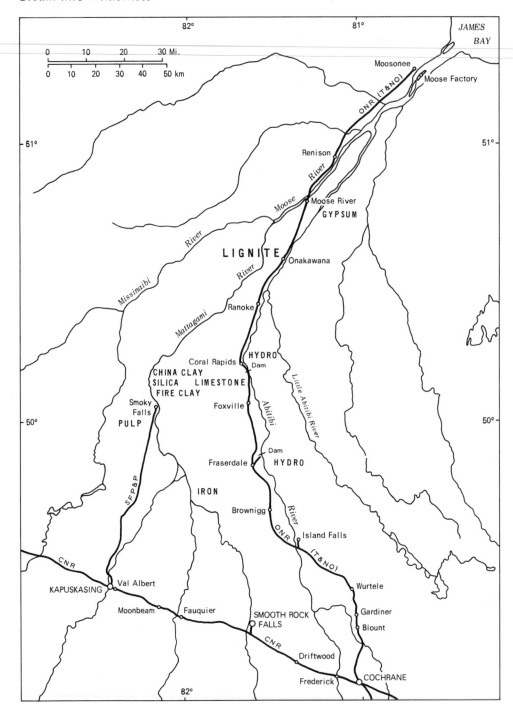

Resources, Cochrane to Moosonee. The resources north of Cochrane were not immediately profitable but the area remains a beautiful and valuable wilderness.

Discouraging reports on resource development did not stifle continuing arguments for an ocean port. In spite of Skelton's statement in 1909 that an ocean port was not feasible within the northern boundaries of Ontario, the idea registered that the province might yet construct its own northern outlet as an alternative to the historic St. Lawrence route. A special committee of the Senate issued a report in 1920 on the navigability and fishery resources of Hudson Bay and Strait. This report concluded that the route was feasible and in time would likely prove to be profitable. Its favourable judgement dwelled impressively on the quantity of fish and marine animals in the tributary rivers and perhaps in the bay itself, though sufficient data did not yet exist on the extent of possible fisheries in the bay.[10]

Propaganda Exceeds the Evidence

Putting together the hard evidence in favour of extending the railway northward, the provincial government of E.C. Drury still harboured serious doubts about accepting so expensive a responsibility. Had the T&NO Commission itself been reluctant, Drury's scepticism might have prevailed. But in the light of possible resources for hydro-electric energy, Lee and his staff grew anxious to extend the line some miles north of Cochrane.

In that area, both industry and the railway could take advantage of the thick forests and the swiftly flowing rivers. Any decision to build beyond the northern edge of the Shield could be deferred till later. In the meantime, the development of hydro-electric sites would benefit the railway if it decided to experiment with electrification. More immediate was the need of power for the pulp and paper industries at Iroquois Falls and Smooth Rock Falls to the west. Demand for energy at these plants would soon exceed the available supplies. So ran the propaganda of the Commission and of the companies which held timber concessions north and south of Cochrane.

As a result of this favourable argument, the Drury government decided in 1921 to withdraw its opposition, and approved an extension northward from Cochrane toward the hydro power zone. The T&NO Commission quickly asked for tenders to construct seventy miles of line. George Lee adopted the rhetoric of northern development in his report for 1921, declaring that the project represented "a further step in a great undertaking." The result would be a port at tidewater and immense expansion of the "mineral, agricultural and forest wealth of Northern Ontario." His exaggeration expressed the ebullience and ambition of business in the 1920s, especially in the North, where urban unemployment and the risks of capital investment were dismissed as problems peculiar to the South of the province. The North continued to be a challenging frontier and the T&NO Railway an essential vehicle for revealing its resources.

In tune with the propaganda of Adam Beck and his ambitious schemes for electrification, Lee's report of 1921 dwelled on the hydro-electric potential of northern rivers. He maintained that sufficient water power could be utilized within seventy miles north of Cochrane to electrify the entire 450-mile system of the T&NO from Moose Factory to North Bay. Additional energy could be developed for "those industries that may naturally be expected to follow the opening of a new country." Pulp mills might well be established where the Moose, Abitibi, and Mattagami Rivers met, since all three rivers afforded smooth-water channels for driving logs over long distances.

To supplement this forest industry, the Lowlands held one of the largest and finest deposits of gypsum and pottery clay on the North American continent. Oil deposits might occur in the Devonian formations. Enormous quantities of iron ore were known to exist on the eastern shores of Hudson Bay. The report concluded that "the vast possibilities contingent upon the completion of the railway are too varied for present review, and will develop only as the road progresses." It is little wonder that George Lee was becoming a popular figure in the North.

His optimistic rhapsodies continued in the *Annual Reports* of subsequent years. That of 1922 repeated statements by consulting engineers: harbour sites were more than possible on the shores of James Bay; hydro-electric power a potential development from the rivers, and forest and agricultural resources present in much of the district between Cochrane and James Bay. By the fall of 1921 the route had been determined, "crossing to the east side of the Abitibi River near the head of the Long Sault Rapids about eleven miles north from Cochrane," then recrossing to the west side of the river about forty-four miles north of Cochrane, and paralleling the west side of the Abitibi River for another twenty-five miles or more.

With approval from Drury and his cabinet, tenders were called in December 1921, at an estimated cost for this first seventy miles of $50,000 per mile. The initial contract was let in January 1922 to Grant Smith & Company, and Mc-Donnell Limited of Vancouver. It was planned to cross the Abitibi River at Mile 44.4 by the end of December 1922, "and the entire seventy miles...to be completed before October 31st, 1923."

They reached the Abitibi River to Mile 44.4 north of Cochrane before the end of winter in 1922-1923. By then the contract for the bridge across the river had been awarded to the Hamilton Bridge Works Limited, of Hamilton, Ontario. This huge structure would meet the highest engineering specifications in Canada. All culverts and trestles were to be permanent steel structures with concrete foundations. Construction proceeded under high standards of supervision. Simultaneously, engineers of the T&NO continued exploratory surveys beyond Mile 70. Their conclusions appeared in the *Annual Report* for 1922, which repeated the ambition to construct the railroad to tidewater at James Bay.

The T&NO Commission obviously took pride in its role as the vehicle of development. In annual reports, in public pronouncements, in correspondence with politicians and the press, its spokesmen repeatedly emphasized material progress, and the settlement of people. Northern resources might even provide alternative sources of energy to alleviate Canada's heavy dependence on American coal. The self-proclaiming phrases suited the prevailing optimism of the decade of the 1920s. But optimism avoided very real problems. Why, for example, did the route north from Cochrane cost a projected $3,500,000 when an alternate route, not much farther to the west, could have avoided two bridges across the Abitibi River and cost $500,000 less? The Conservative Toronto *Telegram* for February 23, 1923 raised the question publicly:

> The U.F.O. Government finds itself in a predicament today that will require a good deal of explaining before T. & N.O. Railway extensions are completed. Accusations of incompetence and waste of public funds, of intolerably bad judgement in deciding the route of extensions...are already being made against the Drury administration and the T. & N.O. Board, of which Geo. Lee is chairman.

The reporter for the *Telegram* stated that official maps of the area east of the Abitibi River indicated "great stretches of muskeg and equally extensive areas of burn." Attempting an explanation for constructing the line through unsuitable terrain, the newspaper argued that the T&NO Commission hoped to forestall the building of a competing line by the Abitibi Pulp and Paper Company which had already constructed a railway through its timber concessions from the CNR south to its plant at Iroquois Falls. Since the company held extensive timber rights north of the CNR, it could be expected to extend its line farther north unless the T&NO Commission managed to build first through that particular region.

The reasoning was plausible. It reflected the tendency of the railway to build only where proven resources would be available for shipment, providing almost immediate returns on construction outlay. The same rationale already entered into plans for the easterly extension from Swastika to the Québec boundary. Lee's annual reports on the northerly extension of the railway are singular in their undue optimism, and in their extravagant expectation that wealth must automatically materialize once the line reached tidewater. The *Annual Report* for 1922 includes the following paragraph, almost certainly written by Lee himself:

> Hudson Bay beckons. The programme of construction entered upon last fall will not cease until tidewater is reached and new sources of provincial wealth made available through the exploitation of the natural resources of the northland. There are great fur and fishery possibilities, which the completion of the road will render accessible to the large consuming centres of Ontario, Québec and the Middle West. There are also timber and pulpwood areas of great extent tributary to the Moose, Abitibi, and Mattagami Rivers, and the enormous mineral deposits of the Belcher Islands will provide manufacturing Ontario with a commercial grade of iron ore for the general enrichment of the Province.

Shortly afterwards, Lee wrote a private letter to the other two members of the Commission, Col. J.I. McLaren of Hamilton, and Lt. Col. L.T. Martin of Ottawa. The letter did not ask for their consent or opinion, but simply presented them with his fully documented reasoning for completing the T&NO line to James Bay.

Lee expected Premier Drury to use this letter to defend the project against its critics on the floor of the legislative assembly. In eleven closely typewritten pages he recounted the history of exploratory surveys going back to 1905; listed the potential resources of timber, minerals, lignite, gypsum, fisheries and even agriculture, claiming that for a hundred miles north of Cochrane "the clay land is generally well drained and is very similar to that recently brought under successful cultivation at Matheson, Monteith and Cochrane." But the listing of resources was not enough. He also quoted at length from favourable correspondence.

A.A. Cole, the mining engineer with the Commission, who had worked closely with Lee for at least a decade, was quoted as saying that "this Archaean area comprises 2,000,000 square miles, of which only a few hundred have been worked over in detail." For Cole, it was "natural to expect that further exploration will discover other Sudburys, Cobalts and Porcupines." The Anglican Archdeacon Renison, who had lived for fourteen years on James Bay, wrote that to his mind "the chief argument for the carrying of the railroad down to the shores of the Bay, is to be found in the fact that, that vast inland sea, 1,200 miles long, with a coastline of 3,000 miles, can never be explored thoroughly until it is possible for people to equip themselves at Moose Factory." Experience had shown, Renison continued, "that the venture of faith which led the Commission to go north from North Bay, had given to Canada the greatest silver mines in the country at Cobalt, and the greatest gold mine at Porcupine. These were only discovered as the railroad was built." Lee quoted other correspondents, concluding with the statement that:

> The policy of the Commission has been to go along step by step and be sure of their ground at all times, and we have done so in the case of this Extension – and we have no hesitancy in commending this to the Government; and would recommend that the work be proceeded with at once, to establish Ontario on the shores of James Bay, and in a position to control the greatest undeveloped Country in the World.[11]

But the government sensibly retreated. At the end of October 1923, the T&NO Commission took over the remaining work from the contractors, and itself completed the construction to Fraserdale, just over 68 miles north of Cochrane. A tri-weekly mixed train service then went into operation from Cochrane to Island Falls at Mile 43. Farther to the west, the Spruce Falls Power and Paper Company built its fifty-mile railway north from Kapuskasing to Smoky Falls, enabling that company to haul pulpwood from its northern timber limits, and to service its own hydro-electric power plant on the Mattagami River, as well as other plants belonging to the Ontario Hydro Commission.

A Sensible Caution

In the opinion of the new Conservative government of Howard Ferguson, Ontario railways had already been extended far enough into the northern wilderness of the province. Shortly after his election in 1923, Ferguson with

Lieutenant Governor Henry Cockshutt and George Lee personally inspected the territory between Cochrane and James Bay. While interested in the North, the new premier nevertheless entertained doubts about the value of resources in this particular region. Lee's glowing reports did not convince him.

Following his return, Ferguson announced that further extension of the line must be postponed indefinitely. The expenditure of another $7,500,000 could not be justified given the speculative nature of the financial return. He was more concerned with the transportation needs of northern regions already opened to settlement.

"The Dominion of Canada," said Ferguson in 1923, "is today suffering from the tremendous burden of debt incurred by building railways far in advance of the country's need and we must continue to bear that load of non-productive investment for a great many years." While he acknowledged the potential agricultural and timber wealth north of the Transcontinental Railway and was anxious to use improved transportation in developing northern Ontario, Ferguson held firmly to his conclusion. Emphasizing the limits of provincial government spending, he argued that money spent on further railway extension would result in reduced expenditure among the settled parts of northern Ontario. He intended to give priority to those communities which had already demonstrated the need for improved transportation.[12]

Ferguson maintained this realistic view for the next four years. During the debates on supplementary estimates in the legislative assembly on March 10, 1924, he declared that building to James Bay would be premature. "It will be some years before the road is extended that far. We have unlimited areas now for agricultural and timber purposes. Why should we scatter the settlements more?" The newspapers of the province carried on the controversy with most editors favouring delay. The *Northland Post* of Cochrane proved the exception, arguing steadily for construction as quickly as possible into the James Bay Lowlands, while the *Financial Post* of Toronto echoed the false optimism of George Lee and Arthur Cole, prophesying as yet undiscovered mines which would rival those of Cobalt and Porcupine, though the riches would emanate this time in the Belcher Islands or on the shores of Hudson Bay.[13]

Whatever the course of the debate, the Ferguson government stopped construction at Mile 68. The James Bay line was overshadowed during the next few years by the rapid progress of the Kirkland Lake-Rouyn branch line eastward from Swastika, and by the complex disputes it created between the governments of Ontario and Québec. The scarcity of hydro-electric power in northeastern Ontario continued to be a serious problem. From 1927 to 1930 such wealthy mine-owners as Harry Oakes warned Premier Ferguson that the Northern Canada Power Corporation, controlled through a subsidiary by J. A. Nesbitt of Nesbitt, Thomson and Company of Montréal, was failing to provide sufficient electrical energy.

By 1929 Ontario Hydro had to purchase power from Québec companies through contract in order to meet demand in the south of the province. Delays were caused by debate over whether Ontario or Québec had jurisdiction to develop hydro power on navigable rivers. Though the means he adopted suggested a taint of collusion and monopoly, Howard Ferguson opted for the building of the Abitibi Canyon power dam with supplies, equipment, and labour brought to the site by the T&NO Railway.[14]

It is possible to exaggerate a direct connection between the building of the power dam in the Abitibi Canyon and the T&NO, but it was no mere coincidence that the governments of Howard Ferguson and George S. Henry, from 1929 to 1932, supported the building of both. The railway and hydro-electric energy were linked together as instruments of northern development. Eventually, the thrust farther north originated with Ferguson himself. Despite his decision to halt construction at Mile 60 north of Cochrane in 1923, the North remained a significant factor in his economic policies. Sensing the premier's eventual support, the T&NO Commission under George Lee steadily pursued its studies of potential resources in the James Bay region.

In 1926, S.B. Clement, the chief engineer of the railway, described extensive deposits of gypsum along the banks of the Moose River. Because of more accessible deposits in Nova Scotia, New York, Ohio and Michigan, he concluded that for the present any processing of gypsum south of James Bay would "not be of sufficient importance in itself to justify an extension of the railway." A further and more elaborate report to the premier in 1929, prepared again by the Commission, exaggerated the old familiar resources, speculated on their extent and value, but offered little of measured or factual information.[15]

In addition to these periodic bolts of propaganda, seemingly larger political and economic reasons were advanced for extending the railway to James Bay. The Lowlands lignite deposits were repeatedly proposed as a substitute for American coal. A strike of American miners in 1922 restricted imports of coal and the provincial government continued to be anxious about this dependence on fuel supplies from the United States.

Apart from uncertainty of supply, imports contributed heavily to deficits in the balance of payments. At the end of World War I, defending the first extension north from Cochrane in 1920, Lee had argued, under Englehart's *imprimatur*, that:

> Our rate of exchange with the United States has become so adverse as to be a grave and serious matter. The only hope of correcting the situation is based on greater production within our borders and fewer purchases from the United States. The result of building this railroad will be an absolute and direct attainment of both these aims...

> Should the United States prohibit coal export Ontario factories would close their doors for thirty days unless they haul 2,000 miles from the West at a cost of three quarters of a cent a ton a mile or $15.00 freight per ton.[16]

Yet another political factor, stemming from the historical boundary dispute in the North between Ontario and Québec, influenced the decision to build the disputed extension. The Québec government was showing interest in developing its own northland along the vast eastern shores of James and Hudson Bays. If the T&NO established a presence on the west shore first, Ontario might then have the capacity to draw on the resources of the entire Hudson Bay area, including those parts within the borders of Québec. If Ontario neglected to push north by rail, Québec would be encouraged to build its own railroad. Such a prospect had been implicit in the arguments since 1920 for extending the T&NO.

A report submitted to Premier Taschereau of Québec in 1923 advocated the development of Fort George, on the northeastern coast of James Bay, as a harbour and railway terminal. The site lay 150 miles north and east from the mouth of the Moose River, closer to Hudson Bay, and was accessible to ocean steamers through Loon Island, a short distance outside the mouth of the river. Publicity emanating from the T&NO Commission argued that if Québec developed its own railway facilities to the eastern shores of James and Hudson Bays, then "our wholesale houses and manufacturers of Ontario will sit by and watch the trade of that great new area being enjoyed by Montréal and Québec competitors."[17]

Then in 1930 a new human factor affected the political contest. With the Depression after 1929, the government found it necessary to create "make-work" programmes for the jobless. The extension of the railway offered a ready-made project. A benevolent public image would gloss over political motives and personal influences. Proceeding with the extension as a "make-work" scheme could also be rationalized as an investment likely to produce profitable returns. Parallels were drawn from the 250 mile line connecting North Bay and Cochrane, where large increases of traffic had occurred, not only in timber, pulpwood and mineral ores, but in local agricultural products and in the number of passengers carried, traffic which brought valuable revenue and provided an essential service in the days before asphalt highways stimulated the competition of trucks and automobiles.

The railway had already been extended gradually north since 1927, from Fraserdale at Mile 68 to Coral Rapids at Mile 96. Completion of the line to James Bay, including the difficult crossing of the Moose River, would take only another ninety miles, making the full extension from Cochrane to James Bay just over 186 miles. After seven years of delay the Commission, with explicit approval from Premier Ferguson, and implicit approval from the provincial government, authorized the final extension of track which would at last fulfill the historic goal of connecting Toronto and its industrial environs to the southern shores of James Bay.

Economically, the extension would prove to be unproductive. But it does not follow that Howard Ferguson was a visionary in his view of the North, or a reluctant victim of the T&NO Commission. Hitherto, he had demonstrated a hard-headed and practical approach to northern development. The enterprise was of intense interest to him and strongly woven into his perception of the province as a whole. Access to northern resources; transportation to mills and markets; the immense wealth added to the brokerage houses and the affluent residential suburbs of Toronto; all had influenced his approach to public policy in the North since his days as Minister of Lands, Forests, and Mines in the Hearst government during World War I. Now, in 1930, he accepted the additional and more specific purpose of sustaining programmes that would keep men at work. On July 29, 1930 he wrote to Lee:

> In view of the present unemployment situation I think this work should be continued this year. If we were to stop work now and turn away hundreds of men, it would only aggravate the present difficult labor situation.[18]

Construction Resumed

This letter resulted from discussions between the two men. Lee received approval at the highest level, which may help to explain his renewal of the contract without calling for tenders. Trouble would surface from that decision years later, with the charge that the influence of Ferguson and the complicity of George Lee had led to the construction of the railroad north from Coral Rapids, including the long bridge over the Moose River, going entirely to one firm – H. F. McLean Limited. Harry McLean and Ferguson were personal friends.

As a contractor and entrepreneur, McLean possessed remarkable abilities. An American by birth, lacking any formal education, his natural ingenuity and administrative skills gained him for three decades a pre-eminent position in the Canadian construction industry. His greatest assets were a shrewd judgement in selecting gifted men to work for him; an ability to maintain their loyalty, sometimes by magnanimous or eccentric gestures; and his cultivation of political contacts which translated into business. A millionaire in 1930 at the age of forty-seven, this lone and singular man built a reputation for projecting contracts on the grand scale.

Ferguson respected McLean for this ability to complete large works of construction. As Vice-President of Dominion Construction Company, McLean was already involved in the $17,000,000 contract for the huge hydro-electric dam in the Abitibi Canyon at Fraserdale, where several hundred workers and their families had to be housed, fed, and supplied for more than two years. The contract was let by a subsidiary of the Abitibi Power and Paper Company, which had leased the site through the influence of Premier Ferguson. More than coincidence is required to explain McLean's monopoly over completion of the T&NO line to Moosonee during those same two years.[19]

Through 1930 and 1931 the laying of track proceeded north, meeting its most difficult task at the crossing of the Moose River. Murray Island divided the river into two wide shallow channels. Workers closed the south channel with earth fill pushed on loaded cars by a locomotive over a temporary timber trestle, while they gradually spanned the north channel by a long bridge of seventeen girders, "two spans of 90 feet and fifteen of 110 feet."[20] It was imperative that the work on the crossing, begun in September 1930, be completed before the following spring, when the swift force and height of the water would crumble temporary forms, sweeping away earth fill unless it was fixed by settled concrete and steel.

Homer Blain, a locomotive fireman and later an engineer, laboured for eight months through that winter of 1930-31, driving a 42-ton crane to install the steel piling and pour the concrete. The work was more complicated and challenging than his usual straight runs between Cochrane and his home at North Bay. Though the contract was held by H. F. McLean, the T&NO supplied the huge derrick and transferred Homer Blain to operate it. He reflected with pride that the bridge still stands, more than forty years after its construction.[21]

The *Annual Report* of the T&NO Commission also paid tribute to the staff of the Hamilton Bridge Company which had the contract for manufacturing this, the third major bridge within a decade, on the line from Cochrane to Moosonee. It was not unusual, said the chief engineer of the Commission,

> ... to unload and place a pair of girders within a period of one hour, and to complete the field bolting and the placing of deck the same day. Within a month the 17 girders were placed and the work was so far completed that track laying could be commenced and continued from the north end of the bridge.[22]

From the Moose River, construction progressed steadily along the west bank to a terminus close to the old trading post of Revillon Frères. The location was chosen as the most suitable site for the eventual construction of a port. There, the river's current was expected to sweep the harbour clear of ice and silt, while the small islands offshore would provide protection. These islands raised a favourable analogy with the port of Montréal, giving to the harbour a protected shipping channel.[23]

With the site decided upon, a name had to be chosen. This time no influence was exerted to name the place after a politician. Instead, native Indian history dictated the choice. Lee instigated research and wrote to Premier George S. Henry, that the word "Moosonee" derived from the Cree word "Moosoneek," translated literally as "at the Moose." He recommended that the northern terminal be known as "Moosonee."[24]

The extension completed, the terminal established, the site named, it remained only to hold the official opening ceremony, which took place on July 15, 1932, though the final track had been laid the year before. Three spikes were driven; one by the Honourable Mr. Justice Latchford, the Liberal who had turned the first sod at North Bay thirty years before; the second by the Honourable E.C. Drury, the former UFO premier, who had turned the first sod of the James Bay extension at Cochrane in October 1922; and the third by the Honourable George S. Henry, the Conservative premier of the province. Howard Ferguson should have been present as the man who authorized construction of the final hundred miles, but he was serving as Canadian High Commissioner in England.[25]

By 1932, then, the T&NO Commission under provincial governments of three different parties, had succeeded in building a railway from North Bay to Moosonee. It had taken thirty years. Northeastern Ontario was now connected with the Great Lakes and with the more complex if depressed economy of southern Ontario. But the extension northward would come under serious scrutiny when the T&NO Railway, like all major public utilities of the time, became involved in the Great Depression of the 1930s.

CHAPTER 10

Chaos and Charisma

Depression in the North

Lee and his colleagues did not foresee the Depression. The campaign of propaganda for extending the railroad to James Bay grew from the pervasive business optimism of the 1920s. In his *Annual Report* for 1928, Lee wrote in words as euphoric as those of many other executives describing the healthy state of their private corporations. "I am," he said, "privileged to record the termination of another year's successful operation...one of the best in the history of the road." All the evidence pointed to increased revenue in 1929, "due to the general prosperity of the country as a whole, and the gradual increasing expansion of the many business undertakings in that part of Northern Ontario tributary to and served by the railway."[1]

The Report for 1928 abundantly documented these claims, showing a net income of more than $1,200,000. This profit had been realized in spite of an unprecedented heavy snowfall through the winter of 1927-28, followed by a rapid spring thaw and steady rainfall, all of which required extra expenditure for repairs on equipment and track. Income for the farming community also suffered, and the Commission continued to subsidize farmers with large purchases of railway ties which were not needed immediately.[2]

Reflecting on the mining statistics for the previous decade, Lee stated that the value of production had shown a sevenfold increase, from $120,000,000 in 1918 to $880,000,000 in 1928. The gold mines at Kirkland Lake were now a substantial part of these figures. Stable values for gold and silver did, indeed, provide a buffer of security for those engaged in northern mining through the 1930s. Lee stated with some pride in his *Annual Report* for 1931, that "Canada now occupies second place in world gold production," which had become "the most important industry of Northern Ontario..." The silver of Cobalt and the gold of Porcupine and Kirkland Lake produced $200,000,000 in dividends alone between 1904 and 1931. Meanwhile, the line to Rouyn-Noranda had recently been completed and it, too, would add to future income from the transport of gold and copper ore.[3]

But these figures from the mining industry were exceptional. In the northern economy, as in Canada generally, the decade after 1929 proved to be a difficult time, when many industries either shut down entirely or were forced by lack of markets into part-time production.

The impact of the Canadian Depression resounded through the country after October 24, 1929, when grain quotations on the Winnipeg Exchange dropped ten cents within three minutes. Five days later the Toronto and Montréal Stock Exchanges followed the collapse of the New York market, bringing the swiftest decline of stock-market values ever experienced in Canadian history.[4]

Most significant for the Canadian economy, with deep repercussions into northeastern Ontario, was the declining world market for western grain. By storing the bumper crop of 1928, and holding it through 1929 for higher world prices, the Wheat Pools of western Canada found their storage elevators in 1930 glutted with wheat. Between 1928 and 1933 the Canadian prairie wheat crop fell by 60 per cent in volume, from 400 million to 160 million bushels. Over the same five years the price to the western farmer declined from $1.60 to 38¢ per bushel. The crops of the United States, Australia, and the Argentine, coupled with high tariffs in traditional importing countries, brought the export of Canadian grain literally to a standstill, reducing farmers to pleas for help from their provincial governments, and cutting seriously into the tonnage carried on Canadian railways.[5]

Over a period of months, this loss of traffic ramified outward from the transportation industry to the manufacturing and service sectors of the entire economy. As an exporting country, with a heavy emphasis on staples such as grain, timber, pulpwood and mineral ores, Canada suffered seriously from the fall in world prices and the decline in world markets. By the spring of 1933 unemployment reached 32 per cent of the labour force. It fluctuated from that figure only slightly during the next six years.

In 1929, on the verge of this national catastrophe, the chairman of the T&NO admitted to little more than a mild recession, a "gradual but general slackening of business conditions throughout the country, which in common with other railroads, was necessarily reflected in the earnings of the T&NO Railway." During this uncertain time, Lee won approval from Premier Ferguson to build the line to Moosonee at a cost of $5,000,000. Together with the huge hydro-electric dam in the Abitibi Canyon, the two projects kept some three thousand men at work.

Neither Ferguson nor Lee made these decisions from any economic theory of using public taxation to maintain employment. Lee, certainly, acted in the conviction that the slump would be of brief duration. A strong economy would continue to expand. Nothing had changed. The function of the chairman continued to be one of directing the means by which northern resources could be tapped and transported. Nor was Lee alone in this view; at the highest level of government, civil servants and politicians were unprepared. Mackenzie King did not consider 400,000 an abnormal number of unemployed in 1929, though the figure represented 10 per cent of the work force, with no cushion of social insurance or welfare. So bankrupt of ideas was the Liberal leadership in Ottawa that King publicly stated he would not give a five-cent piece to a provincial Tory government. But King lost the federal election of 1930 to the Conservative, R.B. Bennett. That same year, Lee found cause to change the tone of his annual reports.

The word "depression" began to appear in conjunction with statements about declines in operating revenue. Though the T&NO did not lose business on the same scale as the CPR and the CNR, both of which relied heavily on grain shipments from western Canada, by 1931 it had experienced three continuous years of a decline in earnings. In 1932 the operating profit fell again, to just over $470,000 – a drop of 60 per cent from the figure for 1928, and nearly 50 per cent from the year 1931.

Despite completion of track to Moosonee and the opening ceremony of July 1932, the ledgers and reports of the Commission could no longer gloss over the fact that the T&NO had been caught in the squeeze of the Depression. So seriously had the earnings of the railway again declined in 1933 – to a mere $32,500 – that the jolting possibility of bankruptcy occurred for the first time. Attempts had recently been made to avoid dismissal of staff by reductions in wages. Now, the Commission had to decide on such sweeping cuts of expenditure that staff dismissals could no longer be avoided. Five per cent of the railway's operating employees, as distinct from clerical and administrative staff, were laid off in 1933. Similar drastic cuts were made by the CPR and the CNR.[6]

Among those suspended were Tom Sykes and Bill Ross Jr., firemen and engineers on the steam locomotives through the 1920s and into the early thirties. Tom Sykes drove a locomotive on the construction to Moosonee. No one thought then of unemployment, but rather of the difficulties of building a road-bed in the valley of the Moose River. Muskeg, swamps, and sink-holes were the most arduous obstacles for everyone who toiled on that line. To obtain a level track they felled trees over the muskeg and piled the gravel on top. Still the tracks would sink, "and the engines used to topple off the tracks over to the side. It would be two, three weeks before we could get them engines back up. The tracks would sink right down into the muskeg."

But he felt that the life was healthy and the labour invigorating, with relaxing times when a man could fish for speckled trout in the fresh streams and fry them for dinner. Tom Sykes compared interludes like that with the cold and snow of winter trips when the line finally came into operation.

> I seen us start out from Cochrane one mornin' – must ha' been early in May...sometime in the thirties. We got stuck in the snow and we stayed there for pretty near 16 hours. Couldn't get the engine backed up..., the snow was that deep. They brought up a snow plough – behind another snow plough – and still they had to hire men to shovel it out – shovel the snow all out. We kept warm by staying in the engine. Then we had to go back and refuel our engine and re-water it – then head for Moosonee. Pretty near all the night on the road going there. Then have to leave the next morning at eight o'clock, back to Cochrane again.

A man worked long hours whether out of Cochrane, Englehart, or North Bay. Only after working the normal twelve hours did he receive time and a half, based on mileage covered rather than on the number of hours worked. But like all firemen and engineers, Tom Sykes preferred railroading to any other kind of work. Laid off in the Depression, he laboured in the mines at Noranda for five years, but was rehired before World War II and worked as a locomotive engineer until his retirement.

Bill Ross, Jr., another engineer, had a similar experience. Like Tom Sykes, he lost his job in the Depression and came back later. Some men, such as his father, were kept on because of seniority, and he knew others who found work in the mines which enabled them to remain in the North. But Bill Jr. had to leave. Others were forced onto relief, he said,

> ...welfare I guess you'd call it but we called it relief in those days...I was able to get a job where some of them weren't. But I tramped the whole city of Toronto on foot – I couldn't afford car-fare – before I did get a job. I shovelled ditches on Cherry Street down there when they were startin' to build that and pave it....

Before leaving North Bay for Toronto and eventually Montréal, he had experience with the jobless men riding the rails. They jumped on and off moving freight cars for free rides long before the Depression, but their numbers increased in the early thirties. He grouped them into three different types – bums, panhandlers, and bindle-stiffs.

> Now the bums, they went and they would just bum something – bum a meal or something like that, from the houses around or wherever they happened to be....And then there was the real hobo. Never worked. That was beneath his dignity. He would go to a door and ask for a meal, but he would not work for that meal. And then there was the bindle-stiff. And bindle in itself means bundle, that they put on a gunny-sack as a rule with two ropes on their back, and they'd have a pair of blankets....And they went from town to town and they would work, long enough to get a stake to move on to another place, but they never settled.

More and more of these desperate men rode the rails as unemployment increased. They had no choice but to keep moving, either to beg or to search for work. If they had no success at either, at least they found companionship of others in the same plight on the rattling boxcars, or in primitive open camps at the edges of towns. Being out of work and riding the rods did not result from some fault of character, but from a disordered economic system in which everyone was caught. The train crews generally turned a blind eye to the presence of these hoboes, knowing by deep intuition that they could one day find themselves in the same cheerless situation. Among the crews, however, a few men could be self-righteous and insist on enforcing the railroad's rules.[7]

Regulations originated at the executive level with George Lee and his colleagues. Though paid as managers of a government Commission, in status not very different from civil servants, they functioned much as businessmen did in charge of substantial companies, considering it a duty to restrict and control the unwanted jobless. The Commission would, of course, be lenient to poor men travelling to new jobs, provided the fare could then be collected from the employers. But this limited sympathy did not extend to the unemployed. "In view of existing conditions," said the *Minutes* of 1931, "it would be very unwise to permit these hoboes to go North." Exaggerating danger to property, the Commission hired constables to police the railway yards, encouraging those members of train crews who disapproved of the hobo. Asked by a superior why he did not take action against these freeloaders, Bill Ross Jr. replied: "Look, I'm hired on here as a fireman. I'm not paid as a policeman." He continued in an interview:

> Furthermore...we were practically asked here, that if they *got* on a train, not to put them off for the simple doggone reason that they wanted to get them out of North Bay. Or Toronto. Or any city or town. Because you didn't have the facilities for looking after the poor devils...

> I could tell you a couple of stories of a couple of men. They were tail-end men. I liked the fellows. But some of the dirty tricks that they played on some of those guys. They were – officious types, if you know what I mean? And they figured it was their duty to put these people off.

> And the method and the manner in which they did put them off, a person with a heart would never consider it. When the train was moving...dropping the red flaming stuff that runs off a fusee down onto their fingers. That I know happened....Two men I know did that, and when they were caught by the rest of the train crew, they were jolly well put in their place.

This scale of unemployment, with its attendant tragedy and potential social danger, prompted the dominion and provincial governments to launch a programme based on a northern frontier that was still sparsely settled. As the Depression deepened, thousands of people were converging on the cities and towns, creating urban slums with increasing demands on public welfare. Anxious to check this influx and to reduce relief expenditure, governments decided to institute a resettlement programme. Its slogan: "Back to the Land."

In April 1932, the federal government of R.B. Bennett passed the Relief Land Settlement Act, under which Ottawa would co-operate with the provincial governments, and with municipal authorities, by granting $200 per head to men from depressed southern areas to assist them to settle on northern lands. The federal government's contribution would be matched by the two other levels of government, giving each settler a total of $600 in aid. The grant could be used for transportation, land purchase, building and costs of equipment. The provincial government administered the scheme, assisted by a joint board of the three governments which screened prospective settlers. Crown land agents selected the areas for settlement in Ontario, concentrated in the districts of Thunder Bay, Hearst, and Kapuskasing. Since these territories contained so few people, it was hoped in Ottawa and Toronto that the plan would revive the traditional "pioneer spirit" with its appetite for opening new farms and tracts of timber. Settlers were obligated to purchase their lots, but no payments were due for two years. Given this incentive, politicians and civil servants hoped to attract settlers to parts of New Ontario still in a state of comparative wilderness.

In 1932, 210 families from twenty-six municipalities in the South were sent to northern Ontario. In 1933 the Ontario government placed a limit on expenditure for the programme of $75,000. Such limited financial aid contributed little to solving either the problem of unemployment in the South or the problem of settlement in the North.

The Conservative government of George S. Henry met defeat at the polls in 1934, to be replaced by the Liberals with Mitchell Hepburn as premier. By that time the northern settlement programme already appeared headed toward failure. The farming experience of the settlers was limited. Some had had experience with the cleared lands of southern Ontario, but many came from towns and cities. More telling than any factor against the plan, however, was the lure of the city, since markets for farm produce continued to be depressed through the decade of the 1930s. Hepburn extended the programme until 1936, when he announced that "we are going out of the business of colonization. It is unsound in principle and simply throwing good money after bad." By admitting failure of the policy he was being realistic. Since 1932 a total of six hundred people had been settled under the programme. Seven years later only half of them still remained on their land.

This scheme initiated by Bennett in Ottawa and George S. Henry in Toronto was the last concerted effort to colonize northern Ontario. Its failure destroyed any further hope of enabling the T&NO to recover from the Depression through provision of extensive transportation services for a large influx of settlers. The entire project had been unrealistic. Earlier attempts to settle discharged soldiers on these lands had usually led to abandonment after a few years, unless quantities of marketable timber were available or new and promising mines had been found in their vicinity.[8]

The Relief Land Settlement scheme can be explained only by the desperate search for palliative measures at a time of crisis in urban employment. Depression lay like a grey, pervasive cloud over the economic life of every region of Canada, including those settled communities of farms and towns which interrupted the northern wilderness from North Bay to Cochrane.

The T&NO Railway was just as vulnerable as municipal corporations and private enterprises to this decline of prices, of purchasing power and of traffic. Net income again fell drastically in 1933. Them, with the election of Mitchell Hepburn as premier, the Commission came under close, investigative scrutiny. For the railway and for northern Ontario, Hepburn's partisan inquiries during the summer of 1934 dramatically intensified the politics of the Depression.

Hepburn's Revenge

The Liberal party, led by Mitchell Hepburn, won a surprising majority in the summer of 1934. Nothing like it had been seen in Ontario politics since the Conservative victory under James Whitney in 1905. From then until 1934 the Conservatives had ruled the province with only one short interruption from 1919-1923, when Drury and the United Farmers of Ontario had held a restrained and temporary dominance over the provincial government. The UFO had come to power lacking a determined or coherent party organization; they had gone out of power in 1923 to disintegrate as a political unit, with their members caught up in the Progressive movement or joining the Liberal party. The Conservatives once again dominated Queen's Park from 1923 to 1934.

Hepburn's victory in 1934 had the quality of a political crusade. He dominated the Liberal party before and after the campaign. At the age of thirty-eight his partisan loyalty seemed to have merged with a higher loyalty, a dedication to the cause of common people suffering from unemployment and low wages, whose condition was often so desperate that they organized hunger marches, one of which ended at Queen's Park during that very summer of 1934. Hepburn in those early months appeared to be a man of action, one who would make decisions and recover for ordinary men the dignity of work and the power to earn; a man who would revive the farming and industrial economies of the different regions of the province; a leader whose sympathy with the common people would bring about a humane system of public relief. In the victorious and heady summer of 1934 he was the darling of the Liberal press.

The Toronto *Globe*, still owned by William Gladstone Jaffray, the son of Robert Jaffray who had chaired the T&NO Commission under the Liberal government of George Ross in 1904, printed a eulogy of Hepburn in August 1934. The *Globe*, like the Toronto *Star* under the editorial direction of Joseph Atkinson, modified its support because of Hepburn's affiliation with the "wet" or liquor interests; both papers traced their Liberal sympathies back to the days of a rural, Protestant, Orange, and "dry" Ontario. But the election of 1934 astonished and delighted Liberal newspaper editors. After twenty-five years in the political backwater as a splintered small-town party, the Liberals now commanded a majority of sixty to the Conservatives' seventeen in a legislature of ninety members. The decisive victory had been achieved by Hepburn's colourful leadership, by his "pep and ginger" oratory, by his vibrant personality and campaigning style. The *Globe* called it a "dynamic campaign," conducted by a "man of action," whose sincerity was beyond question.[9]

In office hardly more than a month, Hepburn appointed three commissions of inquiry, one into Ontario Hydro, a second into the Niagara Parks Commission, and a third into the T&NO. All three of these investigations had one purpose in common – to publicize and document Hepburn's pre-election charges that the previous Conservative government spent lavishly in a time of Depression, that collusion existed between Conservative ministers and private business, especially in northern timber and pulp concessions; and that too many civil servants and commissioners of public utilities collected inflated salaries on the strength of association with the Conservative party.

The first commission concentrated on the guaranteed purchase of power by Ontario Hydro from the new dam in the Abitibi Canyon. To chair the commission, Hepburn appointed F.R. Latchford and Robert Smith. Latchford, an elderly Chief Justice of the High Court of Ontario, had long ago graduated from his days as an undistinguished provincial Liberal politician to a prominent career on the bench. Robert Smith was a former Judge of the Supreme Court of Canada. Both could be trusted to probe for collusion between the previous Conservative government and the Abitibi Power and Paper Company.

To promote the processing of pulpwood, the Abitibi Company had been granted 4,500 square miles of timber lands in northeastern Ontario, in the region of Iroquois Falls, Matheson and Cochrane. The company had acquired this timber concession in 1919 from Howard Ferguson when he was Minister of Lands and Forests. His policy then and after 1923 encouraged the extraction and manufacture of resources on a large scale, by granting monopoly timber rights to a few stable companies employing local labour. The provincial legislature usually passed his proposals with little or no debate, though he faced a political scandal when the Drury government in 1920 investigated his concession of large timber tracts in the northwest of the province. Ferguson survived that setback and became premier in 1923. For the next seven years he did not alter his methods in any way. He accepted a close connection between the government railway and the operations of the Abitibi Company, which supplied an important percentage of the pulp and lumber hauled on the flat cars of the T&NO.[10]

Power resources in the Abitibi Canyon were made accessible by extension of the T&NO north of Cochrane. Yet the actual market for electrical energy from remote northern rivers lay 250 miles to the south in the Sudbury region. Both the provincial government and Ontario Hydro rejected plans to develop energy sources in the far North until more certain markets could be assured. For the time being, they left the issue to Abitibi Power and Paper, which depended for transportation facilities on the T&NO Railway. The railway, too, might be electrified and itself provide an additional market for the power of the Abitibi Canyon.

Through a subsidiary, the Abitibi Company in 1929-30 offered to sell hydro-electric power to Ontario Hydro on condition that the provincial government lease the site of Abitibi Canyon rent-free to the company for ten years. Acting personally, without consulting other than a few cabinet colleagues, Premier Ferguson approved these terms. The Latchford-Smith Commission used that agreement as its point of departure.

How vulnerable were Howard Ferguson and the Conservative party to charges of collusion between private companies and crown corporations such as Ontario Hydro or the T&NO Railway? By allowing himself to become involved in such transactions, Howard Ferguson may have been properly concerned only with future needs of electrical energy among communities in northeastern Ontario. Hydro sites in the South were already utilized to the full; the provincial government was in fact purchasing power from Québec companies. Moreover, negotiation between the provincial government and private corporations could be justified by historical precedent, going back to the days of Oliver Mowat and practised by every premier of the province since, whether Liberal, Conservative, or United Farmers.

But Premier Ferguson's executive power had not been sanctioned by debate in the legislative assembly. Even the cabinet had acquiesced in merely nominal consultation. During the 1920s, Ferguson's authority expanded, leaving him open to suspicion of collusion with private interests. That suspicion carried over into the premiership of George S. Henry, who simply approved the arrangements already made. According to the Latchford-Smith Report, Henry had gone still further. To encourage the sale of Abitibi bonds in the early years of the Depression, he authorized Ontario Hydro to purchase the bonds at prices well above their market value. This intervention became doubly suspect when investigation revealed the premier's own portfolio held $25,000 of these bonds.[11]

Newspapers across the province covered the hearings of the Latchford-Smith Inquiry through the summer of 1934. When the report appeared in October, it dramatized in the public mind Hepburn's pre-election charge of questionable connections between government and its public utilities on the one hand, and large private corporations on the other.

The North in the Cabinet

During his campaign, Hepburn had confided to political friends his desire to investigate the T&NO. They had advised against public statements on the subject at that crucial time. The railway was not only strongly supported in the North; it had become a vital part of the region's history. Liberal votes could be lost by any premature attack.

The Liberal sweep of northeastern constituencies posed a problem for him. He needed a man to do for the Liberals what Frank Cochrane had earlier accomplished for Whitney and the Conservatives, someone with that blend of political experience and administrative talent which makes a senior cabinet minister. None of the new members qualified to serve as his political lieutenant in the North. Three were French Canadians. Edmund Lapierre had been elected for Sudbury; Theodore Legault for Nipissing; J.A. Habel for Cochrane North. W.G. Nixon of New Liskeard took the constituency of Timiskaming, and John Rowlandson of Porquis Junction won Cochrane South. From this wealth of numbers Hepburn came under pressure to make a cabinet appointment.[12]

As Minister of Mines he appointed Paul Leduc, representing Ottawa. He could not afford politically to appoint another French Canadian. But neither Nixon nor Rowlandson carried the weight that Hepburn wanted at Lands and Forests, and in Northern Development. In those departments he required further close inquiries, to answer such questions as whether civil servants continued to act on behalf of the Conservative party and how much speculation and defaulting had taken place in the awarding of timber licences. Work of this magnitude lay beyond the talent and the political experience of the newly elected members from the North. Instead, Hepburn turned to his long-time friend, Peter Heenan, a Liberal-Labour MP in Ottawa, where Hepburn himself had represented the federal constituency of Elgin West since 1926.

Twenty years older than Hepburn, Heenan's knowledge of the North came from experience. A Roman Catholic of Irish birth, he had lived and worked for part of his life in Kenora as a locomotive engineer. For eight years he had served as chairman of the Brotherhood of Locomotive Engineers. Mackenzie King had appointed him as Minister of Labour from 1926 to 1930. Now, with the federal Liberals ousted from office, Heenan could accomplish more for labour and for the North by assuming a senior portfolio in Hepburn's government. The incumbent Liberal MPP for Kenora, Earl Hutchinson, who shared Heenan's labour sympathies, resigned his seat for the good of the party and the prospect of an appointment to the Workmen's Compensation Board, or possibly to the T&NO Commission.

Heenan was acclaimed the representative for Kenora in August 1934. Hepburn immediately made him a member of the cabinet as Minister of Lands and Forests, with responsibility also for Northern Development. In his new post Heenan at first emerged as a powerful figure in the cabinet, a man from whom Hepburn took advice on northern affairs. At the beginning of Hepburn's administration, none of the new members from the North could compare with his influence. He might have become the premier's closest consultant on affairs of the T&NO Railway. He could, indeed, have become the minister to whom the Commission reported, removing it from the immediate and direct authority of the premier.

But history did not follow that course. Hepburn mistrusted men who disagreed with him, and within two years he and Heenan differed in their attitude to labour. Though Hepburn championed the "common man" as an individual, large trade unions evoked his suspicion. Heenan became associated in the cabinet with David Croll and Arthur Roebuck, whose attitudes Hepburn found too soft on labour and on the left in general.

But in 1934 this alienation lay in the future. During that summer Hepburn exuded confidence in the men around him. Having appointed Heenan, he was now much clearer in his own mind that changes would have to follow in the management and operation of the T&NO Railway. Speaking of the extension to Moosonee, for example, the North Bay *Nugget* reported him as having said in Toronto:

> That extension should never have been built. It starts nowhere and ends nowhere. It's just a bill of expense. The extension to Abitibi Canyon might have been justified, but beyond that it was just a contractor's proposition.[13]

Leaving his readers to draw their own conclusions about what lay behind "a contractor's proposition," Hepburn proceeded to name a one-man commission to investigate the politics of the T&NO. The decision constituted a further step in his vengeful pursuit of government agencies dominated by Conservative appointments.

CHAPTER **11**

Under Attack

For more than thirty years, from 1902 to 1934, the T&NO functioned without the clearly defined position of general manager. The original Liberal Commission had been preoccupied with construction rather than organization. Englehart had assumed and maintained a direct role in the railway's executive management, requiring that all departmental reports be forwarded to him in Toronto, with copies for the Provincial Secretary. George Lee informally combined the posts of chairman and general manager at North Bay, concentrating authority so rigidly that other members of the Commission were reduced to nominal colleagues. Englehart and Lee had each sustained regular contact with the office of the premier or his delegated minister. Both were Conservative in their political affiliations.

This partisan nature of the T&NO Commission had been obscured by the long tenure of the Conservative party, and by expansion and efficiency in the railway's operations. But the bitter political contest of 1934, a Liberal victory and an immediate probe into the affairs of Ontario Hydro forcefully reminded people that no one political party could forever control a publicly owned utility. It came as no surprise that the new Liberal premier should announce an investigation into the management of the T&NO. With assets considerably smaller than those of Ontario Hydro, the railway was nevertheless the oldest and second largest public utility in the province.[1]

Its affairs, moreover, had never been thoroughly debated in the legislative assembly. In general, politicians indifferently left the T&NO within the closed correspondence of the cabinet and the premier's office. Loose, ill-defined notions of accountability had enabled George Lee and Howard Ferguson to establish an easy, amicable relationship by telephone and letter. Throughout the 1920s, the premier's authority over the railway resembled that of a corporate president.

Hepburn did nothing to change this absence of a clear and open legislative procedure. He assumed the executive mantle as other premiers had before him, expecting the T&NO to report directly to his office. Meanwhile, he appointed a Liberal barrister from Windsor, Armand Racine, as investigator of the T&NO. Racine had previously served on Hepburn's commission of inquiry into the

110

Niagara Parks Commission, and that report had pleased the premier. Its recommendations of a new membership and practical methods to institute meaningful economies suited the image Hepburn strove to create in the public mind.[2]

Ironically, at the very time that Hepburn announced Racine's appointment by an Order-in-Council, the newly completed section of the Trans-Canada Highway opened from Ottawa to North Bay. Peter Heenan, accompanied by other northern politicians, presided at the official ceremony. All the speakers expressed enthusiastic support for the first paved highway connecting North Bay with the Ottawa Valley and the Temiscamingue District of Québec. Newspaper reporters accompanied the official party on a well-publicized visit to the home of the Dionne quintuplets near Callander, just outside North Bay. Editors in their offices dwelt on more serious aspects of the event. They forecast expanded trade between Northern Ontario and Québec, while further construction would keep six hundred men at work. None observed that this asphalt road, carrying cars and buses as well as trucks loaded with freight, would prove to be a far more serious threat to the T&NO Railway than the critical questioning of the Racine Commission.[3]

The Racine Inquiry

The very existence of the Racine Inquiry disturbed people in the North. An editorial in the North Bay *Nugget* voiced widespread support for the railway just as Racine began his hearings:

> It may be that the T. & N.O. and its officials, like many government utilities, have been subjected to an overdose of cabinet influence. [But] Northerners for the most part placed explicit trust in the directors of "their" railway, and will demand that they be given a fair trial and not placed on the political sacrificial altar before guilt is unquestionably established.[4]

The "cabinet influence" referred to Howard Ferguson's policies and directions, but the men most vulnerable now were George Lee and his colleagues in the executive offices of the T&NO. Racine's charges appeared to have some validity as he proceeded with the inquiry which opened in the head office of the T&NO Commission at North Bay on August 14. He called witnesses and examined them publicly during the next four weeks, completing his inquiry on September 12 and submitting his report to the Lieutenant Governor in Council early in October.[5]

The hearings provided news for papers all over the province but the North Bay *Nugget* reported them most prominently. Racine's questions and the replies of his witnesses competed on the front page with Adolf Hitler's conduct as Chancellor of Germany; the kidnapping of the London brewer John Labatt; the final ambush of the Dillinger gang in Chicago; and the statement of Prime Minister R.B. Bennett that he hoped to continue paying federal relief for the camps of unemployed single men.

Reporters and editors alike saw the Racine Inquiry for what it was, an investigation into financial and economic problems on the T&NO, with incriminating issues of politics and patronage beneath the surface. Racine's questions fell into three categories – those which dwelt on the methods used to finance the railway and whether or not such methods drew heavily on provincial taxation; those which solicited information on the Moosonee extension; and those which directly concerned the quality of management, including possible connections between government and members of the T&NO Commission.

Racine's figures on financing of the railway indicated that the T&NO Commission had never paid interest on a total government investment of $30,207,934, the figure fixed by Premier Ferguson in 1924. Additional investments were made after 1927 – a Serial Bond for $6,000,000 and an advance of $7,000,000 from the Provincial Treasurer, the latter used to finance the Moosonee extension.[6] The Commissioners had provided for interest payments on this additional $13,000,000, but no provision had been made for a sinking fund to retire the capital over a fixed period of time, as required in the original legislation.

As a result, Racine concluded that the annual reports of the T&NO Commission had misled the public. The reports repeatedly indicated an annual surplus which had been remitted to the Provincial Treasurer, right up to the early thirties. George Lee had persistently contrasted the problems of other Canadian railways with the efficient operation of the T&NO, enabling it each year to produce a profit which yielded revenue to the government.

Calculating the interest which should have been paid, and which would have been a normal yearly expenditure had the railway been a private corporation, Racine arrived at a deficit of $8,000,000 accumulated since 1905. Adding the costs of the Nipissing Central Railway and the losses accruing from the Moosonee extension, the total deficit could be interpreted as more than $9,000,000.

But it was a paper figure. No previous government had even asked the Commission to establish a sinking fund, or to make annual interest payments. Neither George Ross nor James Whitney as premiers at the beginning of the century, or Ernest Drury and Howard Ferguson in the 1920s, had ever pressed their cabinets on the issue of interest payments or a sinking fund to retire the railway's debt. The original and overriding function of the railroad had been to colonize and develop the North. Returns to the government and the people of the province could be seen in terms of settlement, of mines and mills and factories manufacturing pulp and paper, all of which provided work and taxes.

Moreover, the Consolidated Revenue Fund of the Ferguson government during the seven years from 1923-30 had received annual cheques totalling close to $7,000,000 – an average payment of nearly $1,000,000 a year, or a return of 3.3 per cent on the government's fixed investment of $30,200,000. These reliable payments help to explain the easy relationship between Ferguson and Lee. They also make plausible the change in the premier's attitude which prompted his approval to finance the extensions, first to Rouyn and later to Moosonee.

Racine condemned the Commissioners of the T&NO for "condoning the practice of permitting the publication annually of a financial statement that did not represent the true position on the railway..." He continued:

> This matter was apparently brought up and discussed several times at meetings of the commission, but no proper action was taken. Although year after year the commissioners advertised to the people of the Province of Ontario that the T. & N.O. was the only railway in Canada earning money, actually huge deficits were being accumulated. Had this fact been generally known, undoubtedly public opinion would have demanded a reorganization of the railway at a much earlier date than this, with consequent savings of public funds.[7]

Having issued a public reprimand, Racine withheld reference to this particular issue in his specific recommendations. Nor did the government of Mitchell Hepburn subsequently demand annual reports of a different nature from those of previous years. Surpluses continued to appear as assets, though the Commission retained them after 1935 instead of making annual payments to the Provincial Treasurer. Subsequent annual reports made no further mention of interest payments on the fixed capital debt. To all intents and purposes, that debt had disappeared. The specific amount simply appeared year after year under liabilities in the annual reports. Those reports became brief statements of account, checked eventually by the provincial auditor.

As for the extension to Moosonee, Racine could appreciate and accept the southern part of the line from Cochrane north to the power plant in the Abitibi Canyon. The traffic here produced about $40,000 of revenue a year at the time, and it was likely to justify itself even more substantially in the future. Beyond the canyon, from Fraserdale to Moosonee, stretched a huge area of low-lying swamp which Racine examined for himself. Timber, pulpwood, and minerals appeared in such slight quantities that their commercial development could only be a visionary's dream.

As for a port at tidewater, where was it? Racine pointed to the obvious reality that no such port had been constructed or was being contemplated. The extension of the railway at Moosonee ended fourteen miles south of James Bay. Shallow water prevailed at the estuary of the Moose River, with a narrow ship channel, while out in the bay navigation at most could move only two months of the year. Floating ice and shifting sand bars offered constant hazards to commercial shipping. In his reports on the Moosonee extension, Racine stated that none of the evidence justified the haste with which the line had been built nor the assumption of profitable traffic.

He heard statements from George Lee, from L.T. Martin of Ottawa and J.I. McLaren of Hamilton, the other two members of the Commission; from the chief engineer of the railway, S.B. Clement; and from Arthur Cole, the mining engineer. All five men left the impression that the "final decision to commence construction was made by the Government of the day." Racine had no reason to doubt their word. The decision to build north from Abitibi Canyon had nominally emanated from the Conservative cabinet; in fact, the decision had been taken by Howard Ferguson as premier in 1927, then again in 1930. Acknowledging this information as a part of recent history, Racine expressed his opinion that the T&NO Commissioners had nevertheless "failed in their duty by not opposing this construction."

The Power of the Premier

Racine blunted the effect and significance of his report by failing to develop its constitutional implications. Instead, he left it simply as an implicit condemnation of Lee and his colleagues. No one could deny that Lee had promoted the extension, persuading Martin and McLaren to his view, and probably directing Clement and Cole to submit their earlier favourable reports on mineral and timber development.

The profound question remained unanswered. How could the chairman of the T&NO Commission contradict directives from the premier of the province? If Howard Ferguson depended on Lee after 1923 for information on the management of the railway and looked to the chairman of the Commission for accurate and sound advice, it was Premier Ferguson who made the final decisions. He decided also on the granting of large timber licences and the leasing of power sites, though his advice on these matters came from other departments of government. Such decisions affected the direction and expansion of the railway. Ferguson consulted his cabinet by token gestures. In practice he alone directed the relationship between the provincial railway and the development of regional resources. In the middle, but outside the cabinet, stood the chairman of the Commission.

Some indication of this powerful influence of the premier of the province emerged at different stages of the Racine Inquiry. Questioning the salary and expense accounts of the chairman, for example, at a period when wages and salaries had been reduced on Canadian railways, Racine inquired why Lee should have been allowed to charge additional expenses over and above those of his private railway car, the *Temagami*. That account neither initiated with nor was approved by the T&NO Commission.

As illustration, Racine introduced a number of letters from Premier Ferguson to Lee – the first dated October 21, 1928, which began:

> The policy of the government in more recent years has been to make known our north country to visitors of influence and importance who may visit us from time to time.

> You are called upon to spend a great deal of time in charge of various parties showing them about and entertaining them. This entertainment, of course, should not be done at your own expense.[8]

Ferguson followed this by authorizing an expense account of $2,500, a figure which he raised to $3,500 in 1930, just before resigning as premier to become High Commissioner in England.

As Racine pointed out in a nice point of constitutional procedure, the members of the T&NO Commission should have been asked to grant their approval, since the amounts were charged directly against the accounts of the railway, not to those of the government. In fact, the other Commission members had expressed only mild curiosity about the expense account. Though $3,500 was two or three times what thousands of workingmen earned in 1932, it never appeared in the publicly audited books of the T&NO. Racine concluded that the amount could only be interpreted as "a secret allowance to a servant of the government by letter." Arbitrary procedure led to no serious discussion in meetings of the Commission, any more than did unusual bonuses paid to senior executives of the railway between 1930 and 1932. J.I. McLaren summarized the common attitude throughout the management of the railway when he said to Racine "...I took it that the Premier of the government had authority to order almost anything he wished."[9]

The active and considerable power of the premier would be demonstrated anew over the following months by the decisions of Hepburn himself. People writing to him from all over the province, once the Racine Inquiry had begun its hearings, assumed that the real head of the T&NO Commission was Mitchell Hepburn. In terms of public ownership, the railway theoretically belonged to the people of the province, and particularly to the people of the North; but men and women of various political persuasions easily accepted direct executive leadership by the premier over the railway, assuming his nominal consultation with the cabinet and his obligation to present significant changes to the legislative assembly. Short of minimal consultation and legislation, his freedom to make his own decisions on the membership and the functioning of the T&NO Commission went unchallenged. For this reason, the railway could still not be divorced from politics. Racine did not pursue this fundamental issue, well aware that he would not be thanked for doing so and knowing, too, that he was expected to make limited recommendations capable of immediate implementation.

Racine questioned Lee, Martin, and McLaren at some length on the Moosonee extension. Lee now admitted that while the line from Cochrane to Fraserdale had been fully justified, building farther north to Moosonee had proved to be a financial mistake. But he denied that the Commission had made a fundamental error of judgement.

> It's a matter of policy as to whether you are going to boom that country. We tried our best to boom it...There is no mineral development north of there, and I don't know why.[10]

Lee made no reference to the warmth and consistent vigour with which he had pressed the extension on a reluctant Howard Ferguson; sufficient now to argue that the Commission had simply obeyed orders. "We were there to carry out the wishes of the government," said Martin, "and this applies also to the James Bay line." At that time, he added, the premier "had been considered the executive head of the road."

In the eyes of the witnesses, and of northern newspapers, it followed that executives of the T&NO Commission deserved to be exonerated. The Moosonee extension had been authorized by the premier with implicit agreement of the cabinet. Paying tribute to the prominence of Howard Ferguson "in the affairs of this important government utility," the North Bay *Nugget* added:

> The industries...which sustain towns...and settlements along the government railway...are the result of the vision and courage exemplified by those responsible for extending the line piece by piece.[11]

Racine, however, had to find one or more culprits. His criticism came back to the men who directly managed the railway. The absence of competition in the granting of contracts could be traced back to Ferguson, but Racine lacked convincing proof. He revealed that for the extension north of Fraserdale between 1927 and 1930, five major contracts had been awarded to H.F. McLean Limited for a total sum in excess of $5,500,000. Only one of the contracts had been granted by competitive tender, and even then McLean received an additional unanticipated sum for "hard-pan" excavation. Of the five contracts, four had been awarded to McLean without tender, for a total of $4,500,000. The reason for this arrangement lay in the close relationship between Harry McLean and Howard Ferguson. But Racine did not develop that point. Instead, he wrote that he must "strongly condemn the acts of the Commissioners."

Little evidence could be found to implicate the two Commissioners, Martin and McLaren, but they had to be removed. Both were nominal figures appointed by Drury thirteen years before. Martin resigned voluntarily in October 1934. McLaren, who had achieved the rank of colonel in World War I, had to be removed by Order-in-Council, with some dissent from the Canadian Legion.

Exit George Lee

To Racine, and to Hepburn who read his interim reports, the central figures of controversy were Lee, and W.H. Maund, the Secretary-Treasurer. Both had been associated with the T&NO since the early years of the century. Their careers had probably been promoted by Frank Cochrane, the influential political Conservative voice in the North under the Whitney government in Toronto and the Borden government in Ottawa.

Maund had been the Station Agent at Cochrane when the terrible fire of 1911 decimated the town. By 1915 the annual reports listed him as Secretary-Treasurer. Though lacking expert training in accountancy, he served the Commission as Secretary-Treasurer for nineteen years, preparing not only the accounts for report to the government, but arranging the agenda and taking the minutes at the Commission's meetings. In many ways, he managed the railroad. His position was vulnerable, and Racine quickly seized on the fact that Maund could only claim accounting skills of an elementary kind. It was impossible to determine with any accuracy from his books whether or not the various branch lines of the railway were showing a profit. He did not even know the operating cost of the line from Cochrane to Moosonee.

George Lee held a position of superiority over Maund. He had succeeded Englehart as chairman in 1920, and had served since then in the dual capacity of chairman and general manager. He had maintained close associations within the Conservative party. For that reason Drury had hesitated before appointing him as chairman, but could find no alternative. As chairman, he had served the T&NO loyally through the fourteen years since 1920, earning affection and respect in the North. But his tenure involved working closely with two Conservative premiers: G. Howard Ferguson and George Henry.

Because the railway could not be freed from partisan politics, Lee's Conservative bent made him an almost certain victim of the Racine Inquiry. He was 62, slightly deaf, and only three years from retirement. He could clearly see the determined will of Hepburn and the Liberals in their relentless pursuit of the Hydro scandals through the Latchford-Smith Commission, and he must have felt in his bones that the objectives of the Racine Inquiry had as much to do with politics as with administration and management.

Nothing seemed too small for Racine's penetrating eyes. He revealed that in 1931 Lee and his wife had hosted a dinner-dance for three hundred guests at North Bay in honour of Premier Henry. The affair cost less than $400 in total, including $300 to the North Bay Baptist Ladies' Aid Society for catering the food, and the balance for renting the Masonic Hall and the orchestra. It was trivial stuff. But Racine considered it important to reveal that the entire amount had been charged against the operating costs of the T&NO at a time when George Lee received the large salary of $10,000 a year, plus an annual entertainment allowance of $3,500. Racine also asked why the private car, *Whitney*, had been made freely available to Premier Henry for a trip to Vancouver; and why Maund's assistant, A. Burville Odlum, had burned a large number of files in late June, shortly before the election of 1934. Before long, reporters were asking Hepburn to comment on Lee, which he did at the end of August. "Disclosures so far show that he is not a fit and proper person to carry on. The road is due for a complete over-hauling."[12]

Such a publicly-stated opinion only ten days after Racine had begun the Inquiry seemed hardly forgiveable. But the premier had succumbed to the many requests and unsolicited information he received himself. One man wrote to say that when he had worked with the T&NO at Matheson, George Lee had allowed Conservative banners to hang on the property of the station during the election of 1919. "I am now," he said, "a man of fifty years of age, have my wife and one son age nineteen, all out of work and lost our home recently after having paid $7,560 on it. I am very anxious to get some form of employment …I have been out of work over two years and I do not want to go through life depending on welfare help." During those early months of his premiership, people felt they could write to Hepburn in that way and be understood. They assumed it was natural to write as Liberals to the man who headed the Liberal party in the province.[13]

As premier, Hepburn held responsibility for the North and for the railway which played the foremost role in its economy. His partisan loyalties and his constitutional position should have led him to eliminate the patronage which had accumulated over long years of Conservative ascendancy. But against his own views, other opinions demanded consideration. Among them, newspaper editors were convinced that the welfare of the North and the efficiency of its railway must not be jeopardized by partisan motives. Hepburn's subsequent decisions can only be understood in the light of tension between politics on the one hand and the interests of the railway and the North on the other.

On August 7, 1934, the day before the announcement of the Racine Inquiry, Hepburn wrote to Lee directing him to "transfer all legal business of your Commission to A.G. Slaght, K.C., Toronto." Lee responded the next day, by transferring legal transactions from the Toronto firm of Tilley, Thomson & Parmenter, who had been retained since 1907 at $400 a month plus actual court costs.[14] Slaght, who accepted on the same terms, had long been a prominent and active member of the Liberal party. He began his political and legal career at Haileybury during the days of the silver boom at Cobalt, and had defended the Matheson fire claims of local farmers against the T&NO in the early twenties. A man of this background must surely understand the North, and Hepburn appointed him to the T&NO Commission on August 24, while Racine held his inquiry. Editors and politicians in the North responded favourably even though Hepburn's real reason for such a precipitous appointment probably stemmed from his desire to secure inside reports on meetings of the T&NO Commission until submission of the Racine report.

During the controversy, George Lee received much support. Letters of commendation from such prominent men as the head of Noranda Mines and the president of the Board of Trade at North Bay could not be ignored. Simply dismissing Lee as chairman proved more difficult than the premier imagined. In the first draft of his report, Racine recommended that Lee be retained in some consulting capacity. Hepburn immediately received at least a dozen telegrams of approval. Roy Thomson, the young new publisher of the *Timmins Press*, articulated this general reaction: "Public opinion throughout the North heartily approved Racine Report particularly the generous treatment suggested for G.W. Lee..."[15]

Yet no unified advice emerged from northern Liberal members of the legislative assembly. Meeting in Toronto on October 10, with the report before them, they could not agree on the question of dismissing Lee. Hepburn and Racine decided that, given the premier's public statements, retaining Lee in any capacity would appear inconsistent. When the Racine Report finally became public on October 15, the second recommendation read: "that Mr. George Lee, the present chairman, be retired with the railway pension to which he is entitled." Lee's pension amounted to $2,000 a year from the Civil Service Pension Fund plus $1,000 from the T&NO.[16]

Enter Arthur Cavanagh

No public protest followed and Hepburn moved quickly to appoint a new Commission. Lee resigned on October 20 and an Order-in-Council announced the new membership the following day. The Commission was enlarged to five men. Hepburn appointed himself chairman. The other four were Arthur Slaght, Armand Racine, C. V. Gallagher, and Malcolm Lang, all loyal and committed members of the Liberal party. Hepburn, Slaght and Racine were already publicly associated with the affairs of the railway, but they resided in the south of the province. Gallagher, a surveyor and contractor, had lived in South Porcupine since 1912. He had served for thirteen years as Reeve of Tisdale Township, and according to the North Bay *Nugget*, had been a "staunch Liberal for the fifty-five years of his life as was his father before him."[17] Malcolm Lang, an even more important member of the Liberal party in the North, had served as an MPP at Queen's Park until 1926 and as an MP in Ottawa until 1930, where he had shared an office with Hepburn. On December 1, Hepburn resigned as chairman, appointing "Mac" Lang in his place, with Gallagher as vice-chairman. Both appointments met with approval in northern communities.

None of the newly appointed commissioners knew anything about running a railway. Their first task was to select a general manager. Racine had been critical of combining the chairmanship with the post of general manager, as Lee had done for fourteen years. He recommended that the new general manager be experienced in the operation of a railroad and not a member of the Commission. Hepburn received a number of suggestions, most of them with political overtones. Peter Heenan recommended M. S. Campbell, chief labour conciliation officer in Ottawa. Powerful Toronto Liberals such as Percy Parker, J.H. Gundy, Frank Denton, Smirle Lawson, Arthur Slaght, and Ian MacKenzie unanimously recommended their own candidate – Latham P. Burns, a professional engineer who had once worked on construction of the T&NO, and who had recently opened a small brokerage business in Toronto. Urging his appointment, Ian MacKenzie wrote to Hepburn: "you owe it to younger business Liberals of Toronto who supported you."[18]

In the North, two candidates led the field. Earl Hutchinson who had surrendered his Kenora constituency for Peter Heenan had experience as a locomotive engineer, but he would be rewarded by a post in the Department of Lands and Forests. Most northern newspapers pressed the premier to appoint the mayor of North Bay, W.G. Bullbrook, who had worked for twenty years with the CPR. Bullbrook's salary as mayor came to $800 plus a living allowance of $400. Lee's remuneration in 1934 amounted to $9,000 (after a 10 per cent cut on all Canadian railways), plus an expense allowance of $3,500 and an additional $600 for his automobile. Little wonder that Bullbrook was anxious to become general manager. If successful, he would gain promotion socially as well as financially. His name was widely supported by local Liberal associations in Mattawa and North Bay, by J.R. Hurtubise, the federal Liberal MP for the constituency of Nipissing, and by the sitting Liberal members from the North in the provincial assembly – J.A. Habel, W.G. Nixon, and Theodore Legault.

Had the premier been solely influenced by public pressure expressed in letters and editorials from the North, Bullbrook would have been his first and compelling choice. Public testimonials, however, did not always coincide with private opinion. W.G. Nixon, the MPP for Timiskaming, confided to Hepburn that despite his endorsement of Mayor Bullbrook, he preferred "a really competent business man," who would help to keep politics out of the affairs of the road "to the greatest possible extent."[19]

Hepburn met with Bullbrook in Toronto, then chaired his first and only meeting of the new T&NO Commission on October 30. He announced the next day that the new general manager would be Arthur H. Cavanagh, who would assume office immediately. Here Hepburn illustrated the kind of dramatic gesture, with its element of surprise, that he loved to arrange and at which he excelled.

Who was Cavanagh? His name appeared nowhere in the correspondence recommending men to the premier, nor had he been mentioned in speculative newspaper reports and editorials. Since the final choice was Hepburn's, what had influenced his decision? The Commission and the cabinet would follow his lead, as they had those of Ferguson and Henry before him. The action followed the pattern of Hepburn's conduct in retaining a firm hold on the party leadership while attempting to fulfill his election promise of abolishing patronage, inefficiency, and wasteful expense in the management of public utilities. Appointing Bullbrook or Burns at this point would confirm the impression in the public mind that Hepburn was doing no more than substituting Liberal for Conservative patronage. The appointment of a general manager must be seen as a non-political move.

Cavanagh would surely appear to the public in that light. At forty-seven, he had worked on railroads all his life, starting with the T&NO in 1905 when he was eighteen. He then moved to the Canadian Northern and remained when it became part of the CNR, serving at Sudbury, Capreol, Toronto, Hamilton, Hornepayne, and Allandale, where he had been superintendent since 1931. He was due for further promotion to General Superintendent of the CNR in North Bay. Cavanagh's career had so far been devoid of politics. Party affiliations did not interest him. He passionately and thoroughly involved himself in his work as a railroad manager.

But politics are pervasive. Cavanagh's wife was a sister of J.M. Cooper, Liberal MPP for Sudbury. Cooper in turn was a good friend of Malcolm Lang, who took Cavanagh to Toronto to introduce him to Hepburn. While the three men sat in his office, Hepburn telephoned S.J. Hungerford, President of the CNR. Hungerford had no wish to lose Cavanagh, whom he considered one of their promising men. But for the sake of good relations with the T&NO he offered to grant a four-year leave of absence. Cavanagh thereupon accepted Hepburn's offer at a salary of $10,000, with no contract, no expense account and no pension, but with free passes on the two national railways.[20]

The two men quickly established a mutual respect. Each admired the other's capacity for efficient administration and firm decisions. Hepburn would support Cavanagh from the premier's office over the next eight years, confident in his delegation of authority to a man he could trust. Cavanagh returned that trust, working full time as a professional railroad man, the first to be appointed general manager of the T&NO.

Northern newspapers received his appointment with warmth. North Bay saw him as a "fellow citizen" with a fine record of service as superintendent and manager on the CNR. His selection seemed to be non-partisan and in the best interest of the railway. The political crisis resolved, it would now be Cavanagh's responsibility to tread the delicate line between efficient management and the recurring influence of partisan politics.

120

CHAPTER 12

Continuity in a Political Frame

Management from Queen's Park

Hepburn acted on receiving the Racine Report by forcing George Lee into early retirement and demoting W.H. Maund from his position of Secretary-Treasurer. That was the sum total of his decisions against the management of the railway in the fall of 1934. He had to tread carefully. Extensive political interference by the premier could arouse resentment in the North. Despite this political risk, however, Hepburn's authority over the T&NO continued undiminished. There is no evidence that he practised less control than did his political enemy, Howard Ferguson, in the 1920s.

As premier of the province, as head of the provincial Liberal party, as a man supremely confident of his abilities, Hepburn wielded remarkable power over the railway from the fall of 1934 until his resignation from office in 1942. No criticism of this concentrated control was voiced at the time, either in the press or in political correspondence. The deafening silence was itself a pointed commentary on Canadian attitudes toward politics, patronage, and business enterprise. Indeed, correspondence to Hepburn confirms the impression that people preferred to deal with the premier, rather than with the executives of the Commission. The latter themselves felt reluctant to take action in areas of capital expenditure, or economy and employment, without the personal approval of the premier.

The public generally assumed that the cabinet and the legislative assembly imposed genuine limits on the power of the premier. In reality, Hepburn's consultation with the cabinet or with colleagues in the affairs of the T&NO seems to have been perfunctory, despite its profound influence throughout the northeast of the province.

He alone determined the composition and powers of the new Commission. Malcolm Lang became chairman on December 1, 1934, one month after Hepburn had appointed Cavanagh as general manager. Then, early in 1935 the premier requested and received the resignations of the other four Commissioners: himself, Slaght, Racine, and Gallagher.[1] An Order-in-Council altered the wording of the original Act of 1902 which had defined the Commission as comprising "not less than three nor more than five persons," to read simply "one or more persons appointed by the Lieutenant Governor in Council." The change enabled Lang to function as a one-man Commission at a salary of $9,000 plus expenses.

But Lang's powers were restricted. Hepburn made it clear that he expected Lang to confine his work to public relations while Cavanagh, in consultation with the premier's office, managed the railway's operation. Fortunately for the railway, Lang proved a congenial and tactful man who at first accepted these limitations, listening to the grievances of employees, while keeping open his contacts with local politicians. He maintained his own political interests by contesting the federal Liberal nomination for Timiskaming in 1935, which he lost to Walter Little, the head of a small transport company in Kirkland Lake. Like so many other provincial Liberals in the three or four years after 1934, Lang played the game as Hepburn called it. Only gradually would he become disillusioned and resign from a position too directly under Hepburn's tutelage.

Three examples illustrate Hepburn's power over the railway in the period following the Racine Report. They indicate how politics could impinge upon the operation of a government-owned transportation system when that system lacked a clearly defined protection against partisan interference.

The first example involved the purchase of major new equipment. Racine had reported deterioration in the rolling stock of locomotives and of freight and passenger cars. Of a total of sixty-three locomotives, only forty-five were classed as in good or fair condition. The last purchase of freight cars in 1923 had brought the total to three hundred, many of which were so badly in need of repair that other lines refused to use them, while the Commission paid out $160,000 a year renting "foreign" cars.[2] Racine pointed out that it would be cheaper to borrow the necessary $800,000 for the purchase of about two hundred new cars and pay the interest, a step that would not be taken until 1947. In the years from 1935 to 1937, four expensive locomotives and ten modern passenger cars were ordered instead, with the approval of the premier of the province.

The Vice-President of the National Steel Car Corporation in Hamilton wrote to Hepburn, thanking him for an interview, and telling him he had called Cavanagh in North Bay to say "that I had conferred with you and that I had your assurance that you would assist" in obtaining the contract.[3] The order for ten new coaches then followed, six of them air-conditioned. Employment was thereby stimulated in Hamilton, as it was in Kingston at the plant of the Canadian Locomotive Company by the purchase of four "Northern" type locomotives, all of the 4-8-4 wheel arrangement and drive wheels 69" in diameter. These were the largest as well as the last steam locomotives bought by the T&NO Railway, costing altogether more than $560,000. The recommendation to purchase originated with Cavanagh. Delivery was spread over three years, so that payment came from current revenue, avoiding the necessity to borrow. Even so, Lang had to write to Hepburn requesting his personal approval before placing the figures for these purchases in the estimates on capital expenditure.[4]

A second illustration of Hepburn's power over the railway arose out of the request of workers in the general office in North Bay for the right to bargain collectively. Racine's Inquiry created apprehension not only throughout the

T&NO system but in the town itself. A number of Railway Brotherhoods at North Bay corresponded vigorously with Hepburn on the outcome of the Racine Report, and particularly on the appointment of Cavanagh. They wanted assurance there would be no arbitrary dismissals of workers, since they feared that Cavanagh might find a conflict of interest in his role at the T&NO so long as he was only on leave from the CNR.

In the spring of 1936 representatives of at least seven railroad unions wrote to Hepburn: the Brotherhood of Locomotive Engineers, Brotherhood of Locomotive Firemen and Enginemen, Brotherhood of Railroad Trainmen, Brotherhood of Maintenance of Way Employees, Order of Railway Conductors, and Commercial Telegraphers' Union. They all supported the attempt of employees in the T&NO general office to achieve the right of collective bargaining through the International Brotherhood of Railway and Steamship Clerks. George Lee had told Racine that he opposed collective bargaining for the office workers. "I was bucking the labour organization," he said. "I am more or less inclined to do that all the time."[5] It was understandable that after his resignation the office workers should renew their efforts.

There is no evidence that Hepburn answered the union leaders in the North. But relevant correspondence went directly to him, and he held a meeting in his office with Peter Heenan and three representatives of the Brotherhood of Railway and Steamship Clerks, including its Vice-President, F.H. Hall of Montréal. Hall was one of the ablest negotiators among all the railway unions in Canada. Over the next year he did in fact make his Brotherhood the bargaining unit for the office employees. During the very week in April 1937 when Hepburn intervened personally to suppress the Congress of Industrial Organizations (CIO) in the Oshawa General Strike he wrote to Hall:

> I have no objection to collective bargaining, nor the right of the T. & N.O. organization of railway clerks to be members of the standard international railway unions.[6]

Five days later the premier received a strong letter of protest from A.R. Mosher, President of the All-Canadian Congress of Labour and also of the Canadian Brotherhood of Railway Employees. The latter considered itself a national alternative to Hall's International Brotherhood of Railway and Steamship Clerks which had its head office in Cincinnati. Mosher claimed:

> For many years, clerks and several other classes of employees on the T. & N.O. have been members of the Canadian Brotherhood of Railway Employees...F.H. Hall and his organization...have for more than fifteen years sought...to disrupt the Canadian Brotherhood of Railway Employees, and, at the present time, he is collaborating with a group of Communists, in Toronto, who are trying to induce the membership of the Brotherhood to transfer their allegiance to the Brotherhood of Railway and Steamship Clerks. I believe that, on investigation, you will agree that this organization should not be given any recognition on the T. & N.O.[7]

Mosher's charge exaggerated the role of the Communists. Hepburn continued to give his approval to Hall, which automatically carried with it the approval of Lang and Cavanagh.

The third illustration of Hepburn's participation resulted from serious efforts by Cavanagh to introduce economies in the operation of the railway. The T&NO maintained separate yards from those of the CNR at Cochrane. Cavanagh drew up a plan that would amalgamate the two yards with a minimum of interference and displacement for the workers on both railroads. Nevertheless, some redundancy of employees might result from the change. Cavanagh had been with the CNR for so long that his proposal was viewed with suspicion as potentially dangerous to job security. Letters of protest were dispatched to Hepburn both before and after a public meeting in Cochrane. There, the townspeople drew up a list of objections, based on their claim that Cochrane had originally been surveyed with a view to the town becoming and remaining a large T&NO centre. At first, Hepburn sided entirely with Cavanagh, who promised savings of $50,000 a year through his plan. A month later, after vociferous public meetings and critical letters from the North, Hepburn wrote to Cavanagh:

> I would ask you to hold your plan for amalgamation in abeyance until I have had an opportunity of discussing the matter with you. There is a certain angle of the situation that I want you to know about.[8]

Cavanagh postponed the amalgamation indefinitely.

These examples indicate how politicians, the presidents of local Liberal associations, the branches of the railway unions, the people generally and Cavanagh as general manager, all assumed that the premier of the province would make the final, hard decisions. The chairman of the Commission might be a discreet and humane man, but he was simply by-passed when any vital problems demanded executive decision. During the late thirties Mitchell Hepburn effectively supervised the administration of the T&NO, but he had to proceed cautiously in order to maintain morale on the railway while holding political support in the northeast of the province.

Some of the bluntest counsel came from Cavanagh at the time of his appointment as general manager. In 1974, at the age of 87, Cavanagh could still remember with some detail those months after the Racine Inquiry, the report of which, he said, was sent to guide him in his early administrative action:

> I couldn't see the justification of it, and I told Mr. Hepburn that if... these men were to be dismissed and replaced by men without experience or qualifications for railway work, then I wasn't prepared to take his job. He had the wrong man. But if he wanted it run strictly as a railroad, by railwaymen, I would take the position. But there would be nobody dismissed because of their political views...He took my advice and kept me on and there was nobody dismissed...True, there [were] some changes made but...not...in the way of dismissing people.[9]

Hepburn did remove the manager of the James Bay Inn, a Conservative who had actively campaigned in the election of 1934. He also ordered the Inn to be sold in 1937 for $10,000 though it had cost $56,000 to build.[10] Hepburn had already transferred the legal business of the T&NO to Arthur Slaght. Now he withdrew the auditing of the books from Edwards, Morgan and Company of Toronto, who had audited annually since 1910. The business went first to C.A. Houghtby of London, Ontario, on the advice of the editor of the *London Advertiser*, a daily newspaper which offered the only Liberal competition to the Conservative *London Free Press*.[11] When Houghtby died within the year the contract went to Black, Hanson and Company of Port Arthur, where Harry Black supported Hepburn during the election of 1937. In a letter to the premier, Black declared his loyalty: "I refused to move in any direction...until I had received word from you." He added that the T&NO audit was his only government work, and since "the appointment came to me directly through you...I presume that it cannot be changed without your consent."[12] His company continued to audit the books until the election of a Conservative government in 1943, when George Drew as premier returned the auditing to Edwards, Morgan and Company. In 1947 the railroad's financial statement was finally transferred to the Provincial Auditor.

The issue of morale concerned others outside the railway and even outside the North itself. Howard Fleming, publisher of the Owen Sound *Daily Sun-Times*, who had an interest in a printing contract for the T&NO, expressed a view currently held among many businessmen in North Bay, when he wrote to Hepburn on behalf of the senior administrative staff. They should, he said,

> ...be given an opportunity under new management the same as you have given Hydro employees under [Stewart] Lyon...They do know the North country. They have given their lives to the railway...They had poor direction from the late Commission, but...till some dishonesty...is shown, they should be given the opportunity of proving their worth under the proper direction of the new Commission.[13]

On the whole Hepburn followed this advice. S.B. Clement stayed on, as did W.H. Maund and others who had been severely criticized in the Racine Report. Clement, indeed, remained until his retirement in 1943, having served thirty-two years as chief engineer. Archibald Freeman, another senior member of management, suspected by some local Liberals of incompetence and Conservative partisanship, became Secretary-Treasurer and assistant to Cavanagh when Maund died in 1941.

By then, of course, the wheel had come full circle with the election of George Drew as premier. But it is significant for the history of the railway that through the political controversies of the 1930s and the early forties, Hepburn's interference led to no serious loss of morale in those areas of management which were vital to the executive direction and consequently to the stability of day-to-day operations.

125

Maintaining Solvency

The new Commission after 1934 found itself bound by old practices even in finance. Attempts to float a debenture issue in 1934 elicited only limited response among the bankers and brokers of Toronto. Uncertainty prevailed as to whether the Hepburn government would honour the obligations of previous Conservative administrations. Contracts had been signed to purchase hydro-electric power from Québec companies, at prices which Hepburn considered far too high. Was he simply scoring political points, or would he renege on those contracts? The question hung ominously over the financial sources of capital for the T&NO Railway.

Racine's sharp criticisms of inadequate presentation of financial detail in the annual reports compounded the Commission's difficulties. He censured especially the deficient auditing of losses and debts over the previous decade, the absence of a sinking fund, and the failure to allow for depreciation and replacement of equipment. As a result, Hepburn concluded that the T&NO would not likely attract private capital in large amounts. His government had no option but to continue carrying the railway's long-term capital debt.

In January 1935, a month after Malcolm Lang had been appointed chairman, Cavanagh as general manager wrote to inform the premier that any immediate effort to pay interest on the $30,200,000 of capital investment would result in a deficit, "as the earnings of the Railway are not sufficient to take care of such a charge." A week later Hepburn replied, not to Lang but to Cavanagh:

> I have decided for this year at least to continue the practice of the former administration. The surplus earnings, if any, will be turned over to the Provincial Treasurer, and credited to the consolidated revenue fund.[14]

Accordingly, the *Annual Report* of the T&NO for 1935 showed the loan from the province of Ontario, divided as follows:

Non-interest bearing loan	$30,207,934.92
Interest bearing loan	7,000,000.00
	$37,207,934.92

The rate of interest on the $7,000,000 was 4.56 per cent which the railway paid during the next fiscal year ending March 31, 1936. But the government and the Commission both were intent on reducing the principal of this loan as quickly as possible, while recognizing by statute that the government would continue to carry the non-interest bearing loan of over $30,200,000. An Order-in-Council dated April 22, 1936 directed the Commission to list this continuing capital debt as not bearing interest.

Meanwhile, $800,000 of its operating surplus went to reducing the principal of the interest-bearing loan. The balance of $6,200,000 was then transformed into a bank loan, and the auditors stated in the *Annual Report* of 1937 that the

$6,200,000 could no longer be considered a government responsibility. This portion of the railway's debt now became a demand loan from the Bank of Nova Scotia, the principal of which the Commission gradually whittled down from the proceeds of profitable business during World War II.

In addition to these particular amounts, there still remained the Long Term Debt undertaken to help finance the Moosonee extension, in the form of another debenture at $6,000,000 dated February 1, 1928. The *Annual Report* for 1936 clarified the status of this particular bank loan: "the first payment of principal, amounting to $107,000, falls due on February 1, 1939, and thereafter the principal is payable annually in increasing instalments until the final date of maturity, February 1, 1968." Until 1939 interest on this $6,000,000 debt was paid annually, but in that year additional payments began which steadily reduced the principal. By 1946, as a result of annual payments, the outstanding debt on both these bank loans totalled well under $5,000,000.

The Commission did not begin acquiring new capital debts until 1947, by which time the railway was becoming a transportation system, acquiring bus, boating, and trucking companies, together with equipment for telecommunications. After 1946, the Commission began a program of conversion to diesel engines. New bank loans then were made generally in smaller amounts of from five to seven million dollars, the interest and principal of which were payable over relatively short periods of time. The Commission never defaulted on these payments. Its credit remained stable and reputable once the Racine Inquiry had been placed in perspective. Henceforth the railway management negotiated all its loans with the chartered banks rather than with the government.

Traditional annual payments to the Provincial Treasurer ceased after 1935. In that sense, Hepburn established a precedent. Henceforth the railway's net earnings were retained as surplus income, stated in the audited annual reports but never paid to the government. The amounts could simply be interpreted as equivalent to a percentage return on the non-interest bearing provincial loan of over $30,200,000. That figure remains on the account books. It has been listed in the annual reports of the Commission ever since 1924, the sum of successive provincial, non-interest bearing loans for construction of the road between 1904 and 1923. The annual increase through the years of construction and the acquisition of equipment grew substantially after 1904, reaching $20,000,000 at the time of World War I. Then came the extension to Fraserdale, followed by the lines eastward to Kirkland Lake and Rouyn. When the Ferguson government came to power in 1923, inheriting a large debt from the United Farmers' Government of Ernest Drury, Ferguson halted construction north of Cochrane and in 1924 fixed the provincial non-interest bearing loan for the T&NO at $30,207,934.92. Hepburn's Order-in-Council of April 22, 1936 stipulated that this debt would continue to bear no interest. Thereafter the figure never changed.[15]

At the same time, the gross assets of the railway in terms of the assessed value of road and equipment, beginning with a figure of $7,400,000 in 1905 steadily increased in tandem with the non-interest bearing provincial loan to reach the same book value of just over $30,700,000 by 1924. But while the government

127

loan continued to be stated at the same figure for the next forty years, the gross assets steadily appreciated due to the railway's own investments and borrowing until in 1970 they stood at well over $80,000,000.

Loans with chartered banks have been made over short periods and paid back, but the provincial loan remains the largest and most significant of the railway's liabilities. As a sum which historically has required neither interest nor repayment of the principal, it has provided a basis of financial stability. Because the provincial government has made it possible to state the original investment as simply a figure of record, year after year, public ownership has provided a very clear advantage, enabling the railway to withstand periodic slumps and unusual costs while adapting continuously to the demands for transportation and communication services throughout northeastern Ontario.

The $30,000,000 loan could have been repaid at any time since the mid-thirties from the gross assets of the Commission, together with its steadily accumulating retained surplus revenue. That the Commission has never been required to pay interest, nor to make any remittance to the Ontario government since 1935, undoubtedly constitutes a subsidy of the railway by the taxpayers of Ontario. But for half a century, the non-interest bearing loan has become an investment and, with the exception of four years in the mid-sixties, the provincial government has never been compelled to cover a burdensome deficit, such as the federal government has for the Canadian National Railway. All of Ontario has benefited from a transportation system which opened the resource industries of the North. Businessmen in those industries have derived substantial profits from the inexpensive and reliable carriage of goods. For good reason, the people of the northeast have identified the publicly-owned facilities with their vital economic and social interests.

In 1920, northern newspapers and the provincial government fought against the absorption of the T&NO into the CNR. In like manner workers on the T&NO did not allow the declarations of the Racine Inquiry in 1934 to interrupt the basic continuity of service and development. Having precipitated the crisis, the premier now had to resolve it amicably for both the Commission and for the North. Once Hepburn accomplished that necessary aim, the T&NO turned to the vexing problems of operating effectively through the remainder of the Depression and World War II.

13

Adaptation and Experiment

Economic Recovery

The appointment of Arthur Cavanagh and the acquiescence of the provincial cabinet settled political battles on the T&NO for a time. Lang and Cavanagh were free to explore new problems of investment, expansion and adaptation to modern, competing forms of transportation. Without flexible and imaginative policies, the T&NO could not have developed as it did into a more complex network of transport and communications. Growth was slower and goals less grandiose than in the past, but gradually, step by step, the Commission acquired the means for potential if not actual repayment of its continuing debt to the provincial government.

By 1936 the provincial economy generally, and the T&NO in particular, showed signs of recovering from the bleakest years. Net earnings that year rose to more than $790,000 – an increase of 200 per cent since 1934. Though losses had resulted from previous financing of the Nipissing Central Railway, which ceased operations entirely at this time, that particular problem lay in the past. Now, the Commission could maintain the level of its freight and passenger service while expanding into forms of traffic that would enable it to compete on the new highways. The value of its freight traffic increased from $2,600,000 in 1934 to $3,626,000 in 1937 while revenue from passenger fares in the same period moved upward from just under $600,000 to more than $740,000.[1] The amounts were not large but they showed a slight surplus of revenue over expenditure.

Unfortunately, the annual reports give no employment figures for this period. Racine estimated the work force of the T&NO in 1934 at approximately 1,500 during the winter months, and 1,700 in the summer, suggesting a stable population of 7,000 dependent on wages and salaries of the Commission. This figure probably increased slightly in the following three years. The financial statements show a higher tonnage of pulp, timber, and ore being carried by the second half of the decade, resulting in more employment and higher pay. Net earnings rose to more than $1,369,000 in 1937, greater than the profit for 1928, before the harmful effects of the Depression had been felt.

The recovery proved to be short-lived when a brief but severe recession occurred throughout the Canadian economy in 1937. Cavanagh described its repercussions in the North and particularly its effect on the T&NO in the *Annual Report* for 1938. First, he said, higher wages resulted when the T&NO restored wage reductions in line with other Canadian railways. Secondly – again following the practice of other Canadian railways – free pick-up and delivery services had been instituted without imposing comparable rate increases, the railways themselves absorbing this new expense.[2] Thirdly, the imbalance between northbound and southbound traffic proved still more costly. Northbound freight continued at a high level while trains returning south could not be loaded to capacity because of serious declines in the production of forest products, especially of pulpwood and paper.

It was some consolation that this recession did not fundamentally alter a pattern of recovery on the T&NO Railway. The *Annual Report* for 1939 confidently stated that "forest products, including lumber, pulpwood, wood pulp and paper are again moving in good volume." But one significant downward trend could not be reversed. While traffic might be restored for bulk and heavy freight, new roads and highways allowed cars, buses and trucks to provide alternative means of travel for larger numbers of people. Passenger revenues declined. The *Annual Report* for 1939 referred to this challenge and added resignedly: "with highway improvements being made, this condition tends to become permanent. It is not likely that passenger traffic will ever again equal the travel of a few years ago."

Still, even as the number of passengers declined, two events already forecast the adjustments that would be implemented by the Commission through the decade to come. One was the beginning of its own bus service; the other was the outbreak of world war in September 1939 and the mobilization of the entire Canadian economy which followed. Out of these contrasting events, from small and pragmatic beginnings, the T&NO took its first tentative steps toward transforming a publicly-owned railway into a comprehensive transportation system.

Road Transport

Since its inception in 1902 the rail service of the T&NO Commission had been complemented by other means of transport. Most notable had been the wagons, sleighs, and horse-drawn pack trains which hauled supplies and people from Englehart through Charlton to the Gowganda gold mines. Those mines never developed into major producers of gold, though the T&NO extended tracks westward from Thornloe to Elk Lake, reducing the distance to be travelled by wagon and sleigh. Some three thousand people earned their living by providing hotel and restaurant service for this traffic in the two decades before 1930. After discovery of the Dome and Hollinger mines in 1909, horses hauled supplies and equipment from Kelso to Porcupine and Night Hawk Lake, until the railway reached the new town of Timmins.

Later, to cover the distance from Kirkland Lake to the main line of the T&NO at Swastika, Walter Little turned his wagon, sleigh, and then his truck service into a private transport company, based at Kirkland Lake. A similar combination of primitive vehicles had connected Cheminis with Rouyn until completion of the branch line into the province of Québec. Ore valued at millions of dollars had been carried by these supplementary means to the main line of the T&NO. Until the 1930s, therefore, without plan or policy, the railway had assumed complementary means of transport, when and as they appeared necessary. Then, in 1936, the Commission acquired its own small fleet of buses. Vehicles powered by internal combustion engines, running on rubber tires on the new asphalt highways, henceforth offered an attractive alternative to passengers who previously travelled by rail.

Lang wrote to Hepburn in March 1936 explaining the need for bus service to transport miners from the Pamour Mine for six miles to their homes in Porcupine; and from the mines of Larder Lake for twelve miles to the town of Kirkland Lake. At the same time he was in touch with Arthur Slaght, the legal counsel, on amendments to the T&NO Act. Additional clauses incorporated into the Revised Statute of 1937, enabled the Commission to,

> ...purchase or otherwise acquire motor vehicles and trailers as defined by The Highway Traffic Act...lines of buses, coaches, trucks, and aeroplanes...[with the right to operate these vehicles]...for the purpose of carrying on or upon the highway and elsewhere the business of a public carrier of passengers and freight.

A second amendment exempted the Commission from the licensing requirements of the Commercial Vehicle Act, the Public Vehicle Act, and the Municipal Act of the Province. The exemption bore a significance far beyond that of a convenient legal amendment. Since 1902 the railway had developed as a monopoly. No one objected because no one wanted to compete. Now, however, a statute of the province placed the Commission in a privileged position by comparison with private transportation companies. Both then and since the privilege seemed justified by the absence of any significant profit in a sparsely populated and relatively remote area of the country. Even so, the addition of this new form of transportation illustrated again the tensions which could arise for the Commission from its provision of a public service, while pressure from government and public alike insisted that the service pay for itself.

Between 1936 and 1938 eleven buses were acquired. Manufactured by the Ford Motor Company and holding twenty-one passengers, they travelled over slightly longer routes than those Malcolm Lang had originally described in his letter to Hepburn. The move reflected a significant change initiated by Cavanagh in train service. Only three months after becoming general manager in February 1935, he changed the northern destination of Train No.47, the main through train which originated in Toronto, from Cochrane to Timmins. For more than twenty-five years it had gone north to Cochrane. Now from Porquis it would turn west to Timmins, and the Porquis to Cochrane track would become simply a branch line. Cavanagh made this change to obtain greater revenue by providing more direct service to Timmins, now a booming centre of the highly prosperous gold mining industry, while Cochrane, with the decline in forestry and agriculture, had become almost solely a railroad town, most of whose workers held some form of free pass. Lang defended both the altered route and timetable to Hepburn. No. 47 now could leave Toronto somewhat later – at 11:10 p.m. instead of 9:30 p.m. – so that "the people from the North have the advantage of a full evening in Toronto to attend theatres, hockey games, etc."[3]

This change did not significantly affect the citizens of Cochrane and other small communities. Most people in these towns could not afford such trips. For them, efficient local transportation was a more relevant need, whether for work, school, or recreation. Cavanagh and Lang started the bus service in 1936-37 with this local traffic in mind. In addition to the short runs from the mines at Porcupine and Larder Lake, the bus lines also offered more flexible timetables than the train.

In that isolated region between Timmins and Cochrane the highway was little more than a gravel track during the late thirties, marked by potholes and deep ruts. The passengers bounced and rolled about in the seats. But henceforth the buses would become familiar sights on their routes to and from points where sparse population no longer justified the continued operation of an extensive rail passenger service, at least not in the summer months.

In the early days of road transport, winters presented far more serious problems for the buses than they did for the trains. From November through April buses stood idle because the roads were not regularly cleared of snow. The buses had to be designed to withstand rugged terrain rather than to make speed or provide comfortable passage. In wet weather male passengers sometimes would push and heave the bus – if it could be moved at all – out of deep mud ruts caused by the melting snow or by days of rain. As manufacturers gradually adapted the buses for cold winter travel, slippery conditions on snow-packed inclines still made short trips a trying ordeal for passengers who were often required to get out and push.[4]

Gradually, the quality of highways improved. Asphalt and pavement, together with more adequate winter care, made it possible to offer bus travel the year round. In 1939 additional buses came into service and a new bus garage was built at Kirkland Lake.

By then, too, a subsidiary company had been formed. In March of 1936 when Lang advised Hepburn of the introduction of the buses, he also indicated his desire to operate them as a private company because "railways in the United States which have entered into trucking and bus business have preferred to operate under separate companies." On January 6, 1938 another Order-in-Council of the provincial government incorporated Northern Canada Transportation Limited, with its head office in North Bay; and a month later the Secretary of State in Ottawa also granted the application of the T&NO under the laws of the Dominion of Canada, to incorporate this new company for the purpose of operating its bus and truck lines.

A connection may have existed between these events and the determination of Malcolm Lang to absorb the bus line operated out of Kirkland Lake by the McLellan family. This small business provided local hourly service between Kirkland Lake and Swastika, with seven buses owned and driven by the four

McLellan brothers. Their father had acquired the business in 1923 from Walter Little Transport Ltd., purchasing the passenger and baggage service of that pioneer company. A convenient and useful system, it had operated at a small profit for almost fifteen years. Malcolm Lang's interest was stimulated by the knowledge that the McLellan family were known supporters of the Conservative party. Essentially a politician, a colleague and personal friend of Mitchell Hepburn, Lang sought to absorb them by purchase or effective competition.

Cavanagh disagreed. He considered that the interests of the T&NO were better served by leaving the small bus line of the McLellans alone. With their family operation, they could run their buses far more cheaply than could the T&NO, which was bound by unionized rates. But Lang overruled Cavanagh, and told the McLellans that as of September 1, 1938, the T&NO bus service would be extended westward through Kirkland Lake to Swastika and the main line train.

It was an unwise move. Bethune Smith, the secretary of the provincial Liberal party, visited Kirkland Lake and wrote to Hepburn that the people of the community resented Lang's intimidation of the McLellan brothers, and his refusal to buy out the McLellans at a fair price. Their attorney complained to the premier, who supported Lang but also stated he was satisfied the Ontario Municipal Board would renew the McLellan licence.[5]

There the matter ended, with the T&NO operating a costly and competing bus line, until Cavanagh became chairman in 1940 and ended the service on the grounds that it was uneconomical, leaving the McLellan brothers in sole possession of the local routes in the vicinity of Kirkland Lake. Cavanagh in his second *Annual Report* for 1941 as Chairman, referred to new economies secured from the "elimination of some Passenger Schedules without impairment of service by the improved co-ordination of bus and train transportation." In that year the T&NO still owned and operated twenty buses – too many for the realization of even a limited profit. By the following year the total had been reduced to seven. There it remained while the war continued to impose restrictions on highway travel, and forced increasing numbers of people to revert to travel by train.

Gold in World War II

When Malcolm Lang submitted to Hepburn his *Annual Report* for 1939, he made no mention of the outbreak of war. The end of the fiscal year at that time was March 31, and the annual report had to be completed in three to five months after that date for presentation to the legislative assembly through formal address to the Lieutenant Governor.

World War II did not become a feature of the annual reports until the summer of 1940, when the chairman could optimistically tell the government that while "passenger traffic continued to decline," total revenue from operations had increased by more than 8 per cent, and the railway's net profit had improved about 37 per cent over that of the previous year. The reasons could already be traced to the war. From its onset, anticipations of scarcity led to stockpiling which stimulated demand for the resources of northeastern Ontario:

The most notable feature in traffic was the increase in the movement of freight commencing about September 1st, 1939, and being coincident with the outbreak of War. For several months before the War began, freight had been moving in larger volume than in 1938, but during the months of September, October, and November 1939, the increase...was about 40 per cent over the same months in 1938. The greatest increases in car loadings were in lumber, pulpwood, pulp and paper, and ore, while at the same time there was a very heavy movement of general merchandise to the mining communities.[6]

As the Canadian economy moved more dynamically into mobilization for war production, demand increased for the resources of northern Ontario. The T&NO Railway remained the vital link for carrying loads of timber, pulp and paper, iron and copper to the factories of southern Ontario, of Québec, and the United States. The very success of this heavy traffic in freight pointed to a major problem for the northern economy, since the exporting of raw materials did little to encourage development of manufacturing in mining and lumbering communities. In the midst of war, however, this gap could be dismissed as a problem for the future. Far more striking in 1940 was the heightened economic activity and the resurgent hope that replaced ten stagnant years of Depression.

The war stimulated a peculiar if temporary boom in the gold mining industry. From the autumn of 1939 until the spring of 1941 both Canada and Britain were compelled to purchase huge quantities of arms and equipment from manufacturers in the United States. That meant immediate loans from the American government to pay for the materials, and eventual repayment of the loans in gold.

The Canadian government desperately needed all the gold that could be extracted in northern Ontario. Throughout 1940 the federal government urged mines to produce gold to the fullest extent possible, and it gave the managers of gold mines high priority in securing necessary manpower and materials. Mines in the Kirkland Lake and Porcupine areas, which at best had barely maintained solvency in the previous decade, were suddenly spurred to renewed activity. More than 3,200,000 fine ounces of gold were produced in 1940, with a value of well over $125,500,000. Almost 25 per cent of this ore came from the Kirkland Lake area, where the mines of Wright-Hargreaves, Sylvanite, Toburn, Kirkland Lake Gold, and Macassa reached peaks of production.[7]

Gold in itself made light demands on railway facilities, but the economic expansion required all kinds of goods to be brought into the North for the miners as well as for the mines they worked. Fewer boxcars returned empty from hauling loads of forest products to the cities in the south of the province. Instead, they came back north loaded with supplies for the flourishing gold mining industry. Unfortunately, the demand for gold proved temporary. Recovery was short-lived. The experience demonstrated once again how vulnerable are primary, extractive industries to forces beyond the control of people in the North.

Canada and the United States agreed on a mutual defence policy in the Ogdensburg Agreement of August 1940, signed by Mackenzie King and Franklin

Roosevelt. That treaty encouraged the purchase by Canada and Britain of American arms and supplies. Then, in April 1941, the prime minister and the president signed the Hyde Park Declaration, a document which instituted lend-lease with the United States. For all practical purposes, the Hyde Park Declaration became a commercial treaty, under which each of the two countries – Canada and the United States – provided the other with those war products which its own factories could produce most efficiently and economically. Britain was the largest customer, paying in lend-lease dollars both for American goods and for American parts used in Canadian manufacturing. Governmental purchases of gold to repay American loans were no longer required.

Finally, any further doubts about British and Canadian purchases and debts ended when the Japanese attacked Pearl Harbor in December 1941. That event brought American ships, planes, armour and men fully into the war for the first time, and added the enormous production of American factories to the cause of the allied powers. Gold was no longer needed to pay for goods purchased from the United States. The Canadian government reclassified gold mining as a non-essential industry in October 1942, and withdrew the former priorities. By the end of 1942 the value of gold mined in northern Ontario had fallen to less than half the figure for 1940. In 1944 fewer than 2,100 men were employed in those mines compared with more than 4,700 in 1939.[8]

Before that happened, however, the miners of Kirkland Lake went on strike. That strike holds a significant place in the history of northern Ontario, and indirectly in the history of the T&NO Railway. The workers' action had its roots in the long simmering resentment of miners whose working conditions and wages through the wretched Depression years had compared so deplorably with the enormous wealth of mineowners and brokers, wealth accumulated with an ease in sharp contrast to the danger and drudgery endured by miners for small reward.

On the T&NO, men could organize and present demands for wages according to parallel conditions on the larger railways such as the CNR and the CPR. The Commission assumed that skilled workmen should be treated like their counterparts on the two national railway systems. In northern mining, however, the right of miners below ground to take collective action, to make demands for improved conditions of safety, for shorter hours or better wages, was strongly resisted by wealthy mining companies controlled from Toronto or Montréal by businessmen who seldom or never resided in the North, some of whom were close political friends of Premier Hepburn.

The strike at Kirkland Lake, lasting from late November 1941 to early February 1942, came on the eve of the collapse of Canadian gold markets. It challenged the labour legislation of Mackenzie King's wartime government. The strike was also an omen of the industrial unrest that soon afterwards drove workers and their leaders to affiliation with the growing CCF party in the North.

This liaison, threading its way through the labouring communities of miners, lumbermen, millhands and railway employees, from Sudbury and North Bay in the south to Timmins and Cochrane in the north, carried all five of the north-eastern constituencies for the CCF in the provincial election of 1943. Because

135

of its integration into the economy and society of the North, the T&NO could not remain unaffected by these events.

Lignite at Onakawana

The railway's traditional function of tying together small communities reflected the economy of the North, a reflection intensified by the demands of war. For even in wartime it was evident that the economy of the nation ran on east-west lines, and that the North of the province was simply a vast, sparsely populated expanse from which resources were extracted for transportation southward, rather than for manufacture at their source. In a few succinct sentences, the *Annual Report* of the T&NO for 1943 described what it meant to operate a railroad through undeveloped country while total war had mobilized the industry of the nation.

Commenting on a decline of the T&NO's net profit, Cavanagh pointed to the strongly contrasting results achieved by the two national railway systems, the CNR and the CPR – both of which recorded high levels of rail traffic and increased earnings. To Cavanagh the reasons were "readily apparent":

> No great primary war industries have been established in the territory we serve, neither does traffic between Eastern and Western Canada move by this route to any great extent. Not only is this true, but many Communities served by this Railway have suffered an actual reduction in population, due to slowing down of mining operations.

Some compensation appeared in the greater volume of forest products transported, while passenger traffic remained steady because of restrictions on highway travel. But the railway's earnings, like those for the North in general, did not thrive in step with the rest of the country. The T&NO continued its vital but vulnerable dependence on exporting extracted natural resources while its affairs were subject to the ramifications of provincial politics.

One particular resource, lignite, became closely identified with the fuel requirements of the T&NO's steam locomotives, which burned large quantities of imported coal. During the 1930s and also in World War II the T&NO Commission purchased more than 100,000 tons of coal annually, representing an expense of $650,000. The coal came mostly from West Virginia and Pennsylvania through the Weaver Coal Company in Toronto. By the end of the war in 1945 that company was being paid nearly $1,000,000 a year for coal for the steam locomotives and the plant of the T&NO system. Neither the government nor the Commission happily accepted this dependence on American supplies, which could be restricted at any time by changing American priorities or by coal strikes in the United States.

The closest Canadian sources of coal were in Alberta or Nova Scotia. By the time shipments reached northern Ontario, the cost would exceed that of American coal brought north via Lake Erie and Toronto. But north of Cochrane, in the remote, moist, flat and wilderness country on the way to Moosonee – in the vicinity of Onakawana – enough lignite occurred to produce the equivalent of

35,000,000 tons of coal, if only an economical process of conversion could be discovered.

Lignite derives from the Latin word meaning wood. It is a mineral fuel formed from decomposing plant life, more advanced than peat but too damp and soft to compete with bituminous coal. Its limitations had been suggested as early as 1911 in a report from the Department of Mines.[9] But hopes were revived in the 1920s as the T&NO extended track northward from Cochrane. By then, the prospect of electrifying the railway had clearly been abandoned as too expensive. The motive power for steam locomotives must come from coal, or from a fuel with similar properties.

Accordingly, from 1928, when trains first began to move through the Onakawana region, experiments started in the processing of lignite. The Ontario Research Foundation issued a report in 1933 which stressed the inter-relationship of the railway and the lignite deposits, noting that "fuel is by far the most expensive single item purchased and used by the railways." If processed, lignite could supplant bituminous coal. A market of 150,000 to 160,000 tons per year would be assured on the T&NO alone, quite apart from local demands by the CNR at Rouyn.[10]

Certain problems would have to be solved first. According to the report of 1933, locomotives on the T&NO, heating units in such industries as paper-mills, mines, and smelters; or stoves and furnaces in homes and buildings, had all been designed "for high grade bituminous coal, anthracite or wood."

> Success in the sale of lignite products depends on their ability to replace these fuels with the minimum of mechanical alterations or additions. Speaking generally, the consuming public are satisfied with the quality and price of the fuels obtainable. To associate a replacement programme with a large capital expenditure, even allowing a savings in current expenditure, would condemn the project.

The report further clarified the limitations of lignite by comparing its properties with those of bituminous coal. A locomotive tender filled with processed lignite would generate 43 per cent of the heat supplied by an equal volume of bituminous coal. The high moisture content of lignite, especially in a northern climate with long cold winters, presented additional problems of expensive processing before the fuel could be used effectively.

Whatever the difficulties, the T&NO Railway would be vital to any development of lignite deposits. For the present, it offered the only prospective local market, since the pulp and paper mills in the region used electric boilers powered by the abundant hydro-electricity generated on rivers such as the Abitibi. If other consumption were to develop, the railway must still provide transportation, its freight rate "determining the cost to the consumer of a bulky, low-priced commodity such as fuel" for the entire northeastern region. At the same time, the T&NO could benefit from additional freight and cheaper fuel.

In February, 1936, Lang advised Hepburn that the Commission was still studying the feasibility of the lignite fields at Onakawana. Hepburn took action. He sent L.P. Burns, the engineer who had been supported by Toronto Liberals for the post of general manager in 1934, to compile his own report. Burns confirmed the optimistic prospects when he said in 1938 that within five years 1,000,000 tons could be moving south from Onakawana, reducing the fuel costs of the railway by 50 per cent and earning $630,000 a year from transporting processed lignite to the south. He cautioned the premier that converting the locomotives might prove expensive, but added,

> ...if all the engines in service were converted immediately, the entire cost would be considerably less than the amount saved in one year's fuel bill.[11]

There was no proof for this projection, nor would there be until detailed tests had been made on existing equipment.

The outbreak of war in 1939 stimulated interest in lignite as an industrial fuel; it was already used for industrial heating, mixed with coal, in North Dakota and Saskatchewan. In 1940 the government of Ontario took two steps, in conjunction with the T&NO, to discover convincing evidence as to whether or not lignite could be turned into a practical locomotive fuel. The first step established a separate capital account for lignite research, with authorized appropriation by Order-in-Council, to relieve the limited T&NO revenue from this expensive burden. The second step was to appoint an industrial commissioner with special responsibility for directing this research.

The first man appointed as industrial commissioner was W.G. Nixon, Liberal MPP for the constituency of Timiskaming. In January 1941 he reported to Hepburn that "all our testing should be completed by next summer." The railway would benefit, he asserted, from experiments going forward in Chicago, and in Ottawa, where the Bureau of Mines was testing drying processes using either steam or oil.

That spring Cavanagh ordered the modification of Engine No. 306 to burn lignite, and a test run between North Bay and Englehart took place in July. The lignite was prepared at North Bay by the Fleissner process of steam drying, three parts lignite being mixed with one part soft coal. The report noted that "...this was the first time in North America that Fleissner lignite had been burned in a locomotive." The temperatures in the fire bed were lower than that secured from soft coal, but "combustion and heat transfer were carried well forward in the boiler, so that steaming was maintained in spite of lower furnace temperatures." In fact, the test run had not provided evidence to inspire the heavy capital investment required if lignite were to be made commercially feasible.

Another report of 1941, prepared by Archie Freeman, Cavanagh's secretary and assistant at the time, stressed the inefficiency and economic waste of using lignite. Existing locomotives would have to be replaced, rather than rebuilt, at a cost of $3,500,000. The fuel could not be used during the winter because of its moisture. Only a limited market existed apart from the railway, and the Commission would find that any savings would be more than offset by higher costs of operation.[12]

Because of the continuing expense and the lack of clear conclusions, Hepburn removed the experiments from the jurisdiction of the T&NO. He transferred responsibility in 1942 to the Department of Lands and Forests, where it properly belonged. Through the war years, interest persisted and Hepburn visited the fields in the summer of 1942. At that time the provincial government announced a $250,000 project to extract and process limited tonnage of lignite for commercial testing. The Hamilton *Spectator* reported "that it may prove a boon to the people of this province, for the difficulties of the fuel situation of today only faintly foreshadow the troubles of tomorrow."[13]

The *Northland Post* of Cochrane advanced a more immediate reason to encourage the project, observing the stimulus it would bring to the economy of that region. In 1946, Leslie Frost as Minister of Mines wrote to Harold A. Wills, publisher of the *Northland Post* and President of the Cochrane Board of Trade, saying that the Ontario government had spent more than $1,000,000 between 1928 and 1946 on experiments with lignite. Frost himself had studied the three major reports which had been made in that time, the last one from a Select Committee of the legislature in 1945 which said in its conclusion it did not believe,

> ...that the development of the lignite deposit at Onakawana is economically sound, particularly in view of the lack of evidence of any substantial backlog of industrial markets.

In the light of these reports, Frost informed Wills that his department viewed the whole project of extraction as too costly in comparison with the possible industrial use of lignite. The deposits at Onakawana might contain 100,000,000 tons in raw form, but they would cost $28 to $30 a ton to mine and process, compared with $8.00 per ton for coal, and even less for oil. Such a figure was out of the question for the railway. Cavanagh had summarized the conclusion of the T&NO in 1944 when he told the Department of Mines that "...in any consideration of the future development of lignite, the Railway should not be counted on as a potential consumer in its locomotive operations."[14]

The decision not to proceed was a fortunate one, for after the war the T&NO began phasing out its steam locomotives and replacing them with diesel-electric engines. If the huge investment required to develop and use lignite had been made, either of two results might have followed. The railway could have proceeded with its transition to diesel-electric power, writing off its investment in lignite-fired locomotives as a further burden on its public debt. Only the government could have covered a capital loss of such magnitude. Alternatively, the T&NO might have decided, in view of its large investment in lignite, against proceeding with the conversion to diesels. The railway would then have been denied the economies resulting from diesel-electric operations, and would have been hard-pressed in the post-war world to maintain a satisfactory earning position. Cavanagh undoubtedly made the correct decision in 1944.

CHAPTER 14

The Premier versus the Chairman

From the Depression of the 1930s through World War II, the T&NO remained a stable but barely solvent railway system. Politics did not extend below the executive level of the Commission. Older men rejoined the staff as younger men left or were called up for military service and both freight and passenger traffic improved.

On the eve of the war new rolling stock had been acquired – four locomotives and ten modern passenger cars. Expansion into trucks and buses was just beginning, but oil shortages due to the war restricted these early moves into highway travel. Box cars and flat cars were repaired rather than replaced, giving employment to North Bay workers but driving up costs to hire additional freight cars to a record $467,900 by 1946.[1] These increases, together with higher wages and compulsory cost-of-living allowances during wartime, inflated the operating expenses of the railway.

At the same time, though the T&NO held a monopoly of transportation throughout the northeastern region, the prospects for growth were hampered by operating in an area of such limited expansion. The northern economy remained essentially an appendage to the industrial cities of southern Ontario and the United States. Total population in the three provincial Districts of Cochrane, Timiskaming, and Nipissing stood at 175,000 in 1941. By 1951 the population had reached only 182,000 – an increase of 4 per cent. In that same decade, the population of the District of Sudbury increased by nearly 40 per cent, from 85,000 to 115,000. But Sudbury and Sault Ste. Marie were served by the main line of the CPR. Their burgeoning economies did not spill over into the regions north of North Bay.[2]

There, the provincial railway had its own special services to perform. On the whole, it sustained those obligations without subsidy, and without imposing any further debt on the provincial government. The Commission had attained a remarkable degree of financial independence for a railway which had to function in a colonial environment. Despite declining profits between 1940 and 1945, caused by the financial squeeze between fixed freight rates and spiralling costs, the Commission managed to maintain a sound monetary position to the end of the war.

Adjustments to a peace-time economy then demanded new plans for the transportation system of the North. Once more, however, the planning and adjustment took place in the context of political change that reached into the North as a result of dramatic events at Queen's Park.

Resignation on Demand

Mitchell Hepburn's leadership showed signs of weakness by 1940. Because of the prominent role played by the premier in the highest administrative affairs of the T&NO, this deterioration influenced the Commission in ways that were decisive.

Hepburn's drinking, his poor health, his lack of discipline or routine, robbed him of that "pep and ginger" vigour which had characterized his performance in the early years of his premiership. His strong sense of leadership was unfortunately flawed by an absence of system and of sustained organization. As a result, decisions were often erratic and unpredictable. Above all, his continuing quarrel with Mackenzie King and the federal government tended to distort his political judgement. Hepburn rose in the legislative assembly on January 18, 1940 to move a motion of censure against the prime minister of the country. Supported by George Drew, the provincial Conservative leader, the motion easily passed. Of sixty-six Liberals, only twenty-six supported Hepburn and fourteen of them were ministers and officeholders. Ten Liberals actually voted against their own leader, while the other thirty either abstained or were absent. Hepburn's extreme action began a serious if silent questioning of his capacity to lead.[3]

Circumstances following this dramatic incident form part of the political background leading to significant changes at the top of the T&NO Commission – first in 1940, then in 1944. Though all four of the northeastern provincial constituencies were held by Liberals, not one supported Hepburn's motion of censure. The member for Cochrane North, J.A. Habel, actually voted against Hepburn in the assembly, yet still considered himself a loyal member of the provincial Liberal party. W.G. Nixon for Timiskaming and C.V. Gallagher for Cochrane South both abstained, while J.E. Cholette for Nipissing stated publicly that he would have added his own negative vote to that of Joe Habel's had he not been obliged to catch a train.[4]

These attitudes, acknowledging the leadership of Mackenzie King, reflected the strong hold of the federal Liberal party in the North, as distinct from the Hepburn organization. In the ensuing federal election of March 26, 1940, all eight of the constituencies in northern Ontario elected Liberal candidates. J.R. Hurtubise was re-elected for Nipissing with the largest majority in his long political career; Walter Little returned for Timiskaming; J.M. Cooper (Cavanagh's brother-in-law) for Sudbury; Joseph Bradette for Cochrane; and Bradette was a close political friend of J.A. Habel.[5]

Hepburn had been seriously rebuffed. He had lost the loyalty of the provincial party in the North. This outcome should not be exaggerated, but the events belong to the political history of the North, and help to explain the environment in which Hepburn forced the resignation of Malcolm Lang and appointed Arthur Cavanagh to the combined office of chairman and general manager of the T&NO Commission.

On March 19, 1940, two months after the motion of censure, and one week prior to the federal election, Hepburn wrote to Malcolm Lang:

> I deeply regret...I have arrived at the conclusion that in the interests of efficiency and economy in the management of the T.&N.O. Railway, it will be necessary for me to ask for your resignation as chairman of the Commission.

The premier considered his wording carefully. He referred to "circumstances with which you are quite familiar," and then offered Lang a position especially created for him – industrial commissioner for the T&NO – so that he could continue his "valuable contribution toward the development of the natural resources of Northern Ontario." The proposed job had never existed before. Its purpose was to resolve the problems of processing and using lignite.

Lang considered the letter and sent a firm reply one week later:

> You will appreciate...that since I assumed the chairmanship...I have at all times directed the policy of the railroad to these ends [efficiency and economy] and, as results have shown...with considerable success. Your letter asking for my resignation therefore comes to me as a surprise.

> The importance of the office of chairman is such as would, I think, warrant an interview with you in regard to the affairs of the railroad, before your request for my resignation was sent forward. It seems to me that had this course been adopted it would have been more in keeping with sound business practice where...matters of policy affecting the enterprise of considerable magnitude are involved. In my letter of January 31 to you, I asked that I might have an interview with you at your convenience, but I received no reply to this communication.

The tone of the letter was bitterly consistent. Lang could see little point in accepting the post of industrial commissioner, when Hepburn gave such meagre recognition to his previous performance as chairman. He declined the offer and resigned.

The dispute and resignation became public on April 1, with a press statement issued by the premier's office. The statement said that when Lang had been appointed in 1934, "his duties were outlined as being in the capacity of more of an industrial commissioner and general public relations official" owing to his lack of previous railway experience. Nothing in the correspondence of 1934 supports the truth of this allegation, but the rationalization suited Hepburn's purposes in 1940.[6]

The statement also referred to the composition of the Commission sanctioned by the Order-in-Council of 1935, when the previous three-man Commission had been replaced by one commissioner and a general manager. Relations between the two men proved amicable for a short time. But "friction developed when Colonel Lang sought to interfere with the duties assigned to the general manager," and reached a climax when Cavanagh reported he "would no longer be responsible for management." The statement concluded:

> ...the Cabinet was faced with the problem of accepting Mr. Cavanagh's resignation and securing some other experienced railway man to carry on his work or to submit a proposal to Colonel Lang, which he ultimately rejected.

Hepburn's press release, his letter to Lang, and Lang's reply, all were printed in northern and Toronto newspapers on April 1, the day on which Cavanagh officially became chairman as well as general manager. With that appointment the T&NO Commission reverted to the self-same condition in the top administration which had led Racine and Hepburn to their criticisms and changes of 1934.

Cavanagh managed the railway more efficiently and professionally than George Lee had done, and he kept his activities free from politics. But combining the two positions implied from the beginning a concentration of power in the hands of one man which Hepburn would have resisted six years before, and which would certainly arouse suspicion and resentment among employees. What reasoning led Hepburn to this decision? How had he arrived at grounds for dismissing Lang, and why did he not appoint a new chairman?

While political influences can be exaggerated, they cannot be discounted. Whatever other considerations lay behind his actions, Hepburn treated Lang arbitrarily for reasons which cannot be separated from the political atmosphere of late 1939 and early 1940. Lang suffered from ill health, but he suffered in another sense from his close ties with the federal Liberals in the North, and from doubts that he would support Hepburn in the mounting quarrel with Mackenzie King. A distance had opened between the two men, which left Hepburn even more dependent upon Cavanagh for assurance that the railway would not lead him into financial or political trouble. In the undefined relationship between the government and the T&NO which allowed the premier of the province to function almost as chairman, the position of Malcolm Lang had become ambiguous, if not untenable. Cavanagh's vigorous and thorough administration, his intimate knowledge of every detail of the railway, and his sound relations with Hepburn, all coalesced to reduce Lang's position to that of a redundant chairman.

The Role of the Trade Unions

These strained relationships were brought to a breaking point by the trade unions, which provided the immediate cause for Lang's dismissal and Cavanagh's appointment. Unions had grown both in size and power through the thirties. Local union chairmen had insisted on being consulted at the time of the Racine Inquiry. By 1940 most of the 1,700 employees were organized and represented by seven major railway brotherhoods. Collectively, the unions referred to themselves as the Federated Trades, System No. 86, in the American Federation of Labour.

Negotiations over wages, seniority, and hiring of employees from outside the T&NO system, were all watched carefully. Wage contracts could be settled within the Commission, but disputes over seniority and hiring often ended in the office of the premier. When this occurred, Hepburn's secretary, Roy Elmhirst, asked either Cavanagh or Lang for information and advice. Their responses would then be incorporated into the premier's reply. As a result, Hepburn became aware of the conflicts between the chairman and the general manager over union matters.

Employees generally had been recruited with little dissension into the international brotherhoods. The Commission gradually came to accept collective bargaining, moving sensibly away from the earlier reactionary attitudes of George Lee. But labour on the T&NO could be divided, first by seeking to define which union had the right to organize, according to definition by craft; and secondly, by rivalry between the international brotherhoods and the national unions. These divisions were not serious among the employees; most of them hardly knew that dissension existed. But union leadership could be involved, which in turn affected management. If the leaders of the unions failed to obtain satisfaction from management, they contacted the premier directly.[7]

One example involved the attempt by the Brotherhood of Railroad Trainmen to organize the bus drivers in 1939. The head office of the Brotherhood in Cleveland had appointed A. J. Kelly as its Dominion Legislative Representative in Ottawa. Kelly wrote to Lang, who responded himself, instead of turning the query over to Cavanagh. The chairman and the general manager consulted amicably together on this occasion. Lang told Kelly that since the Railroad Trainmen could organize only the bus drivers, while the T&NO planned to include truck drivers and the men servicing both trucks and buses, the Trainmen might not be the most suitable union. Lang then advised Hepburn that the Brotherhood of Railway Employees seemed to be the most likely union on which the Commission would agree. Kelly took his appeal to Hepburn, protesting that Lang was procrastinating; but the premier willingly left the matter in the hands of the Commission.[8] In fact, the original inquiry should have gone to Cavanagh alone, allowing him to exercise his executive judgement as general manager, with appeal from either party to Lang if grounds for grievance persisted. The premier need not have been involved at all.

Hepburn could have confined his action to reminding Lang and Cavanagh of their respective jurisdictions. For confusion certainly existed. That became manifest in another labour dispute of 1939 when a brakeman, dismissed for being drunk on the job, appealed to Malcolm Lang and was reinstated by an arbitrary decision of the chairman. Cavanagh disapproved but kept his silence until the man insisted on having his seniority restored and turned to the Canadian Association of Railway Employees to defend his case.

This latter organization was a breakaway group headed by a mediocrity named Charles Beattie, who also held office as vice-president of the All-Canadian Congress of Labour. Beattie pounded home the nationalist theme with unconvincing and limited intelligence when he appealed to Hepburn. He defended the fair-minded attitude of Malcolm Lang, but attacked Cavanagh for insisting on the letter of the contract with the international brotherhoods. "A controversy has arisen," said Beattie, "and the International Unions are using their influence with the General Manager to keep the closed shop proposition...as it is to their benefit and not to the benefit of the employees."[9] Cavanagh correctly assessed Beattie as a nuisance rather than a competent union leader. Across the country, railroad workers had shunned his Canadian Association of Railway Employees. Beattie had taken up the case, hoping to involve the chairman and the premier, in order to enhance the prestige of his ineffective union. But Hepburn refused to be drawn in and the attempt did not succeed.

More serious for labour relations on the T&NO was Lang's peremptory decision to reinstate the brakeman on his own authority, despite the fact that, as Cavanagh wrote to Hepburn, "we have a signed agreement with the various labour organizations with whom we have contracts...to the effect that employees dismissed for violation of Rule 'G' [liquor cases] would not be reinstated in the service."[10] The case exhausted Cavanagh's patience. He did not write Hepburn a formal letter of protest, but complained to him personally about Lang's far too frequent interference in areas properly the responsibility of the general manager. The number of unions the T&NO had to deal with made it imperative that formal procedures and contracts be strictly adhered to.

Through the early months of 1940, Premier Hepburn received letters from union representatives and politicians, defending Lang's impartiality, commending his willingness to meet with the men at any time, and extolling his good relations with the unions. One of the letters, signed by six local chairmen of the railway brotherhoods, said:

> At the present time, and for some time past, a great deal of unrest has existed in labour circles on the T. & N.O. Railway, due entirely to the Management's persistent unfair attitude in dealing with even minor problems affecting employer and employees. In cases of this kind we feel that it is our right to appeal to Col. Lang as the highest official of the Railway in order that fair dealing may prevail.

The chairmen of these local brotherhoods desired a meeting with Hepburn. When he failed to respond, they persuaded three of the four northern MPPs to send their own letter. W.G. Nixon, J.A. Habel, and J.E. Cholette signed a letter to Hepburn which stated:

> We know that at the present time there is a difference of opinion as between the Chairman of the Commission and the General Manager.

145

> We believe we are correct in stating that the great majority of the
> employees of the road are behind the Chairman of the Commission...
> We appreciate the railroad ability of the Manager but the consensus
> of opinion is that he is inclined to be arbitrary, has at times pushed
> his efficiency program to the extreme, resulting in bad feeling among
> the employees.[11]

The extent of this critical disapproval did not become immediately apparent.
The letters may have been solicited by Lang; more likely they expressed genuine
discontent. Conflicts within the labour movement on the railway would remain,
to re-emerge after the provincial election of 1943. But in 1940 reporters noted
that the statement published on March 30 announcing Lang's resignation occa-
sioned little surprise among employees:

> Views expressed by the T. & N.O. men indicated that Mr. Lang has
> been held in high regard, but it is considered impractical to have two
> heads who do not agree on policy, particularly when and where it
> affects unionized employees.[12]

In order to sustain a rational and efficient management, Hepburn may have
had no choice but to dismiss Lang. Rules of procedure could be seriously under-
mined by his humane inclination to act personally on individual grievances. But
Lang often acted also from political motives. Suspicion grew that he used such
issues as a means of frustrating both Cavanagh and the premier with whom he
felt less and less in sympathy.

The manner of Lang's forced resignation, however, without even the courtesy
of an interview, spoke volumes on Hepburn's decline as a politician and administrator. The two men had once been friends. Now, Lang could only reply
through the press. Nor did the premier bother to look for a new chairman.
Rather than chance another political appointment, considering the acute dis-
affection among northern Liberals, Hepburn simply appointed Cavanagh as
chairman while retaining him also as general manager. The cabinet accepted his
decision. For the next three years, as Hepburn's leadership descended to chaotic
collapse, Arthur Cavanagh made all the important decisions of policy and administration for the T&NO Railway Commission.

15

Toward a New Commission

Trade union leaders could not casually telephone or simply talk to Arthur Cavanagh with the same ease as Mitchell Hepburn could. But they shared the premier's respect for him. Lang, with his slight talent for administration, could hardly have managed the transportation system alone. In contrast, Cavanagh was capable of decisive, professional, even innovative leadership which maintained stability through the difficult years of World War II. No one since Englehart and George Lee had commanded such total executive authority over the T&NO. Cavanagh *was* the Commission, with a direct line to the premier.

Hepburn, in turn, functioned in many ways as a chairman, when and as he chose. Without consultation, for example, he proceeded immediately to implement his idea of appointing an industrial commissioner. As Lang refused the post, Hepburn offered it to W.G. Nixon, another Liberal politician and the MPP for Timiskaming. Nixon would probably have preferred to be named chairman, but readily accepted what was offered. The T&NO Act required amendment so that Nixon could be paid a salary in his new capacity while retaining his pay as an MPP.

Again, Hepburn had no difficulty making the necessary change. For the next two years Nixon reported to the premier on research into the use of lignite.[1] When Lands and Forests took over the research in 1942, Nixon communicated with that department. He ceased to function in this dual role after being defeated by the CCF candidate in the provincial election of 1943.

A Concentrated Authority

The events which made possible this concentration of power revealed the solid substance of prime ministerial government behind an insubstantial parliamentary form. A premier who could make such major decisions displayed powers not far removed from those of a corporate president. There had been little evolution in political and constitutional forms since the days of James Whitney and Howard Ferguson. The T&NO was still little more than a semi-independent agency of government. It functioned without any clear distinction between policy and operation, or between public service and financial solvency; and also without any practical awareness of its subordination to the legislative process.

By legislation the Commission came under the authority of the Lieutenant Governor in Council – meaning the cabinet – which in turn was responsible to the legislative assembly. In practice, not merely the highest appointments, but a remarkable number of administrative details and policy questions could still be decided by the premier. He might consult with individuals of his choice, but his executive authority had strength enough to ensure that discussion in cabinet or well-prepared presentations to the legislative assembly were only nominal requirements.

After Hepburn's resignation in October 1942, a gradual change developed in relations between the premier and the Commission, a change marked by the gradual substitution of more efficient bureaucracy for the direct intervention of the premier. But this transition again must be explained within the ebb and flow of politics.

Before Hepburn's decline and final resignation, he raised Cavanagh's salary as chairman and general manager to $15,000 in 1941, the highest amount to that date ever paid an administrator on the T&NO system, placing him on the same level as regional vice-presidents on the CPR or the CNR. Cavanagh, who had requested this increase, received a copy of the implementing Order-in-Council. He thanked Hepburn personally but he could not obtain a contract giving him security and the pension to which he felt entitled as head of an agency of government which in the past had amply demonstrated its vulnerability to the flux of politics. Apparently, Hepburn dropped that part of Cavanagh's request because it raised complications which the premier could not resolve without a probing discussion in cabinet.

Cavanagh renewed his request with Hepburn's Liberal successor, Gordon D. Conant. Bland and indecisive, the temporary head of a caretaker government, Conant adhered more readily to cabinet consultation. First, the Attorney General's office advised him that any contract between Mr. Cavanagh and the Commission would not accord with the latest Act governing the T&NO Commission. That statute contained a clause prohibiting any member of the Commission from entering into a contract which involved the payment of money under the control of the Commission. At last Cavanagh's position had to be clarified. He had never been formally appointed as general manager by the T&NO Commission. Now, as chairman he was not entitled to be paid also as general manager. Hepburn had never bothered to legalize an apportionment of salary between the two positions.

The premier and the provincial treasurer recommended to the cabinet that the T&NO Commission be authorized to enter into an agreement acceptable to the chairman and general manager. The contract stated that the T&NO Commission agreed to employ Arthur Cavanagh as general manager, while remaining as chairman of the Commission, "without remuneration except for his services as General Manager..." The salary was to be not less than $15,000, and his allowance on retiring would be the normal one-fiftieth of annual salary multiplied by the number of years of full service. The period of Cavanagh's engagement would extend for ten years from December 1942, but the contract "may be terminated at any time upon notice in writing from the Commission to the general manager."[2]

Constitutionally, Hepburn had created an anomalous situation. How could the chairman of the Commission dismiss the general manager if they were one and the same person? To arrive at a contract, the body referred to in the documents as the Lieutenant Governor in Council, meaning the cabinet, in this particular decision had to assume the functions of the T&NO Commission. Fortunately, the tangled confusion did not extend further. Cavanagh continued to function as both general manager and chairman, reporting directly to the premier. But the anomaly could not continue indefinitely. George Drew would have to face it when he became premier following the election of August 4, 1943.

The Election of 1943

The provincial Liberal party in that election collapsed throughout the province generally, but particularly in the northeast. All five constituencies from Sudbury north to Cochrane returned candidates of the Co-operative Commonwealth Federation. The CCF, founded barely ten years before, had emerged dramatically to become a dynamic force in Ontario politics. Party standings in the legislative assembly now totalled thirty-eight Conservatives, thirty-four CCF, and eighteen Liberals.[3]

The decimation of Liberal representation from sixty-six in 1937 to a mere eighteen in 1943 did not come as a complete surprise. Hepburn had seriously divided the party since 1940. After his resignation no forceful leader had emerged to replace him. No Liberal programme had appeared with appeal for the discontented ranks of labour. Membership in trade unions, together with the trials of war, had crystallized the discontent of miners, industrial workers, and railwaymen over low pay, inadequate pensions, and an uncertain future. The CCF, which had nominated only thirty-seven candidates in the election of 1937, and elected none, put forward eighty-six candidates in 1943 and elected thirty-four. Under the leadership of E.B. Jolliffe, the party formed the official opposition in the provincial assembly, with close to 15 per cent of its membership from northeastern Ontario.

George Drew and the Conservatives formed the new government. For the next two years his leadership exhibited moderation, careful listening, and caution in making decisions and appointments, as he worked toward another election at the end of the war. In Drew's mind the election of so many democratic socialists could be interpreted as only a temporary protest. Against skilful Conservative organization, the CCF might well be defeated in a year or two, while the Liberals were unlikely to recover from the chaos which Hepburn had left at the constituency level. This confident anticipation of a more promising outcome had some bearing on Premier Drew's decisions as he formulated his own approach to the T&NO Commission.

Like Hepburn in 1934, he could be expected to make changes, though the circumstances and the political climate differed greatly. Drew's election took place in wartime, not during the economic slump of the Depression. George Drew, moreover, was a man of strong military associations. With the country at war he would hardly adopt methods of confrontation. Nor could he have scored advantages from charges of patronage or wasteful expenditure, since corruption seemed minimal on the T&NO and controversy would have given the advantage to the lively CCF opposition in the North, tied as it was to the trade unions. From the outset of his régime, relations between Drew's government and the Commission quietly continued as though no serious interference with the railway would occur.

Behind the scenes, however, Drew moved gradually toward the appointment of his own members to a new Commission. He completed this transformation in the summer of 1944. The steps he took to arrive at these decisions are clearly evident in some respects; in others, where the material has either been removed from the files, or was never committed to paper, the historian is forced to rely upon incomplete evidence.

New Pressures, New Solutions

Drew faced four problems on the T&NO Commission shortly after attaining office as premier. The first was the continuing confusion between policy and operation resulting from combining the offices of chairman and general manager. This situation bore no relationship to the personal integrity and efficiency of Arthur Cavanagh. He directed the railway with an informed and professional hand, but his concentrated power intimidated its employees. With no Commission over him, how could one appeal his decisions? Grievances and criticisms had to be contained within the system, unless those who made them were prepared to appeal to the cabinet and the premier.

This sense of being forced to extreme procedures annoyed and frustrated the trade-union leaders. Their complaints constituted the second influence on Drew, one which drove him to define anew the constitutional relationship between chairman and general manager. Union complaints in turn illustrated more specifically the third problem – those pervasive pleas and requests which hang about any premier newly elected to office, pressing him from many directions, each demand reminding him of his political obligations and his resources of patronage. Finally, as the time of decision approached, George Drew held strongly to the notion that at the end of the war, with thousands of young veterans returning to an economy still unable to employ them, a new scheme of settlement in the North – one that would succeed where others had failed – could combine northern development with an economic safety valve by relieving pressure on factories in the South of the province, which might need time to absorb additional manpower.

In October 1943, barely two months after the election, Drew received a strongly worded resolution passed unanimously by the General Chairmen's Conference Committee, composed of the general chairmen of all thirteen unions who now represented the employees of the T&NO. The debate over the resolution included some harsh references from one union to the "totalitarian form of administration...introduced on the T&NO Railway by Mr. Mitchell Hepburn," at a time when sons of employees were fighting fascist governments in Europe. But the final wording of the resolution simply asked Premier Drew to,

...set up a Commission to administer the Temiskaming and Northern Ontario Railway, AND that employees on the property and in the employ of the Railway be accorded the privilege of electing representatives on the Commission equal numerically with the number appointed by the Government.

The accompanying letter added that "such a move would be a true step towards that industrial and economic democracy which we feel sure you are anxious to assist in establishing."[4]

Drew did not respond immediately; he delayed even a polite acknowledgement. It could be argued that the war effort demanded more urgent attention and the railway did not seem to be in any difficulty, either in its operation or in its relations with the government. But the resolution was troublesome. Its wording appeared to be moderate and reasonable but in reality it asked for a concession unprecedented in the forty-year history of the T&NO Commission.

From the standpoint of Queen's Park, appointing northern members to the Commission seemed generous enough, without allowing employees to elect their own representatives. But behind the wording of the resolution lay the personal weight of three union leaders who were not only well established employees of the T&NO but also prominent members of the CCF in the North. Two of them could directly confront the premier from the opposition benches across the floor of the legislative assembly. Calvin Taylor, chairman of the Brotherhood of Railway Employees, was the newly-elected MPP for the CCF in Timiskaming as well as the mayor of Cobalt. Arthur Casselman, chairman of the Order of Railroad Telegraphers, had won an overwhelming majority for the CCF in Nipissing. And Cecil McLaren was both chairman of Systems Federation No. 86 and one of the most active members of the CCF in North Bay.[5]

Drew had good reason to be cautious. In January 1944, the chairmen's committee approached him again and this time they asked for a meeting. The premier met with the executive of the conference committee shortly afterward when they had modified their proposal, arguing that the men themselves should choose at least one representative to the Commission. The notes for the meeting indicate, however, that equally urgent in the minds of the men was the establishment of a Commission that would offer them a centre of appeal beyond the general manager. Drew felt compelled to appoint a Commission over Cavanagh. The problem would be to decide on its composition.[6]

At the same time that he received suggestions from the unions, Drew conferred with George Lee, who had been retired from the Commission for ten years.[7] From the New Liskeard Board of Trade and from individuals came specific names, in letters which assumed that the premier would likely appoint a Commission composed of a chairman, a labour representative, and a commissioner for public relations.

These unsolicited applications – all based on rumours – are the only apparent evidence that Premier Drew was contemplating a new Commission. He wrote no notes on the subject, and no record exists of his conversations. But Drew probably discussed the T&NO with A.D. McKenzie, chief organizer of the Progressive Conservative party, and the premier had clearly decided he would not be rushed.

In March 1944, Drew ordered that a new file be opened on the northern Clay Belt, as a step to establishing a policy on the settlement of veterans whose return from the war was imminent. Leslie Frost, the Minister of Mines, submitted two reports from his department, both negative in their conclusions. Drew felt a commitment to restore the pre-war level of mining activity and to expand northern farming. But he found little encouragement from those in a position to give him advice. Frost submitted reports full of information and sensible judgement but not of encouragement.

Any policy of northern development, Frost said, must recognize the reasons for previous failures. In the past, governments had refused to acknowledge that some races were more suited to settlement than others; that group settlement was more effective than individual efforts; that settlers needed constant supervision by government technicians. Agricultural development of the 16,000,000 acre Clay Belt had failed because forestry had not been combined with agriculture, and because more than half the Clay Belt consisted of rock, peat, and low nutrient soils. These limitations, together with short frost-free periods and the lower costs of agricultural production in the South, inhibited settlement by other than the two thousand or so families who currently lived on a few hundred farms along a three-hundred-mile frontier.[8]

These discouraging facts would not change significantly over the next thirty years in the north-south corridor between North Bay and Moosonee. But Drew believed in 1944 that the conclusions of people like Leslie Frost were based on historical precedents. The future of settlement might now be projected differently. He was unwilling to give up his dream.

Interwoven with this ambition to project his own notion of northern settlement was the determination of George Drew to appoint a partisan T&NO Commission, as most premiers had before him. The exception had been Ernest Drury in 1920, who could find no alternative to George Lee. Howard Ferguson in 1923 had inherited an essentially Conservative chairman with two congenial, acquiescent colleagues who formed an acceptable and comfortable Commission. Drew faced a different situation.

In Cavanagh he had a one-man Commission and the confusion between policy and management could not be allowed to continue. In addition, while no one questioned Cavanagh's ability, he contributed little to cementing political relations between the Conservative party and northern communities. To small-town politicians and chambers of commerce, Cavanagh was a remote figure preoccupied with running an efficient railway.[9]

That was insufficient for George Drew. A Commission should reach out and strengthen relations for the Conservative party in the North. In 1944, he settled on Lt.-Col. Charles Edward (Ed) Reynolds as the new chairman. No one in the North had been consulted – neither Arthur Cavanagh nor the chief Conservative organizer in North Bay, Harry J. Reynolds, a distant relative of the newly-selected chairman.[10] Party leaders in the North reacted quietly but Cavanagh had reason to ponder if political manoeuvring would finally undermine his own position.

Building the long bridge across the Moose River on the way to James Bay, 1930. This accident was caused by collapse of supports on the trestle bridge, toppling cars and their loads of ties down the side of the steep embankment.

Top: Hay meadow and reapers. *Below*: Hay stacks and farmers. Both photos were taken at Ship Sands, Moose Factory, in 1911. They illustrate the repeated attempts of the T&NO Commission to promote agriculture in northern Ontario, even to the edge of James Bay.

Top: Encampment of Cree Indians at Moose Factory, early in the twentieth century. Below: Official opening ceremony for the Moosonee extension, July 15, 1932.

The Hollinger gold mine in the 1920s. Ore cars at the 425 foot level, and pouring gold into moulds. A bullion shipment left Timmins every ten days on the T&NO Railway, for the Mint in Ottawa.

Aerial view of the ONR railway yard, the diesel shop and round house, at North Bay.

Left: Arthur H. Cavanagh, general manager 1934-1947; chairman of the Commission 1940-1944. Appointed by Premier Hepburn, Cavanagh concentrated a remarkable degree of power over the railway. But he was always the professional man. In 1936 he ordered the four last and biggest of the steam locomotives.

68

No. 1102, a "Northern" type (4-8-4) made in Kingston, and operative until steam was replaced by diesels entirely in 1957.

Preparing the "centennial" steam locomotive in the repair shops at North Bay, 1967.

Receiving a new diesel locomotive from General Motors, in the shops at North Bay, October, 1953.

From inside the cab, the operations for the engineman on the diesel are simpler and smoother, if also less exciting than the fire-box and the valves of the steam locomotive.

The Commission of the ONTC, meeting at the head office in North Bay, 1959. Left to right: R.S. Potter, W.A. Johnston, S.W. Gowan (secretary), C.E. Reynolds (chairman), A. Jardine (general manager), R.A. Aubert, and A.R. Herbert. By this time it was not unusual for members to be MPPs, as Johnston and Herbert both were. The Kirkland Lake *Daily News* said of the Commission in 1950: "In these days of 'big business' with its sedate panoply of dignified board room ceremonies and pontifical verbiage, it's as refreshing as a spring breeze to see how the ONTC operates. We in the North may occasionally differ with its decisions... but we'll always admire its method of approach...The ONR...operates with the...stress on the human and personal element in its negotiations and business." (May 13, 1950)

By the 1960s the ONR was entering a new phase in its history, acquiring trucks, buses, and boats to justify its new title as the Ontario Northland Transportation Commission. *Below*: A unit diesel train transporting pellets from the Sherman iron mine at Temagami.

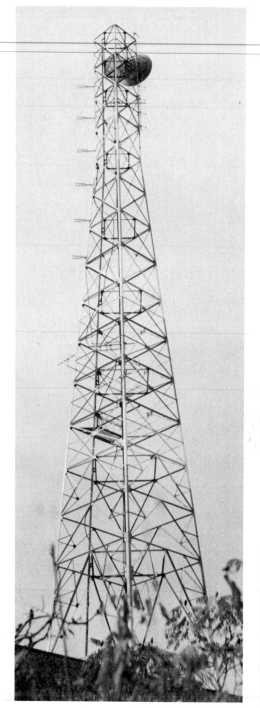

Towers of Ontario Northland Communications, which have become a vital part of the Commission, providing telecommunication through cable and microwave for the entire northeast of the province.

SAFETY FIRST

TEMISKAMING & NORTHERN ONTARIO RAILWAY

NORTH BAY DIVISION

TIME 75 TABLE

Taking Effect at 12.01 A.M., Sunday, December 2nd, 1934

SUPERSEDING TIME TABLE No. 74

FOR THE INFORMATION AND GUIDANCE OF EMPLOYEES ONLY.

CHECK DAYS OF THE WEEK WITH EXTREME CARE.

GOVERNED BY EASTERN TIME

EAST OR SOUTHBOUND TRAINS, AS INDICATED BY TIME TABLE HEADING, ARE (UNLESS OTHERWISE SPECIFIED) SUPERIOR TO TRAINS OF SAME OR INFERIOR CLASS RUNNING IN THE OPPOSITE DIRECTION IN ACCORDANCE WITH RULE No. 72.

THE RAILWAY'S RULES ARE PRINTED SEPARATELY IN BOOK FORM. EVERY EMPLOYEE WHOSE DUTIES ARE CONNECTED WITH THE MOVEMENT OF TRAINS MUST HAVE A COPY OF THEM AND OF THE CURRENT TIME-TABLE ACCESSIBLE WHEN ON DUTY.

A. H. CAVANAGH,
GENERAL MANAGER.

W. A. GRIFFIN,
SUPERINTENDENT.

TIME TABLE No. 75—EFFECTIVE DECEMBER 2nd, 1934

TEMAGAMI SUB-DIVISION

Station list (Miles from North Bay)

Stations	Miles from North Bay
NORTH BAY C.P.R.	
NORTH BAY T. & N. O.	1.3
C. N. R. CONNECTION	0
C. N. R. CROSSING	0.4 / 0.5
TROUT MILLS	8.7
FERONIA	
WIDDIFIELD	13.5
MULOCK	18.1
TOMIKO	27.3
RIDDLE	
OSBORNE	37.7
DIVER	39.8
OTTER	41.6
BUSHNELL	
KENNEY	48.4
REDWATER	55.5
DOHERTY	63.4
TEMAGAMI	71.8
GOWARD	75.6
OWAISSA	78.5
RIB LAKE	83.0
JOHNSON	
LATCHFORD	94.
SOUTH GILLIES	97.7
CASSIDY	
LORRAIN (Junction with Lorrain Sub-Division)	
COBALT	102.8
NORTH COBALT	105.7
HAILEYBURY	107.4
NEW LISKEARD	112.6
UNO PARK	118.4
THORNLOE	124.8
EARLTON (Junction with Elk Lake Sub-Division)	128.6
HEASLIP	134.9
ENGLEHART	138.5

★ No Passing Track

SPECIAL INSTRUCTIONS
TEMAGAMI SUB-DIVISION

Registering Points ... North Bay C.P.R., North Bay T. & N. O., North Bay C. N. R. and Englehart.
Comparison Clocks ... C. N. R. and Englehart.
Bulletin Points ... North Bay T. & N. O., North Bay C. N. R. and Englehart.

Speed Restrictions
Passenger Trains .... 55 miles per hour
Freight Trains .... 40 miles per hour.

Except southbound trains between Mulock and Trout Mills; passenger trains 40 miles per hour; freight trains 25 miles per hour.

The following special instructions will govern trains moving between North Bay T. & N. O. yard office and North Bay C.P.R. Passenger Depot.

Without special instructions, no light engine, irregular train or extra section of regular train shall exceed the running time of the fastest time table schedule.

Special attention is directed to Rule 102, "General Train and Interlocking Rules."

All trains must reduce speed and use extra precaution approaching Golf Street.

All trains between Regina Street and North Bay C.P.R. Station will be governed by C.P.R. signals.

Movement of westbound trains between Regina Street and C.P.R. Station will be governed by block protection signals. Distant signal is located at Regina Street, and controls the approach of T. & N. O. trains to home signal. The home signal is located about eight hundred (800) feet west of Regina Street, and governs two routes. The upper arm governs the approach of T. & N. O. trains entering C.P.R. passenger yard, and the lower arm controls approach of C.P.R. trains entering same yard.

Movement of trains between C.N.R. Connection and North Bay C.N.R. Passenger Station governed by Electric Train Staff System. "See Rules Governing Movement by Electric Train Staff System," page 10.
Special attention is directed to "Rule 102 General Train and Interlocking Rules."

Semaphore signal located at Commercial Street, west of North Bay C.N.R. Passenger Station, and the two-arm semaphore bracket signal, located 2,000 feet east of North Bay C.P.R. Passenger Station, are for the protection of trains occupying the main tracks at the station.

The northerly arm of the bracket semaphore signal governs the approach of westbound trains on C.N.R. main track. The southerly arm governs the approach of westbound trains on the T. & N. O. exclusive track. The northerly arm of the semaphore bracket signal, located at Commercial Street, are interlocked with the first crossover switch east of the station. The normal position of these signals is "proceed". Trains finding semaphore signals in "stop" position must stop clear of the signal and not proceed until signal is changed to normal position.

The position of the first switch west of the North Bay C.N.R. Passenger Station is normal when set for the northerly track which track is the C.N.R. exclusive main track. The southerly track from this switch to connection with T. & N. O. is T. & N. O. exclusive main track.

Operator at C.N.R. Crossing, M.P. 0.5 will register all first class trains, except where train orders are displayed by any section thereof, in which case trains Nos. 46 and 47 must register.

Conductors of trains Nos. 46 and 47 will hand Identification Ticket Form 1415 to Operator C.N.R. Crossing.

All trains will approach and pass through North Bay T. & N. O., Cobalt, Earlton and Englehart Yards prepared to stop unless main track is seen to be clear.

Junction with Canadian National Rys. (Interlocked) at M.P. 0.4.

Railway Crossing at grade with Canadian National Rys. (interlocked) at M.P. 0.5.

Train No. 6 will register at Cobalt.
Trains Nos. 60, 61 and 9 will register at New Liskeard.
Trains No. 17 and No. 18 will stop on flag at the following places only in addition to flag stops indicated on schedule: Holdens Spur, Jocko, M.P. 43.8, M.P. 50, M.P. 60.3, Gillies Depot and Maybrook.
Train No. 6, 60, 61 and 9 will stop on flag at the following places: M.P. 132.9, M.P. 131.5, M.P. 130.6, Maybrook and M.P. 115.2.
Train No. 9 will stop on flag at Maybrook.
Southbound freight trains between Tomiko and Trout Mills must not follow any train until twenty minutes have elapsed.

Spur Tracks	Mileage
Wm. Milne & Sons	73.5
Temagami Timber Co. Ltd.	80.1
Dynamite	104.0
Nipissing Central Ry. Transfer	121.5

Spur Tracks	Mileage
Wm. Milne & Sons	2.7
Public	10.4
Wm. Milne & Co.	13.5
Canadian Timber Co. Ltd.	44.0
Public	50.0
Rabbit Creek Pit	58.7

TIME TABLE No. 75—EFFECTIVE DECEMBER 2nd, 1934

RAMORE SUB-DIVISION

NORTHBOUND TRAINS — INFERIOR DIRECTION

THIRD CLASS		SECOND CLASS			FIRST CLASS				STATIONS	Telephone Calls	Miles from Englehart	No Passing Track	FIRST CLASS				SECOND CLASS			THIRD CLASS		
87 Freight / Daily	85 Freight / Daily	23 Mixed / Daily ex. Sunday	11 Mixed / Saturday only	9 Mixed / Saturday only	71 Passenger / Daily	19 Passenger / Mon., Wed., Fri.	17 Passenger / Daily ex. Sun.	47 Passenger / Daily	STATIONS				18 Passenger / Daily ex. Sun.	20 Passenger / Tues., Thur., Sat.	46 Passenger / Daily	72 Passenger / Daily	8 Mixed / Saturday only	10 Mixed / Saturday only	24 Mixed / Daily ex. Sunday	96 Freight / Daily	94 Freight / Daily	

Special Instructions

RAMORE SUB-DIVISION

Registering Points — Englehart, Swastika, Porquis and Cochrane.
Bulletin Points
Comparison Clocks

Speed Restrictions

Passenger Trains .... 55 miles per hour
Freight Trains 40

During the hours that operator is not on duty at Swastika, the Train Register will be kept in a cabinet in front of the freight shed.

All trains will approach and pass through Englehart, Swastika, Porquis and Cochrane Yards prepared to stop unless main track is seen to be clear.

Train No. 18 will wait connections with Nos. 50 and 31, unless otherwise instructed.

Train No. 17 and No. 18 will stop on flag at Spur M.P. 10.9, Goldthorpe, Vimy Ridge and M.P. 107.

Train No. 19 will wait connections with No. 54 and No. 37 at Porquis unless otherwise instructed.

Train No. 46 will wait connections with Trains Nos. 52 and 33 at Porquis and Train No. 71 at Swastika unless otherwise instructed.

Train No. 47 will wait connection with Trains Nos. 35 and 52 at Porquis unless otherwise instructed.

Train No. 72 will wait connections with trains Nos. 46 and 17, unless otherwise instructed.

All trains from Kirkland Lake Sub-Division may leave Swastika Junction without obtaining Terminal Clearance and will register at Swastika.

Spur Tracks	Mileage
Public	6.5
Public	6.5
South Mindoka	10.9
Goldthorpe	31.4
Public	47.0
T. S. Woolling	52.0
Vimy Ridge	61.5
Public	70.3
Public	78.1
Nellie Lake Pit	90.8
Public	107.0

★ No Passing Track

TIME TABLE No. 75—EFFECTIVE DECEMBER 2nd, 1934

SPECIAL INSTRUCTIONS ISLAND FALLS SUB-DIVISION

Registering Points
Bulletin Points } Cochrane, Fraserdale.
Comparison Clocks

Speed Restrictions:
Passenger Trains .... 30 miles per hour.
Freight Trains .... 30 " "

All trains may leave Moosonee without obtaining Terminal Clearance.

Railway Crossing at Grade with Canadian National Railway (not interlocked) at M.P. 0.4.

Junction with Canadian National Railway (not interlocked) at M.P. 0.3.

Freight trains must not run any one mile in less than two minutes and thirty seconds.

Permanent "STOP" sign-boards indicated by red lights at night at the Railway Crossing at Grade with Canadian National Railway M.P. 0.4, Island Falls Sub-division, are located as follows:

300 feet North of Railway Crossing, and
300 feet South of Railway Crossing,
on the Temiskaming and Northern Ontario Railway Main Track, and
300 feet East of Railway Crossing, and
300 feet West of Railway Crossing,
on Canadian National Railway Main Track.

A two-arm semaphore, of the two position, upper quadrant type, is located at the southwesterly angle of the Diamond crossing at grade with Canadian National Railways M.P. 0.4 Island Falls Sub-division. The normal position of both arms is "STOP."

The lower (or bottom) arm governs trains on the Temiskaming and Northern Ontario Railway main track in both directions:

Indications: Arm Horizontal—Red Light at Night—STOP.
Arm 90° above—Green Light at Night—PROCEED.

The upper (or top) arm governs trains on the Canadian National Railway main track in both directions:

Indications: Arm Horizontal—Red Light at Night—STOP.
Arm 90° above—Green Light at Night—PROCEED.

All trains and engines must stop before reaching the permanent "STOP" sign-boards. A Trainman will then proceed to the crossing, determine whether there are any trains approaching from either direction on the Canadian National Railway Main Track, and if that route is clear, will set the lower arm at "PROCEED" position for the movement of train over the crossing. When train has occupied the crossing, he will then return the lower arm to normal or "STOP" position.

Strictly observe General Rules Nos. 98 and 106.

Switches and other fixed signals, Larocque to Moosonee, inclusive, are not provided with lights. Trains run during hours from sunset to sunrise will be governed by day indications.

	Mileage
Spur Tracks	
Public	17.4
Ballast Pit	94
Ballast Pit	94.7

ISLAND FALLS SUBDIVISION

Northbound 103 (Mixed, Wed. Only)	Northbound 101 (Mixed, Wed. and Sat.)	Coal, Water / Wye / Tel. Offices	Miles from Cochrane	STATIONS	Telegraph Calls	Passing Tracks	Other Tracks	Southbound 102 (Mixed, Thur. Only)	Southbound 104 (Mixed, Wed. and Sat.)
	9.00 A.M.	Y W C D N	0.0	COCHRANE	● C N	Yard	Yard	8.30 P.M.	6.20 P.M.
	9.07		0.3	.C.N.R. CONNECTION				8.23	6.10
			0.4	C.N.R. CROSSING					
	f 9.24		5.7	LAROCQUE	Q	55		f 8.06	f 5.53
	f 9.34		8.2	GENIER	J R		9	f 7.56	f 5.43
	f 9.50		9.8	CLUTE	C U	68	4	f 7.40	f 5.27
	f10.14		15.2	BLOUNT	B N	68	8	f 7.16	f 5.03
	f10.30	W	18.6	GARDINER	M F	37		f 7.00	f 4.47
	f10.49		22.4	WORKMAN	W			f 6.41	f 4.27
	f11.03	W	26.2	● WURTELE	● W U	68		f 6.27	f 4.13
	f11.20	W	31.7	MAHER	M A	68		f 6.10	f 3.56
	f11.37		36.8	TRAPPERSVILLE	V	69		f 5.58	f 3.39
	f11.51	D	42.1	McGINIS	G			f 5.39	f 3.25
	s12.20 P.M.	Y D	43.1	ISLAND FALLS	R V	24	9	s 5.10	s 3.10
	f12.40		48.9	HOMUTH	H U	69		f 4.50	f 2.53
	f 1.00	W	55.9	BROWNRIGG	B O	68		f 4.30	f 2.33
	f 1.17	Y	62.6	BURNWOOD	W D	62		f 4.13	f 2.16
1.37 P.M.	s 1.33 P.M.	Y D	69.2	● FRASERDALE	● F R	Yard		s 3.55	s 2.00 P.M.
f 2.08			78.3	THERRIEN	H X	71		f 3.28 P.M.	
f 2.28			85.7	FOXVILLE	F X	75		f 3.08	
f 2.45			91.9	SEXTANT	S A	54		f 2.51	
s 2.57		W Y	96.3	● CORAL RAPIDS	C R	Yard		s 2.39	
f 3.19			104.4			42		f 2.17	
f 3.40			112.0			43		f 1.56	
f 3.58		W	118.8	ONAKAWANA	K A	44		f 1.38	
f 4.18			126.1			42		f 1.18	
f 4.37		W	133.0	MOOSE RIVER CROSSING	M V	43		f12.59	
f 5.02			141.9			43		s12.34	
f 5.20			148.5			40		f12.16 P.M.	
f 5.40			155.9			44		f11.54	
f 5.58			163.1			43		f11.34	
f 6.10			171.0					f11.12	
f 6.41			178.9					f10.50	
7.00 P.M.		C Y W	186.2	MOOSONEE	M H	Yard		10.30 A.M.	

★ No Passing Track.

Friends and Partisans

Drew had known C.E. Reynolds as president of the Canadian Corps Association, a position in which Reynolds had spent years of dedicated work. A veteran of four years on the western front in World War I, where he had been awarded both the DSO and the MC, he had remained intensively active in all issues affecting the veterans of that war. George Drew felt an intuitive sympathy for such a man. He himself had been wounded in the same war, and by 1944 the two men held the same military rank.

Reynolds, moreover, could claim a northern background. Born and raised in Sault Ste. Marie, he had attended high school in Owen Sound, and worked in a lumber mill at Blind River before moving to Vancouver, where he lived with his parents until he enlisted to serve in World War I. After his return to Canada in 1919 he owned and operated a sawmill in British Columbia for five years. He returned to Ontario in 1925 and by 1929 had founded a cement contracting company – Ontario Transit Mixers of Canada Limited – which provided his main source of income for the next fifteen years.[11]

But he spent most of his time with the Canadian Corps Association, travelling back and forth across the country to investigate and attempt to resolve some of the grievances of veterans. His business failed to expand and provide income in proportion to Reynold's notion of his status and position. He readily accepted the new appointment. As chairman his salary would be $6,000, later raised to $9,000, plus expenses, which enabled him to live a moderately comfortable style of life with his wife and three children in North Bay.

Reynolds was fifty-seven at the time and he remained chairman for the next eighteen years. In 1945 he found a post on the T&NO for his old friend, Owen T.G. Williamson, secretary of the Canadian Corps Association, who had a talent for writing historical journalese. While not appointed to the Commission, Williamson was listed and paid among the top administrative staff of the railway for the next ten years. As its first public relations officer, he also pleased Premier Drew by writing propaganda in the form of pamphlets and articles that publicized the history of the railway and of the North.[12]

Then, to avoid Hepburn's mistake of creating a one-man Commission, Drew decided to revert to the earlier Conservative practice of appointing a three-man Commission. As the other two Commissioners he selected Robert S. Potter from Matheson and Reginald A. Aubert from Englehart. Potter qualified as a prominent Conservative who owned and operated a successful farm in the Matheson area, with regional business interests in mining and lumbering. His previous experience as a prospector gave him an intimate knowledge of the region, while his contacts through business and farming made him a "Mr. Northern Ontario" for the Conservative party.

Aubert could be touted as a representative of the employees and the unions, since he worked on the railway and had for some time been local chairman of the Brotherhood of Firemen and Oilers. But his real qualification was political, since he also functioned as president of the local Conservative Association in Englehart. Once appointed to the Commission, he could not easily sustain identity as a representative of the employees. Both he and Potter remained on the Commission for as long as Reynolds, until 1962. Each received $2,000 a year plus expenses, though Aubert received assigned tasks which justified an additional $1,500 annually by an Order-in-Council renewed each year.

By August 1944, then, the T&NO Railway had a new Commission with a chairman of equable temperament, possessed of methodical routine administrative abilities, and loyal with a soldier's sense of duty to the Conservative government. The CCF accepted his appointment with apparent composure, despite their majority in northern constituencies. But, then, what could they do, given the modest expectations among the people of northern towns, together with the political inexperience of new MPPs? What could they criticize, except that the Commission had again become a political body? Drew could readily reply that Aubert satisfied the unions' request for an employees' spokesman; Potter had extensive local interests and many friends in lumbering and mining; while Reynolds brought no previous commitments to the partisan politics of the northeast. The CCF in the North seemed satisfied that summer when their trade-union demands were met by the appointment of two employees to an enlarged pension board. For most workers, pensions meant more to them than the politics of the Commission.

An argument could be made that Drew had avoided controversy by waiting, then acting as quickly as he did; also passing over certain Conservative figures in the North. He could have chosen Harry J. Reynolds, a federal judge who had extensive contacts throughout the Conservative party from his base in North Bay. Or he could have called upon Colonel E. J. (Ernie) Young, the defeated Conservative candidate for Nipissing in the election of 1943. Young had lived most of his life in North Bay, had once worked for the T&NO, and been ousted from a local civil service job after Hepburn's victory in 1934. He and his wife symbolized total commitment to the Progressive Conservative party. As a full Colonel he had been serving in England at the time of the 1943 election. But Young had neither Reynold's prestige nor his experience; his income derived from a dry-cleaning establishment in North Bay. Nor did Young possess the implied political neutrality which C. E. Reynolds brought to the new Commission. As compensation, and as a means of drawing him eventually into the inner circle as one of Drew's most important executive assistants, Young was appointed liaison officer between Queen's Park and Ontario House in London, England, to aid in the return and settlement of war veterans. The appointments of both Reynolds and Young appeared in the same public announcement for press and radio on 15 August 1944. The wording included no mention of party patronage.[13]

Given the circumstances, response in the North proved favourable and re-markably unquestioning. The Conservatives would not hold a single seat in the northeast until after the election of 1948, yet Drew could appoint an obviously partisan Commission without protest either from the opposition parties or from the press.[14]

One reason may have arisen from the recent history of agencies and commissions of the provincial government. Whether the aim was control of liquor, or compensation for injured workmen, supplying electricity as a public utility, or

154

governing the parkland of Niagara, the public service was directed by a party which had gained power through the active support of members and followers. People accepted that the party in power, and especially its leader, had the right to appoint to semi-independent agencies of government party members who could be trusted to carry out party policies. Because Drew faced no public debate on this issue, he felt free to appoint a partisan Commission, one which gradually became identified with the lengthy rule of the Conservative party in the province.

Another more specific reason for the absence of controversy appeared in an editorial published by the North Bay *Daily Nugget*:

> The T. & N.O. Railway, which is synonymous with the history, growth and development of the north country, again has a commission after being without one during the past few years. The railway appears to have been operated in a highly efficient manner and for this reason it is unlikely that this newly created commission will assume an extremely active role in the actual operation of the railway.[15]

That view paid tribute to the management of the railway by Arthur Cavanagh, who now reported to a Commission composed of members with little or no knowledge of transportation.

Cavanagh had defended the jobs of employees at every level in the Hepburn purges ten years before; he had tightened the administration of the railway; purchased equipment equal to that of the CNR and CPR, and directed the economies which had maintained financial stability through Depression and war. In light of this contribution it was all the more remarkable that Drew did not consult him when appointing the new Commission. Whether from reluctance to confront a strong-willed man, or whether as a deliberate slight, the premier released the announcement to the general public before informing anyone in the North. Cavanagh first heard the news that the Commission had been appointed, with a chairman who would replace him, over CFCH, Roy Thomson's radio station in North Bay. Only later did he receive a curt telegram from Drew:

> Have decided to announce appointment three members T & N O Commission tonight for reasons which I will explain when I see you STOP This in no way affects your own position.[16]

Cavanagh felt puzzled and humiliated. He wrote to Drew the next day, as politely as he could, since the decision had been publicly announced and he did not wish to resign. But how could his position remain unaffected? Reynolds would be his superior and the T&NO Act empowered the Commission "with full jurisdiction over all matters pertaining to the Railway, including its operation and maintenance." A week later, Drew replied to Cavanagh, saying:

> I have been satisfied for some time that a very much better relationship will exist on the railway between management and the workers,

155

and also between the railway and the public, if there is a commission distinct from the management as was contemplated in setting up the organization by Statute in the first place.[17]

Evidence had accumulated, the premier added, to demonstrate the need for such a Commission, "and certain events which had occurred made it essential that the decision be made without delay."

Responding to Cavanagh's questions about the status of his position, Drew wrote in terms which sounded like a military order. But his instructions exhibited a sound, administrative sense which added substance to the precedent he was setting and which Conservative governments would follow for the next three decades. To Cavanagh he wrote: "You will retain full management authority, continuing the work which you have done so well. Your position, however, will be divorced from the Commission." The altered arrangement would free the Commission to explore possibilities of development "without involving any members of the operating organization..." In the meantime, Cavanagh's salary would remain at $15,000.

On the same day, Drew wrote to Reynolds to elaborate on his own concept of the role of the Commission. It must continue to play a central role in the development of northern Ontario: "I would like to see every possible opportunity explored with the thought that this road may become the backbone of a greatly expanded system of communication supporting a greatly increased population."

In terms of immediate tactics, Drew advised Reynolds to allow the Commission a reflective period for the next four to six weeks, in which to confer among themselves and learn to know one another. Then they would meet with the premier and the Minister of Planning and Development, the head of a department Drew had just established. Drew concluded this letter expressing concern that friction might develop between Reynolds and Cavanagh:

> The main thing is to assure effective co-operation between the Commission and the management, and to establish a friendly relationship with the employees which will assure their effective co-operation in any plans which may be developed.[18]

This anxiety proved well-founded. At the end of August 1944, Cavanagh could sanguinely assure the premier of his "whole-hearted sincere co-operation with Chairman Colonel Reynolds and his Commissioners." But his past status, his inclination to manage forcefully, his dislike of politics, and his treatment so far at the hands of George Drew, all combined to frustrate co-operation. Over the next few years, as Reynolds sought to implement both his own ambition and the ambition of the new Conservative premier, a festering friction developed in relations between Cavanagh and the Commission.

CHAPTER 16

Efficiency of the Colonels

Reynolds arrived in North Bay on August 16, 1944, the formal date of his appointment as chairman. In an interview he confirmed Premier Drew's policy for the Commission and the North, stating the goals he intended to pursue as though they were his own. Certainly the views which he expressed that day dominated his administration for the next eighteen years. "We are not concerned so much with the operation of the railway," he said, "as with the opportunities it can offer in the development and expansion of the North."[1]

The federal government was still committed to providing men and supplies on a huge scale for the war in Europe and the Far East. Every issue of northern newspapers contained stories and pictures of young men from the North then serving in Europe. Many participated in the D-Day invasion of June 1944. Others were part of the Canadian force that broke through the Falaise Gap in Normandy with heavy casualties and inched its way along the coast to Belgium. The announcement of Reynold's appointment had to be squeezed on the front pages between larger headlines of allied progress and German retreat. Compared to Winston Churchill or Franklin Roosevelt or Generals Eisenhower and Montgomery, readers might naturally ask: who was this Colonel C.E. Reynolds, and why should he be important enough to appear on the front pages?

Less than a Ministry

The question is not entirely rhetorical. Everyone looked with relief to the end of the war, and with curiosity to preparations for peace. Drew wanted Reynolds to speak to this anticipation, to assure the people in the North that the new Chairman concerned himself with their future, which included plans for expanding not only the means of transportation, but the scale of production and of employment in mining, lumbering, and farming. His function would extend beyond that of a part-time chairman of a railway Commission.

Because of the overwhelming number of CCF victories, without a single Conservative member from the northeast, Drew could not appoint a Minister of Mines from the North as he had promised to do before the election. The closest he could come to fulfilling that promise was to select Leslie Frost, the newly-

elected MPP from Lindsay, a rural, small town but hardly a northern constituency. For the time being, Reynolds as Chairman of the T&NO served as a
substitute non-elected minister of northern affairs. But he could never be taken
with the same seriousness as an elected member of the executive council of
government. Nor did he possess the political influence or the intellectual insight
of Leslie Frost. Nonetheless, Reynolds worked assiduously at proposals for
making the North a more expansive economy. In personal terms he and Colonel
E. J. Young were certainly closer to Drew than was Frost as Minister of Mines.

The Commission held its third meeting in the premier's office in Toronto.
Drew directly involved himself in discussions about air service for those parts of
the North then without the means of air communication. He cautioned the
Commission to respond carefully to the request from the city council of North
Bay that the railway begin to pay some form of municipal taxation. When Reynolds asked whether the railway should be made to conform to the demands of
a money-making enterprise, Drew replied: "So long as we proceed on a sound
[efficient] basis we should not limit our vision to plans which might indicate an
immediate profit."[2]

This was the only meeting of the Commission in the presence of Premier Drew
and the last one Cavanagh attended. Henceforth, for as long as he remained
general manager, Cavanagh would take direction from and report to the chairman, who immediately began to seek ways that would implement his own ideas
on development.

Through the winter of 1944-45 Reynolds met a number of times with representatives from the Department of Agriculture, all of whom agreed that the
most effective way to help northern agriculture would be the introduction of
western breeding cattle. By the spring of 1945 he had arranged a scheme under
which the T&NO hired a buyer, purchased the cattle, and absorbed the charges
for freight. In the early spring the railway transported four carloads of breeder
cattle from the West, one of which was unloaded at Earlton, another at Matheson, and two more at Cochrane. The animals were sold to farmers at cost.[3]

At the same time, Reynolds submitted a long report to the premier exactly
one year after his appointment. He wrote it as a memorandum on northern
development, with specific reference to various departments of the provincial
government. Following several months of observation, he concluded:

> I am convinced that this area provides the same opportunities which,
> in times of stress, were afforded to the United States by an ever in-
> creasing development beyond their Western frontier.

According to Reynolds the North of Ontario could expand more rapidly than
the American West because railways and highways were already built and could
be extended. Hydro-electric power abounded, providing accessible energy for
further development of mining, forestry, and farming. In addition, the region's
natural beauty would surely attract recreational and tourist traffic, especially
from the United States, to unspoiled lakes, rivers and woods. Finally, since the
memorandum contained proposals that went beyond transportation, into sub-

jects which could legitimately be described as lying outside the jurisdiction of the Commission, Reynolds explained to the premier:

> As one on the ground and directly responsible to yourself, I do not feel that in dealing with matters, the concern of other departments of government, I am overstepping my prerogatives.[4]

In fact, he was doing just that. Drew sensibly appears to have directed that the memo be filed; it recommended changes which the government could not pursue. Two changes from these discussions, however, affected the public image of the Commission and its relation to the provincial government. The first changed the name of the railway's governing body to the Ontario Northland Transportation Commission; the second change required the Commission to report, no longer directly to the premier of the province, but to a member of the cabinet. Drew sought by these means to place the Commission at a more appropriate level of power and responsibility.

A Change of Name

Cavanagh had first suggested a change of name after Hepburn's resignation in 1942. He talked with Premier Conant in November of that year and wrote afterward: "considerable thought has been given to the selection of a proper name, and I desire to recommend that we change the name of the railway to that of 'Ontario Northland Railway'." Such a move, Cavanagh said, would continue the identification of the railway with the province and especially with the North, while avoiding a limited identity with the District of Timiskaming. The new name would also clear away an expensive, time-wasting confusion with the Texas and New Orleans Railway in the United States. Because both railroads used the same initials, the Ontario railroad lost box cars in the United States, while it received invoices and rental charges which should properly have gone to the Texas company.

Early in 1943 Cavanagh met with the cabinet and argued for the change, but Conant delayed, unwilling to place the proposal before a legislature where everyone knew that an election lay only a few months away. No precedent could be cited for changing the name by Order-in-Council.[5]

The issue remained unresolved until the election of George Drew who raised it during his meeting with the new Commission in November 1944, and asked for recommendations. There was some opposition, for which Col. E.J. Young from North Bay subsequently became the spokesman, though Young should have been preoccupied with his duties at Ontario House in London, England. While the change might remove confusion with the American railway, Young argued, it would entail unnecessary cost. A formal statute would be required, and confusion would be caused among people in the North. More powerful than any of these objections was the historical and sentimental value which the old initials had established throughout northern Ontario. Pondering these questions, Drew's deputy premier – another colonel – G.C. Blackstock, wrote Reynolds that he was "perturbed at the possible reactions which may develop from such a change." [6]

But Reynolds and other members persisted. The new name would be more suited to the expanding functions of the Commission. Yielding to their influence, Drew introduced a bill to amend the Temiskaming and Northern Ontario Railway Act on March 22, 1946 which received formal assent and became a provincial statute on April 5. It was put into effect by an Order-in-Council four days later, when corresponding changes of name were instituted for the rail, highway, navigation and communication services under control of the Commission. Henceforth all letterheads and insignia would carry the title *Ontario Northland Transportation Commission*. [7]

The Authority of the Crown

The Act of 1946 included other changes enabling the Commission to purchase transportation and navigation companies, and to operate them "for the benefit of the travelling public or the residents of that part of Ontario which may be served by the operations of the Commission." A further, wide-ranging clause clarified the legal position of the ONTC with respect to newly-acquired companies or services:

> Wherever in this Act the approval or consent of the Lieutenant Governor in Council is made a condition precedent to the exercise of any power conferred on the Commission, such power may be exercised by any company which the Commission may purchase or otherwise acquire or cause to be incorporated providing the approval or consent of the Lieutenant Governor in Council is obtained. [8]

In other words, as the ONTC expanded over the next two decades, it did so as a crown corporation functioning in the form of a holding company, under the aegis of legislation which gave all its newly-acquired companies the same powers and immunities under the crown enjoyed by a government agency or a public utility. Once under the control of the Commission, these companies, like the railway – now the ONR – would acquire certain privileges not held by private enterprise, not even by the CPR or the CNR. The nature of these privileges made the Commission an even more powerful arm of the provincial government in the northeast. It would need to be wary about exploiting its advantages, since they could raise tensions and difficulties in its relations with small northern communities.

In 1949, for example, the Progressive Conservative Association of South Cochrane wrote to the premier protesting that the ONTC was not liable *in tort*. What did that mean? It took lawyers to explain the meaning to ordinary citizens.

Because the Commission had been designated an incorporated agent of the crown, enjoying the immunities of the crown, it was not bound by a statute unless stipulations binding the crown were expressly stated in the statute. This privilege had been tested in 1934, in a case finally decided by the Ontario

160

Court of Appeal, which held that the T&NO was not liable *in tort* because it was "an emanation of the Crown." For the public, the decision meant simply that passengers had no protection against negligent acts of the ONR which might result in accidents.

The legislation conferred a startling immunity, and the letter from the South Cochrane Conservative Association argued it was wrong in principle "that people suffering damages should be made to rely on the benevolence of a government commission." The Cochrane letter continued:

> While the original purpose of the T.& N.O. Railway was the colonization and opening of Northern Ontario, it is quite clear that the purpose has long since been achieved and that in effect the Ontario Government is now simply in the business of operating a railway which might equally be operated by private enterprise. The position then is this, that the Government steadfastly refused to accept the responsibilities which ordinarily devolve upon anyone operating a business and seek an advantage in the immunity of the Crown *in tort* which is not available to individuals.[9]

The privilege remained, however. Individuals were still compelled to appeal to the chairman of the Commission if their livestock had been killed by trains because of defective fencing along the tracks. In practice, the Commission tried to be flexible and sometimes even generous when deciding such appeals, but it could also stand firm in defending its status of immunity.

The town council of Timmins attempted in 1949 to assert its authority to lay underground telephone and telegraph cables, telling Reynolds that "the Town could and would carry out the undertaking and lease the facilities to the Commission..." Legal counsel for the ONTC advised the Commission it could carry out expropriation of the necessary right-of-way according to two sections of the ONTC Act. One clause allowed the Commission to "acquire the right to convey and transmit electric or other power...through or under land other than the land of the commission," while the other gave the Commission the right to "expropriate any such lands...in the same manner...as is provided in the case of land or property taken by the Crown as represented by the Minister of Public Works under *The Public Works Act*..."[10] These were evident and demonstrable powers of an agency of the provincial government, against which the town of Timmins had no recourse.

An even more blatant illustration of the status of the ONTC emerged in its relations with the city council of North Bay. As an agency of the crown, the Commission had never paid municipal taxes on land which it owned by provincial grant. When the railway had been founded in 1902, the town council and the Board of Trade, in their anxiety that the Commission locate its southern terminus at North Bay, offered a site that would be exempted from taxation for a fixed number of years, only to be informed by legal counsel that their offer was redundant.

As "a body corporate representing the Province," with all its property vested "in trust for the public uses of the Province," legislation from the beginning exempted the T&NO Commission from payment of taxes according to Section 7 of the Assessment Act of the province. Since the Commission could also expropriate land, the original chairman asked the town council to confirm its offer of a financial grant to assist the railway in becoming established at North Bay.[11] Upon receipt of the grant, the Commission located its service and repair shops at the eastern end of McIntyre Street, while the administration building was erected at the corner of Oak and Regina Streets. None of this land could be subjected to tax or rent.

Well before the end of World War II over a thousand employees were working in and out of these buildings in North Bay alone, most of them paying property taxes and supporting an average of three to four dependents. The payroll was spent largely in North Bay. More than any other institution or service, the railway made the town literally a gateway to Temagami and beyond. Unfortunately, no other major industries apart from stations and yards of the CNR and the CPR had located in North Bay. At the end of the war, city officials considered seriously whether the privileged position of the Commission should be allowed to continue. They made their grievances known at Queen's Park, and Drew instructed Reynolds not to become involved in negotiations over payment of municipal business taxes.

At first, Reynolds proposed the contribution of a community building. The city council replied that they preferred a grant from the Commission toward financing an extension to the North Bay Civic Hospital. Reynolds and his two colleagues, with approval from the cabinet, pledged $100,000 in 1946, and in the next session of the legislature the Drew government amended the T&NO Act so that the Commission could, out of its own revenue and,

> ...subject to the approval...of the Lieutenant-Governor in Council ...make financial contributions to or for undertakings or services which are maintained or provided in that part of Ontario which is served by the Commission for the benefit of travellers therein or residents thereof.[12]

When the original pledge was made, the Secretary of the Commission noted that "some contribution to the City could be justified...to compensate for municipal services rendered without payment of municipal taxes." The pledge was honoured in 1949 and charged to the surplus account.[13]

The attitudes developing after World War II, the size of the grant, the formal legislation required to give it sanction, all indicated that for the North the ONR was now big business. It constituted a significant arm of the provincial government. Reinforced by the authority of the crown, its legal status carried privileges in all its relations with northern communities. As government and business enterprise grew more complex, the ONTC could not function indefinitely under the immediate supervision of the premier. Accordingly, George Drew made another decision in 1945 which had far-reaching consequences for the ONTC, and marked a further step toward bureaucratic efficiency.

Relating to the Cabinet

In the provincial election of that year the Progressive Conservatives were returned to power with an overwhelming majority of sixty-six seats in an assembly of ninety. The Liberals merely declined to fourteen seats from the sixteen of 1943, but a stunning defeat hit the CCF. Instead of thirty-four seats, the party retained only eight. Drew's timing of the election, his identification of socialism with communism, his rhetoric about post-war recovery, all worked to make the Progressive Conservatives once again the strongest party in Ontario politics.

The northeast of the province, however, still rejected Conservative candidates. Two seats returned to the Liberals, Cochrane North and Nipissing, but the other three – Cochrane South, Timiskaming, and Sudbury – all remained CCF. Even after the election of 1945, Drew still had no cabinet minister from the North. Either his own good sense, or wise advice, told him that the Commission could not be treated as a ministry of the North, and that Reynolds should cease reporting to the premier. Instead, he decided to include the ONTC among various government commissions which should report in future to a designated ministry of the cabinet.

To implement this change he turned to Roland Michener, who had just been elected for the riding of St. David's in Toronto. A former Rhodes scholar, a lawyer with a successful practice augmented by shrewd investments; a man of amiable temperament with few rough edges, he was then in his late forties and just beginning a distinguished political career. Drew appointed Michener as Provincial Secretary, and altered the scope of that office to include acting as secretary to the cabinet, with responsibility for preparing the agenda and keeping the minutes of cabinet meetings. This innovation brought more system to the centre of government. For three years as a member of Drew's cabinet, Michener organized the secretariat to create a clearer and more efficient handling of affairs in the central executive of the provincial government. Defeated in his attempt at re-election in 1948, Michener then moved into federal politics.

By the time of the change of name to ONTC, Reynolds reported regularly to the Provincial Secretary, as Englehart had reported years before to W. J. Hanna when he held that office. The practice was now conducted with greater formality and definition of function. Michener's deputy minister, Lorne Ross McDonald, screened the reports which came to Michener in his new capacity as secretary to the cabinet. For the next three years Michener attended most meetings of the ONTC in person.[14]

Such a change went beyond mere routine. Though not an actual member of the Commission, Michener took his duties seriously and participated actively in its affairs. His cabinet colleague, G. A. (Tiger) Welsh, another decorated veteran of World War I who represented Muskoka, became a formal member of the Commission. Indeed, to tie the Commission more closely to the cabinet, Drew appointed Welsh vice-chairman of the Commission, and its meetings in Toronto always took place in Welsh's office at Queen's Park. At that time Welsh was Minister of Travel and Publicity, a forthright, outspoken man assigned to encourage tourism and attract American dollars. The Drew government hoped the ONTC could play an active, expanding role in realizing this goal. The premier himself wrote to Reynolds that Welsh's appointment followed the government's new policy "of having a member of the Cabinet sitting on every Commission."

> I feel sure that this will overcome the difficulties which you have encountered in assuring immediate disposition of matters requiring Government approval or Government consideration, and I am satisfied a very simple arrangement can be made between Arthur Welsh and yourself to have periodic meetings at a time that will be mutually convenient in North Bay.[15]

The old direct relationship between the Commission and the provincial premier, going back to the days of Ernest Drury, had ended. Henceforth the Commission would report formally to the cabinet through a minister. While the titles of ministers would change over the years, the procedure of reporting through a ministry would continue.

CHAPTER **17**

Transition in a Post-War World

After 1946 the provincial government interfered less personally, with more of system and cabinet routine. The Commission could not remove itself entirely from political influence, but the flux of politics ran more smoothly as the Conservative party held on to power through one election after another. Reynolds also gave continuity, since he remained chairman for eighteen years, conducting the affairs of the Commission with a bland discretion and less publicity. Before establishing a more settled pattern of management, however, the position and place of Arthur Cavanagh had to be decided.

Cavanagh's Dismissal

At the end of January 1947 the Commission met in the office of Arthur Welsh at Queen's Park with Roland Michener in attendance. The secretary simply noted in the minutes: "In view of certain circumstances which were explained verbally to the Commission, Mr. Arthur Cavanagh was granted leave of absence immediately..."[1]

That same day Michener as Provincial Secretary sent a telegram to Cavanagh, asking to see him in Toronto "at your early convenience." Cavanagh met with Michener and Welsh together, and early in February he addressed to Reynolds a discreet letter of resignation. For some time past, he said, it had been evident that the ONTC was contemplating a reorganization.

> During my years of service with the Railway I have been able to accomplish my ambition and at my present age I do not feel that I could enter into a reorganization with the spirit and enthusiasm that is required.

He added that it would be best for the Commission to "select a younger man." Reluctant to resign, he nevertheless concluded, "I feel it is in your best interests that I should do so at this time."[2]

165

A number of questions surround this dismissal which have never been explained. Why were the reasons not entered into the minutes? Why did it take two cabinet ministers instead of simply the chairman of the Commission to induce Cavanagh to write his letter of resignation? Why did he dwell on his age when in fact he was only sixty, in vigorous health, and would be succeeded by a man hardly four years his junior?

The oral request from Michener and Welsh raised serious issues of temperament and politics, however obscure were the immediate reasons. With all his ability in managing the railway, Cavanagh's self-confidence and tendency to speak his mind created tensions between himself and Reynolds. Opposition existed in various parts of the railway. No one denied the soundness of his professional judgement, but workers found him a formidable person and the unions had complained to Drew that they found him arbitrary. Since 1944 he had grown impatient with a Commission that seemed to him political and amateur compared to his own professional knowledge. From Reynold's point of view, Cavanagh seemed too close to the Hepburn years, an association which had made some men cool toward him ever since his original appointment. With the Progressive Conservatives well entrenched in the province after 1945, it was no accident that Cavanagh's successor should be Archibald Freeman.[3]

Freeman had worked with the ONR since 1911. He was close to George Lee in 1934, when Racine found difficulty finding a definition of Freeman's position and duties. Freeman even then had an influential voice in day-to-day management, but the best title for his work that Racine could find was "Chief of the Wages Bureau, Secretary of the Pension Committee, and Supervisor of Restaurant and News Services."[4] Racine recommended his dismissal, but Cavanagh defended him and in fact made him his assistant in 1940, when Freeman was listed on the books as simply "statistician." After the appointment of Reynolds in 1944, Freeman became assistant to the general manager and secretary-treasurer of the Commission, positions which enabled him to attend meetings from which Cavanagh was excluded. Well before 1947 Freeman attained an advantage over Cavanagh which had some connection with politics.

Freeman soon proved himself a congenial choice. E.J. Young as executive assistant and close confidant of Drew told the premier shortly after that people in the North expressed to him a most favourable response. Freeman, he said, had started under Jake Englehart and had steadily improved his status.

> The fact that a former clerk has become General Manager has made quite an impression on the staff of the Railway. The employees know now for the first time that diligence and industry make it possible for any one of them to attain the highest position on the Railway.

The reasons for promotion coincided with a capacity for sound administration, but two other reasons weighed just as vitally. Archie Freeman, said Young, "is and always has been a supporter of this government." And his appointment "would put the quietus for all time on the rotten Racine Report...which maligned some of the best officials of the Ontario Northland Railway..."[5]

Young spoke here a degree of truth that was pleasing in the minds of northern Conservatives. But behind the partisan prejudice lay Freeman's personal qualities, drawing trust to his judgement and his experienced knowledge of employees. For Reynolds, Welsh, Michener, and Drew, Freeman was more acceptable altogether than Cavanagh. They felt a collegial warmth for his views which they could not feel for the man appointed by Mitchell Hepburn.

But Cavanagh, too, found his own sweet moment of revenge. Given a month's pay and a pension of $4,500, he had to find another position. With a life style based on his salary of $15,000 and an invalid daughter to keep, possessed of a vital physical presence, at the age of sixty he was too young for retirement. He applied for and received a five-year contract as managing director of the Québec, North Shore and Labrador Railway, then being built from the St. Lawrence River north to the iron fields of Labrador. His new salary would be $75,000 a year, five times his earnings with the ONR. The salary, the position, the challenge of the work, all proved more satisfying than the politics of the ONR. Understandably, he left the North both pleased and bitter, though agreeing in principle that Freeman was the most competent person to succeed him.[6]

Review and Reform

Freeman became in time an able and a popular general manager, with the qualities of personality needed for the coming decade of transition. The years from 1947 to 1957 witnessed a reorganization which followed in part from more systematic and formal relations with the cabinet at Queen's Park. Lines of authority from the general manager to the Commission and the definition of functions under the general manager all became clearer. The change of name in 1946 was a mere beginning for this adaptation to the post-war world.

In a wide-ranging transition, which eventually affected the whole of northeastern Ontario, Archibald Freeman directed management, initiated studies, persuaded men to work together, and even led the Commission itself. Reynolds came quietly to accept a more limited authority, acknowledging that Freeman provided the essential qualities of management. The beginning of this change came in 1947 with a study by Woods and Gordon Limited, management consultants of Toronto, who were commissioned to review the whole railway system after Reynolds had consulted with Michener, Welsh, and Freeman.[7]

Reviewing recent history, Woods and Gordon approved the new arrangement "by which the Commission is separate from the management." The Commission should "determine policy and have the means of knowing whether or not policy is being carried out," but it should not interfere in actual management. To ensure the dividing line between the two, the chairman should be part-time, spending a week or ten days a month on his duties. Otherwise he would begin to interfere in matters properly belonging to management. The other commissioners – Potter and Aubert at the time – "need give a very limited amount of time in order to carry out their duties," perhaps one day a month with some extra days for inspection trips.

Having clarified the division between management and the Commission, the consultants found two problems more difficult to resolve. One was of a general nature, the other very specific. The historical records of the Commission revealed nowhere a clear definition of the objectives of the Commission – objectives which should have been given to it by the provincial government. For lack of this definition, questions were left hanging. Was the function of the Commission to promote a particular region, or all of northern Ontario? Were its operations intended to produce a maximum net profit, or to earn a lesser profit and improve the transportation and communication services of the North? To what extent was the Commission entitled to spend on services which were unprofitable, but which served both the North and the province as a whole? According to the report from Woods and Gordon, the government should make these responsibilities clear in its statement of expectations of the ONTC.

The other more specific problem, evident to anyone observing from outside, lay in the wide responsibilities of the general manager. Fourteen department heads reported directly to him, an inheritance from the days when the railway had been a smaller operation. Now, this structure had become too burdensome, giving to the general manager "a responsibility for direct supervision in excess of what can properly be carried out by a single individual." Given his various duties – travelling, meeting the public, dealing with the commissioners, he could not also administer fourteen individuals. Their number should be reduced to seven, with a comptroller reporting to the general manager on the budget of railway operations.[8]

Some of these recommendations were enacted; others were shelved. On the whole, Archie Freeman continued his manifold responsibilities, gradually assigning more authority to his chief mechanical officer, J.W. Millar; his chief engineer, T.D. Saunders; and the superintendent, A. Jardine, the man who would succeed him in 1958. Late in 1947 H.W. Teskey was promoted to the new position of comptroller, and E.A. Frith became manager of communications. All of these men would play significant roles through the transition of the next decade.

A further step toward clearer system and greater efficiency occurred in the fall of 1947, when accounting and audit were brought into the central office from all division points. New machinery was installed for this purpose at the head office in North Bay, and Freeman issued a pamphlet describing for employees the centralization of revenue under the auditor of revenue. At the same time, audit of the annual reports was transferred from a private accounting firm and placed with the Provincial Auditor, while the end of the financial year was changed to December 31, bringing the financial statements of the ONTC into line with those of other agencies of the provincial government.[9]

The year 1947 was therefore a significant one for the Commission, when personnel and their responsibilities changed, influenced in part by more direct control from a secure Conservative government at Queen's Park, but also by the challenge to renovate and to compete in the post-war world. One of these challenges was to build and administer a pension fund that would enable the ONTC to hold its employees in competition with the CNR and the CPR.

The Struggle over Pensions

Few Canadian companies were noted for their employee pension plans in the first third of the twentieth century. The Drury government first introduced a modest plan on the T&NO Railway in 1922, implemented by George Lee as chairman. He modelled the plan on that of the CPR, with which he maintained close personal ties in North Bay. The Commission made an initial contribution of $50,000, a figure which Lee singled out in his annual report because it was made in the very year when the T&NO took a heavy loss from the Haileybury fire. From then until 1934, the Commission transferred $1,000 a month to accumulation of the fund. Employees contributed nothing, and the amounts paid to them on retirement were pitiably small, sometimes less than $100 a year.

Understandably, the unions seized on the issue of a contributory plan in the 1930s, one that would give the employees some right to bargain. The Brotherhood of Railroad Conductors made the first request in 1934. Lee stalled, partly from antipathy to the unions, but partly also because none of the major Canadian railways had a contributory pension plan at that time, and Lee argued that the T&NO was bound by competitive conditions of work and pay.[10]

Cavanagh reversed this stalling, constituting himself a committee of one shortly after his appointment in 1934. By then the non-contributory scheme was twelve years old. Over the next three years, the Commission doubled its contribution, so that at the end of 1938 the fund stood at well over $300,000. Actual pensions paid out that year came to less than $33,000.[11]

Cavanagh witnessed the growth of those figures in reserve and took his time to study the growing grievances of employees. What did solvency matter if some 1,400 men and women workers felt no sense that the fund was in part their own? Their age, too, was advancing; many had been with the railway since the time of World War I. Demands on the non-contributory fund must inevitably increase. The small monthly payments made to retired employees might become even smaller.

Anxiety over retirement affected people seriously because there existed then no supplements through a Canada Pension Plan, while Old Age Pensions were limited to $20 per month for men and women over seventy years of age, subject to a means test. The only reserve for the individual worker came from personal savings or private insurance policies. Most employees possessed neither. Understandably, pensions were becoming central among demands formulated by the unions toward the end of the Depression.

Cavanagh submitted his recommendations to Malcolm Lang in the fall of 1938. Lang forwarded them to Hepburn, asking for approval from the government in principle. Cavanagh and Lang were by then both convinced that the Commission must move to a contributory pension plan, along the lines of the pension plan in Ontario Hydro. The T&NO, said Lang, "is the only road in North American having a retirement plan to which the employees do not make contributions." The officers of the union, he continued, "are urging us to have something done." They wanted the security of an adequate pension on retirement.[12]

Hepburn simply passed the problem along to one of his staff. The document finally approved by cabinet was a contributory scheme which came into effect on May 1, 1939. It followed the model of contributions and payments in the Ontario Civil Service, though the benefits would be less because the new plan had a less substantial reserve behind it. Employees' contributions of four per cent of earnings were matched by the Commission. The minimum pension was $365 and the maximum $2,000 per annum.

For retiring workers the plan did not seem unduly generous, but in fact the pension plan of 1939 accepted more obligations than it could meet. It established no specific funding of pensions for service prior to 1939. In addition, commitments were made to pay pensions to widows and dependent children, and to count military service. Over a period of years a gap would develop between liabilities and reserves, with the Commission itself legally bound by Order-in-Council to make good any deficiencies.[13]

As a result, tensions arose between the unions and the Commission, even among employees themselves. At the beginning of the contributory plan in 1939, close to 80 per cent of employees contributed. Their numbers increased as did the amount in the contributory fund. At the same time, the non-contributory fund declined. Differences inevitably occurred in payments from the two funds. In 1943, for example, fifty-six former employees in the contributory scheme received an average pension of $60.00 a month, while seventy-five received only $36.25 from the non-contributory fund.[14] The older retired employees felt they were victimized by the scheme, while continuing workers, making their 4 per cent contributions, resented those receiving pensions based on the contributory plan, when in fact these pensioners had made only minimal contributions since 1939.

The CPR handled this problem by taking the money for service prior to its contributory scheme out of operating revenue. That model, together with the frustration of employee and pensioner alike, entered into the discontent which union leaders expressed to George Drew after his victory in 1943. From their meeting with him emerged an enlarged pension board – three appointed by the Commission and two "elected triennially by the general chairmen of the organized classes of employees of the Railway."[15] This gain helps to explain acquiescence by the unions and the CCF in the new Conservative Commission appointed in the summer of 1944. At the end of that year the new pension board appointed an actuary to study the whole pension fund.

Their choice was Professor N.E. Sheppard of the University of Toronto, who submitted his report in the spring of 1946.[16] Sheppard concluded that by then 1,626 employees were participating in the plan. Their contributions together with the assets of the fund totalled more than $4,000,000. Over the coming years, however, the fund would have to make payments of about $13,500,000, leaving an "unfunded liability" of $9,500,000. "The truth of the matter is," said Sheppard,

> ...that at the inception of the pension plan there existed a large accrued liability due to the past services of the then existing employees, for which no provision has been made up to date.

On the strength of that conclusion, Freeman as secretary-treasurer recommended to Reynolds that pensions based on service before 1939 be charged to operating expenses, as the CPR was doing. Reynolds telephoned the president of the CNR to discover that they had just added $30,000,000 to their pension fund out of current revenue. Unable to make a decision, Reynolds turned to the premier for advice, and Drew simply handed the correspondence to Colonel E.J. Young, then his executive assistant.[17] Young had neither the capacity nor the inclination to make decisive recommendations.

The ONTC was clearly faced with a serious financial problem over pensions, one which should have been worked out between the chairman and the general manager. But Reynolds delayed, unable and unwilling to work with Cavanagh, until in the fall of 1946 trouble erupted from within the unions. The general chairman of the unions' conference committee, Robert Trowhill, began a bitter correspondence with Reynolds that lasted for the next five years.

Trowhill was the station agent in Haileybury, a man of modest education, firmly dedicated to the trade-union movement and the CCF party. He wrote to Reynolds with no respect for rank, sometimes choosing harsh words that bordered on acrimony. On his side, Reynolds responded with a patronizing condescension which betrayed certain weaknesses of his own. His shy reserve and formal manner were not suited to confrontation, even on paper.

Reynolds insisted that the minimum pension could only be raised to $600 if the employees "unanimously agree to raise their contribution to 6 per cent." Trowhill objected. When Reynolds replied that he based his position on advice from Professor Sheppard, Trowhill sent back a sharply worded letter in which he charged that Reynolds was disturbing the expectations of all union members. The present pension plan, he said, "was set up between this Railway through its General Manager-Chairman, and the whole body of employees through their accredited representatives, all acting in good faith…"[18]

After objecting to "the tone of your letter," Reynolds suspended further negotiations on pension issues. Within the month Cavanagh was removed from office, and discussion with the unions did not resume until 1948, when Archie Freeman as general manager initiated a meeting of the Commission with all of the union chairmen. From this meeting the Commission decided to alter the pension plan, raising employee contributions from 4 per cent to 6 per cent and matching them. Payments could then be more generous to those counting service prior to 1939, with a minimum of $600 for all employees who had worked for more than twenty years.

But the unions still objected to the 50 per cent increase in their contributions, from 4 per cent to 6 per cent. Though the Commission matched that increase, it was still higher than employee contributions on the CPR and the CNR, where pensions based on prior service continued to be paid out of operating revenue. Civil Servants with the Ontario Government still contributed only 4 per cent of earnings. In return for their increased contributions, union members of the ONTC wanted the benefits made more retroactive. In the summer of 1948 Freeman wrote to Lorne R. McDonald, Assistant Provincial Secretary, to tell him that employee representatives on the pension board felt that their extra contributions were only justified if they provided "funds to assist those who are already retired."[19] But the Civil Service Commission recommended, and cabinet agreed, that these retroactive benefits could not be approved for those retired after 1939. As a result, retired employees continued to receive pensions which differed according to time of retirement, though the years of service might be the same. These differences festered among the unions from 1948 to 1951, as the unions argued that their increased contributions should result in improved pensions for those already retired.

Through the pension board the union representatives raised this issue again in 1951. Their proposal went to the cabinet minister responsible, who then was the Minister of Planning and Development, Col. William Griesinger. By then, too, Col. Lorne R. McDonald had become deputy minister to the premier and secretary of the cabinet.

Griesinger presented the proposals of 1951 for the cabinet agenda, but McDonald rejected them as unwise, saying that the minimum pension in the Civil Service did not provide for a retroactive increase. "To do so with one agency of the Government raises the question squarely with regard to Civil Servants themselves, and you will appreciate the difficulty."[20] The result was further delay, with Reynolds, Freeman, and Griesinger all helpless to resolve the grievance. Trowhill became even more militant. In November 1951 he told Reynolds that the employees,

> ...have exactly the same number of dollars in the Pension Fund as the Railway...In effect the Railway is simply using our increased contributions to bolster a Fund that needed bolstering alright, but not necessarily at the expense of the employees without adequate reasonable return...[21]

An element of unreason ran through his letters, a dogmatic, assertive quality, particularly annoying to Reynolds and his Conservative colleagues. Many employees were receiving more in pension than their contributions, and the plan as it existed was not adequately funded. To undertake payment of pensions out of current revenue, or even out of borrowing, would have required cabinet approval, an Order-in-Council, and surmounting objections from the Civil Service Commission. But Trowhill was subject to pressure that reflected also a dissension among employees themselves. Pensions affect workers only less directly than their monthly wages, and tensions could be real between young and old over contributions.

Will Gard, for example, started with the T&NO in 1913 as a hostler at $60 a month; Jim Fletcher as a fireman in 1918 at $162 a month. S.W. (Stan) Gowan became a junior clerk in 1925 at $121.50 a month. Gard and Fletcher became locomotive engineers; Stan Gowan moved up to become secretary of the Commission and director of finances and accounting.[22] All three retired between 1954 and 1967, with well over half their time counting before the beginning of the 6 per cent contributions in 1948. Jim Fletcher explained his point of view this way,

...Mr. Lee said that it would never work. But anyway they finally got the pension...4% of our wages...Then, everything was going good... [when] some of the older members wanted to increase the payment to 6%. Well – then the younger engineers – oh, they raised Cain about it. Oh, we're payin' pensions for them old fellows – for old so-and-so – We're payin' for their pension. But now they're getting a hang of a lot more pension than we get...[23]

Trowhill's tactic was to divert this disagreement between young and old to blame the Commission itself. Dealing with Reynolds, he said, "is simply frustration from beginning to end..." His strident words were an embarrassment to some of his union colleagues; to Reynolds they were again so insulting that he refused to write further, and Trowhill sent all the correspondence directly to the premier, Leslie Frost.

There was nothing unusual in this step; he was doing what other union chairmen had done before him when they corresponded with Drew and Hepburn. But Frost would not be drawn in. He first asked for advice from William Griesinger, who simply scribbled a note that the pension plan probably needed another actuarial study, observing also for Frost that Trowhill was secretary of the CCF for the North and a "Red." Frost decided to pass the correspondence on to his deputy minister, Colonel Lorne McDonald.

Although he was a civil servant rather than a politician, McDonald for the next few years functioned almost as a member of the Commission, continuing that personal relation with the cabinet initiated by George Drew in his directive to Roland Michener in 1945, when McDonald was Assistant Provincial Secretary. He sat with the Commission now on its travels to northern towns, and advised both Reynolds and Freeman on relations with the cabinet. After reading the correspondence from 1948 to 1951 and agreeing with the Civil Service Commissioner that it was "a hell of a mess," he went north to meet himself with the union chairmen. Reynolds and the other members of the Commission did not attend.

McDonald was a man of patience and tact who listened to Trowhill's prepared statement on the grievance of the unions that they were receiving nothing for their increased contributions since 1948. With his expert knowledge of affairs at Queen's Park, McDonald told the union chairmen that it was not possible to incorporate the ONR pension plan into that of the civil service. As employees of a government-owned transportation system, they could be assured, however, that their pensions were secure, whether the money was actually in the fund or not. He elaborated on the responsibility of the ONTC to remain solvent, on its limited resources, on the need to avoid resort to the taxpayers to cover deficiencies, concluding that "the creation of a strong fund by mutual effort of the Commission and the employees was the best and safest course." In short, the government could not agree to additional benefits without another actuarial study of the fund. Trowhill had earlier rejected that proposal when it came from Reynolds; he now accepted it from McDonald, as did all of the other union chairmen.[24]

The second actuarial study was carried out by William Mercer Limited, an English company of accountants and consultants which had recently moved to Canada. Their report was submitted in the summer of 1952. It pointed to an increase of 22 per cent in the number of employees since 1946 – from 1,625 to 1,979; and to a 400 per cent increase in amounts paid out from the pension fund. The deficiencies were becoming ever more serious, with an unfunded liability by 1952 of more than $11,700,000. It was not surprising that this second report came to a conclusion more strongly worded than that of Sheppard six years before.

> Unless the total payroll of contributors continues to increase, it will be only ten or twelve years before the outgo on pensions and other benefits exceeds the income from contributions and interest.[25]

Despite the ominous implications in these words, nothing was done to reduce the growing deficit. Modest improvements were made, however, to lessen the differences among employees, with increased benefits going to those who had put in most of their service before 1939. The militancy of Robert Trowhill was thereby reduced, and the pension plan ceased to be a contentious issue between the unions and the Commission.

But it was L.R.McDonald, deputy minister to the premier, who did the diplomatic and the financial-administrative work with the unions. He had the temperament and the understanding, as well as the experience, going back to the days when he was assistant to Roland Michener and therefore responsible for liaison between the Commission and the cabinet. If in 1953 pensions ceased to be an area of tension between the trade unions and the Commission, the achievement owed far more to the efforts of Lorne McDonald than to those of the general manager or the chairman of the Commission. The role which McDonald played was essential. It pointed clearly to a serious consequence of public ownership. Employees of the ONR were virtually civil servants. If deficiencies in their pension plan had to be covered and payments guaranteed by the Commission, then fiscal responsibility for the plan lay with the provincial government and finally with the cabinet itself.

While the grievances of employees seemed to be settled by 1953, the pointed criticism of the actuaries had not been met. The fund steadily accumulated from increased contributions, but so too did the potential demands which must eventually be made upon it. Another report from William Mercer Limited in 1956 pointed to a further increase in the unfunded liability, which by then had reached $15,400,000. The Provincial Auditor from 1961 to 1964 stressed this deficiency in four consecutive annual reports. By 1965 the figure was a startling $19,400,000. According to the Pensions Act of the province, the Commission was required to pay interest of more than $777,000 on this deficit. Actual payment could not be made that year, and the interest had to be included in the annual report to the legislature as a "current liability." From 1965 to 1973, however, annual transfers were made into the pension fund from current revenue, to a total of well over $12,000,000, which increased the total debt carried by the Commission from year to year.[26]

174

The report and recommendation of 1946 had been well-founded. But the confrontation with the unions, the correspondence between Trowhill and Reynolds, continuous contact on the subject between North Bay and Queen's Park, the direct intervention of the deputy minister to the premier, had all revealed a number of significant characteristics about the ONTC. It was publicly owned, but government would resist liability for any pension plan which involved a subsidy from tax revenue. Yet the confined region of its operations limited its sources of revenue. Finally, the affair over pensions from 1946 to 1953 had revealed that employees of the ONTC were neither full civil servants, nor were they able to negotiate as workers on a privately owned transportation system. They worked instead for a government agency under instruction to function like an independent and solvent business corporation.

CHAPTER 18

A Modern Transportation System

It happened at 6:12 a.m. on the morning of New Year's Day, 1948, when everyone was still asleep or drowsily anticipating the leisure of a holiday. Just two miles out of Cobalt, two trains collided, causing a tragic accident, the most serious in the history of the railway.

The weather was crisp and cold. Three doctors and a nurse had to be awakened and summoned from Cobalt, Haileybury, and New Liskeard. They arrived an hour after the accident, struggling two miles through fields of snow to the scene beside the track where two sizzling locomotives lay on their sides, like black dying monsters. Some men were still trapped among the box cars while others tried frantically to free them. Five carloads of paper were beginning to burn.

Both trains carried freight. No. 416 southbound received permission to pass through Cobalt and shortly after rounded a curve. As the engine came out of the curve:

> Engineman Fletcher and Fireman Edmunds of No. 416...observed the headlight of Extra 312 North emerging from the curve and rock cut about 500 feet south. Engineman Fletcher made an immediate emergency application and along with Fireman Edmunds and Brakeman Phillips, jumped from the cab of the locomotive with the two engines colliding at a speed of...thirty miles per hour....

This account was seen through the memories of the men in the southbound cab who all lived; the three men in the northbound engine lost their lives. Fireman J.R. Newton died within the hour from fractured skull and shock; W.H. (Herb) Lewis died later that morning from multiple burns; and brakeman J.D. Lang dragged out a painful two weeks in hospital before he too expired from pneumonia and toxemia. Premier Drew wrote personal letters to the families of all three men.

Blame for the accident was finally placed on the operator at New Liskeard, who had "highballed" Jim Fletcher south instead of instructing him to hold until the northbound train had gone through. It was a costly mistake. In addition to the loss of life, the large load of paper burned, leaving some salvage for return to the Abitibi plant at Iroquois Falls. As for the engines, they required $100,000 worth of repairs in the North Bay shops.[1]

The engines were both of the 2-8-2 type with 63″ drive wheels, purchased in 1924 from the Canadian Locomotive Company in Kingston. They lasted another seven or eight years and then were scrapped along with all remaining steam locomotives, as the ONR gradually completed its conversion to diesel electric power. That programme was an integral part of the broader, more comprehensive transition of the railway to a modern transportation system, a change essential if the ONTC was to survive within a relatively static northeastern economy.

A Question of Locomotion

The diesel programme had a modest beginning in 1946, when Cavanagh ordered the first three yard switchers of 1,000 h.p. from the Montréal Locomotive Works. Four road switchers were added in 1948. Over the next five years questions had to be resolved on locomotive power which were as fundamental as any in the history of the Commission.

In 1902, the issue had been one of steam or electricity as the form of locomotive energy. Although hydro-electric power could be supplied in abundance along the Abitibi River, and its use remained an option in the legislation for the T&NO, it had in fact proved to be too costly as well as complex.

But coal-burning steam locomotives presented their own problems. The fuel had to be imported from the United States. By 1945 American supplies were uncertain and expensive. Strikes and wartime priorities made it essential for the Commission to plan its orders. The railway had burned 100,000 tons from West Virginia and Pennsylvania in 1933 for a bill of $640,000. In 1947 Archie Freeman as general manager asked permission to order 135,000 tons at a cost of more than $1,000,000.[2] A government agency committed to purchasing Canadian products undertook these costs with genuine reluctance, a reluctance compounded by the high premium on the American dollar. That is why the Commission spent a decade experimenting with lignite.

Added to the cost of the fuel was the financial burden of maintaining steam locomotives. At best they were not very efficient, putting to effective use only 16 per cent of the heat available in coal. In 1947 the Commission owned and operated forty-four steam locomotives, of which thirty-six had been bought before 1930. Given an average service life of thirty-three years, most would have to be written off by 1955 unless they were expensively rebuilt. Replacement could come from new steam locomotives or from a fleet of diesel engines.

Diesels were clearly the dynamic and attractive choice, on which the Commission made a decision in 1950, after three years of study. Three central questions had to be resolved. The first determined the advantages of diesel electric power. The second settled how a programme of major capital costs could be financed. And the third arose from the legislated requirement, repeated in the legislation ever since 1902, that "the railway shall as far as practicable be constructed, equipped and operated with railway supplies and rolling stock made, purchased or procured in Canada…"

The steam locomotives had all been manufactured in Kingston, many of them prototypes of engines produced on a larger scale for the CNR or the CPR. Whether of the "Consolidation" or "Northern" design, or older still, engineers, brakemen and firemen developed an attachment to the engines born of the care needed to make them function. But the very attention which had to be bestowed on firebox and boiler, on valves and brakes, the skills demanded of men who took pride in their work, all augmented the costs of labour. For the accountant with eyes trained to examine profit and loss, the steam locomotive cost more to maintain than the engine powered by diesel-electric energy.

In 1949 Archie Freeman established a high-level committee to clarify the reasons for conversion to this new form of locomotion. Diesels were becoming the motive power for railways throughout the United States as well as in Britain and Europe. They would prove as revolutionary for the hauling of trains in the post-war world as jet aircraft would become for air passenger travel a decade later. Discussions at the ONR were beginning just in time.

The committee recommended an immediate programme of conversion for reasons that were convincing both to Reynolds and the government. Fuel oil for diesels was 16¢-17¢ a gallon, and the ONR could be expected to burn four to five million gallons a year, indicating a fuel bill of $850,000 at a time when the railway was spending close to $1,250,000 for coal. The initial cost of a diesel was certainly higher than that for a steam locomotive. But the latter required watering tanks and coal bins *en route*, frequent stops for lubrication and the cleaning out of fire-boxes. Steam locomotives burned coal inefficiently; repair parts were not interchangeable between types of engine, and extensive inspection and overhauls were needed much more frequently than with the diesel. Long sustained runs and fewer delays for repair would make it possible to perform the same service with fewer engines. These anticipated savings more than balanced the higher initial capital costs.[4]

A main repair and service shop would have to be built in North Bay at a cost of over $800,000. Together with some thirty-six new diesels at an average price of $220,000, investment in the programme over the next five to seven years would amount to well over $8,000,000. With the seven diesels already in operation by 1950, the estimated cost of the programme would be about $10,000,000. A few years earlier, in 1947-48, the Commission had purchased a thousand new box cars from the National Steel Car Corporation in Hamilton at a cost of $5,374,000. Savings resulted of more than $200,000 a year from reduced hiring of freight cars, which comfortably covered the interest costs. The total capital investment in rolling stock, equipment, and building from 1947 to 1957 came to $17,500,000.

In June of 1949 a debenture issue of $5,000,000 was arranged by the brokerage firm of Wood Gundy Limited, guaranteed by the cabinet and payable over ten years.[5] Reynolds pressed on Premier Frost his own overly ambitious notion that thirty-six diesels should be ordered all at once and be paid for over seven years. But Frost was more cautious. As Lorne McDonald reported to Griesinger, the responsible cabinet minister:

The Prime Minister expressed some surprise at the thought of doing the change-over in one fell swoop, and reminded Colonel Reynolds that the Cabinet's decision was a gradual conversion over as short a period as was reasonable.[6]

In this same letter McDonald asked Griesinger to seek advice and submit more information, including "the proportion of Ontario labour involved." Further debentures were arranged in 1952 and 1953, totalling another $12,500,000 – all of them purchased by the Treasurer of Ontario. Almost a third of the total of $17,500,000 was spent on the purchase of the box cars manufactured by Hamilton labour. Where the diesel locomotives were to be purchased would depend also on the volume of Ontario labour employed in their manufacture. This issue was one of careful and serious debate; first, between Freeman and his chief mechanical officer, J.W. Millar; and secondly, within the Commission itself. In the end, it was the recommendation of Freeman and Miller that counted most.

Between 1946 and 1949 there were only two plants in Canada which could provide diesel-locomotives. One was the Montréal Locomotive Works, which contracted with General Electric in Peterborough or the United States for the generating unit. The other was the Canadian Locomotive Company in Kingston, with a history of manufacturing steam locomotives going back to the mid-nineteenth century. Through almost a century the Kingston company had been largely Canadian owned. Now, it was having a difficult time making the transition to diesel engines. For a brief period Fairbanks-Morse bought into the firm, with generators made by Westinghouse in the United States. But the units were not reliable. Since the Montréal Locomotive Works was controlled by the American Locomotive Company, it seemed almost impossible to launch a programme of dieselization and at the same time abide by the spirit and letter of legislation requiring Canadian manufacture.

There was no precedent for this dilemma. Since 1902, except for the first orders for steel rails, all rolling stock and equipment had been manufactured in Canada, most of it in Ontario. At the end of 1947 the problem was serious enough to warrant a delay. Freeman and Millar recommended the ordering of four road-switching diesel engines of 1,500 h.p., but the Commission reviewed the tender and approved the following resolution:

> It appearing that the locomotives offered by the Montréal Locomotive Works will be manufactured entirely in the United States; and an indefinite portion of...making locomotives...by the Canadian Locomotive Company will also be performed in the United States; and further that the monetary situation existing between the United States and Canada makes it imperative that importation of goods from the United States be restricted to the greatest possible extent, it was resolved to take no immediate action with respect to purchase of diesel electric locomotives, pending investigation as to the possibility of manufacture in Canada or Great Britain.[7]

In the past, when purchasing equipment not manufactured in Canada, there had been a definite preference for British goods. Now, Roland Michener as Provincial Secretary, the cabinet minister responsible for the Commission at the time, communicated with Ontario House in London. A number of British companies were prepared to bid, but only the English Electric Company could build the complete unit. Michener reported to Freeman that "accelerated delivery of British-made diesels can now be secured."[8] By then, however, American diesels enjoyed a competitive advantage. The ONR had to meet North American standards, and British prices were high. In 1948 a pattern of orders was established when four road switchers of 1,500 h.p. were ordered from the Montréal Locomotive Works on the understanding that some of the manufacture would be done by Canadian General Electric in Peterborough. The best that the Commission could now achieve was to order diesels made in Canada by branch plants of American companies.

That fact became more pronounced in the early 1950s when General Motors Corporation, encouraged by the Department of Planning and Development in the Conservative government of Leslie Frost, opened a diesel plant in London, Ontario. Production there proved to be the final blow for the Canadian Locomotive Company in Kingston; its diesels were no longer competitive. By the summer of 1950 the ONTC had seven diesel engines in operation – three yard switchers of 1,000 h.p. and four road switchers of 1,500 h.p., all made by the Montréal Locomotive Works. Future orders would have to be divided between that company and General Motors Diesel in London.

The locomotives of the two companies at that time were almost equal in price and performance, but to divide the orders evenly between them would not achieve the desired efficiency in standardization of parts. Since the seven diesel units already operated by the Commission had been made by the Montréal company, Millar and Freeman recommended that "the only practicable method of dividing our order is to secure all our straight Road 'A' units from General Motors Limited and our Road and Yard Switchers from Montréal Locomotive Works Limited," The Commission approved, as did the cabinet on Griesinger's advice. The decision meant that General Motors would receive orders for twenty-seven road units valued at just under $6,000,000, while the Montréal company was to make an additional nine road and yard switchers for approximately $1,650,000.[9]

In fact, from 1950 to 1956, Montréal Locomotive Works made another thirteen locomotives for the ONR, bringing its total to twenty. General Motors delivered twenty-eight Road "A" Units between 1951 and 1957, and in that year the programme was complete with forty-eight diesels in operation. In the fall of 1953 the new service and repair shop was opened in North Bay, and another smaller one in Cochrane two years later. The two buildings together cost well over $1,000,000; both were built by northern contractors. The whole programme, including diesel engines, new box cars, and service buildings easily consumed the total debenture issue of $17,500,000 in the decade after 1947.

It was a major project for the North, supported and guaranteed by the provincial government. Premier Frost presided at the opening of the diesel service building in 1953.[10] The last run of a steam locomotive on the ONR was therefore an event, not only of historical interest for the railway, but of symbolic importance for the whole northeastern region of the province.

Reynolds and the Commission planned the event to coincide with the 50th anniversary celebrations of the town of Englehart in the early summer of 1957. Englehart had been founded as the first northern terminus of the second stage of the T&NO in 1907. Its history had been closely tied to that of the railway ever since. At the end of its last run, to demonstrate these ties, the locomotive – a 4-6-2 wheel arrangement made in Kingston in 1921 and rebuilt in 1940 – was placed on the tracks just south of the station. It was thirty-six years old when it was finally retired, and there it stands today, a black, silent, static, lonely reminder of the half century when such engines had pulled regularly into the railroad yards and the stations of the small northern towns, had whistled and roared through the winter nights, and stopped with a grinding clatter and a constant hissing at the farms to deliver supplies or take on livestock. Those sounds were gone now, replaced by the smoother, more efficient rumble of the diesels which pulled heavier loads with fewer stops. The new engines made the ONR seem more remote from the lives of northern people who had once depended in personal and vital ways on the runs of the steam locomotives.

Electronic Enterprise

The reasons for this historical association had something to do with the distinctive shape and noise of the steam locomotive, with the prolonged roar of its whistle through the silent countryside. But association between train and community rested also on the monopoly enjoyed by the railway for nearly forty years in the region stretching 450 miles north from North Bay.

Monopoly lies at the heart of public ownership for the ONTC. The principle has been the same as that for Ontario Hydro, but on a smaller scale. The distribution and marketing of hydro-electric energy through municipal utilities, brought to agreement under the direction of Sir Adam Beck before World War I, leading then to control of production from a few natural sites, all provided a convenient base for monopoly in a vast province just beginning its industrial expansion in the twentieth century. Premier Howard Ferguson summarized the approach of Conservative Ontario governments when he said in 1929 that while he did not believe in public ownership as a general principle, he fully supported Ontario Hydro as a government-owned and government-controlled commission, because "power is a natural monopoly and it is possible to control the whole situation...We succeeded because of the large market of Toronto for power... In ordinary commercial or industrial enterprises that cannot be done."[11]

From the beginning of the twentieth century to the 1940s, much the same rationale existed for the government-owned railway which transported resources and people throughout the northeast of the province. It was a natural monopoly which could be controlled because there were no competing modes of transportation or communication. Nor was private industry critical of this publicly owned monopoly. It did, after all, make possible the growth of such giant enterprises in mining and pulp and paper as Hollinger, McIntyre, Dome, Lake Shore, Wright-Hargreaves, Noranda, and Abitibi – all names associated with the private brokerage and banking wealth of Toronto, with the imperial position of Ontario in the Canadian economy.

As other forms of transportation and communication developed, however, the regional monopoly became more difficult to defend. Would the expansion of the telephone, for example, require the Commission to enter this whole area of voice communication, controlling exchanges in the North from its ownership of existing poles and overhead wires? When buses and trucks could roll into the northeast along the Ferguson Highway, was the Commission to secure the sole franchise for owning and operating the new vehicles? These became pressing questions during the 1930s, to be resolved only through discussion and agreement. The outcome illustrates the accommodation possible between public and private ownership in a province where the choice between the two has historically been based on convenience and necessity rather than on ideological motives.

But a pragmatic approach to public need, providing the means by which private enterprise could be served and made profitable, contained its own tensions. If the Commission served this need, would its role be simply one of absorbing financial losses in fields where private enterprise was unwilling to place risk capital? If that were so, how was the Commission to remain solvent as a commercial enterprise in its own right? Would it be able to continue meeting the capital cost of linking together the people of small scattered communities, and at the same time to fulfil the expectation of businessmen in a liberal-capitalist society that northern transportation should not involve public subsidy from taxation?

Through the 1920s increasing demand for telephone communication presented the T&NO with the possibility of a profitable monopoly. The railway from its beginning had controlled messages by telegraph as far south as North Bay. From there, for thirty years, the wires out were those of the CPR, until in 1935 the chairman of the Commission signed an agreement with the CNR and the CPR together, giving each company "a share of the outward business to the extent of 50 per cent."[12] But long before then, it was becoming evident that communication by telephone would supersede the telegram. Again, the railway owned the overhead wires for long distance carriage, so that executives of mining and pulp and paper companies could telephone Toronto and other cities over the T&NO lines to North Bay, where Bell Canada connected to carry all calls south or east or west.

Legislation in 1927 enabled the Commission to "construct, complete, equip, maintain and operate telephone and telegraph lines," and to exercise the powers of "a telephone or telegraph company incorporated under the general laws of the Province of Ontario."[13] But by the time this amendment was approved, a small private company was already in the business of providing local telephone service.

At New Liskeard the McKelvie and the McCamus families had prospered since the earliest days of settlement. Profits from their small lumber mill had been invested in a silver mine at Cobalt, and the gains made from that investment enabled them to form Northern Telephone Company after World War I. From the tri-town area they expanded northward, and between 1929 and 1932 the company came into a relationship of potential conflict with the T&NO Commission. In 1929 when Northern Telephone sought a franchise from the town of Matheson to operate its local telephone service, the town council asked the Commission to make its own bid.[14]

Northern Telephone was seeking a larger area to secure a higher return from its initial capital investments. In terms of planning for the future, its arguments were sound. Why should it take the responsibility for establishing local exchanges in such small communities as Ramore, Matheson, and Monteith, without also having the long-distance business between them? For the councils of these small towns, however, at this stage of development in telephone communication, the T&NO Commission presented a clear alternative.

To settle the question, officers of Northern Telephone Company sought control of long distance carriage throughout the whole region. They wished to lease the lines of the T&NO from North Bay to every town in the northeast, including Timmins, Kirkland Lake, Noranda, Kapuskasing, and Hearst. As chairman, George Lee discussed the problem with Premier Howard Ferguson, reporting to the Commission in January 1930 that the premier "quite approved of the Commission buying out or getting control of this company in some way."[15] Faced with the issue of public *versus* private ownership, in other words, despite what he had written about the Hydro monopoly seven months before, Ferguson preferred to sustain the advantages of the publicly controlled Commission, which had a government investment to be protected.

In the immediate environment of northern society, Lee, Maund and their colleagues were sensitive to the need for compromise. The T&NO Commission firmly refused to lease its lines; it even extended them from Kapuskasing to Hearst. But it acknowledged the right of Northern Telephone to handle local business and leased circuits to the company for this purpose.

The Commission and the company came to a negotiated agreement in 1932 by which the Commission continued to hold the upper hand, affirming its refusal to lease lines for long distance calls, but providing "free franking privileges" between offices of the company, and doing whatever else might be possible to improve earnings for the company. A fee would be paid by the T&NO for the company's handling of outgoing calls at its local exchanges. At that time, too, when Northern Telephone applied to Ottawa for a Dominion Charter, the Commission decided,

> ...that every possible effort should be made to prevent this Charter from being granted, as it would be highly detrimental to the Long Distance business of the T. & N.O. Railway.

Within weeks the company withdrew its application and Malcolm Lang, who had roots in the tri-town area, nourished a more amicable relationship with the officers of the company.[16]

At the end of World War II the ONTC established Ontario Northland Communications as a separate division, with E.A. Frith as General Superintendent and Manager of Communications. His knowledge was professional and thorough; he foresaw the complex development of telecommunications and warned the Commission of the likely consequences if disorganization and divided responsibility continued. The people and businessmen in the northeast would only be the losers unless changes were carefully planned. In 1946, with Welsh and Michener in attendance as cabinet ministers, Frith impressed them both when he said:

> If the present complex system is perpetuated and the territory continues to grow, conditions will become progressively worse, until public reaction will force drastic changes.

He concluded that responsibility ultimately would have to be assumed, either by the Commission or by Bell Canada. If the Commission stayed in the business of long distance carriage, then new switchboards would have to be built in Timmins and Noranda at an estimated cost of $200,000 each; and these new switchboards would have to be amalgamated with those of the Northern Telephone Company. "Someone," said Frith, "is in for a long programme of installing new equipment and the building of an organization of trained personnel, whether we take over or not."[17]

Michener agreed that an important question of policy was involved, which the cabinet might have to consider. In the meantime, the Commission again approached Northern Telephone on the question of their selling out. The company refused. Reluctant to take an aggressive stance, the Commission over the next two decades built new exchanges at Timmins, Noranda, and New Liskeard. Finally, in 1966, Northern Telephone Company sold out to Bell Canada. Subsequently, Ontario Northland Communications worked out a series of agreements, including a major one with Bell Canada for connections outward at North Bay on the south and at Flynn Lake in the northwest.[18]

These agreements gradually introduced stability into relations between the Commission and the telephone companies in the region. Ontario Northland Communications has responsibility to provide local telephone service as a public utility at Moosonee, Moose Factory, and Temagami. When added to the contracts with CN/CP for telex messages through North Bay, all of the agreements enable ONC to function as the predominant partner in providing telecommunications for the northeastern district of the province. During the past thirty years its equipment has become increasingly sophisticated, and it has remained a stable source of revenue during a period when earnings from rail service have been adversely affected by fluctuations in shipments of ore and pulpwood, by obligations to provide service between Cochrane and Moosonee, and by consistently poor returns from passenger traffic since World War II.

Branching Out

Of necessity, the Commission has become more than a railway, the function of

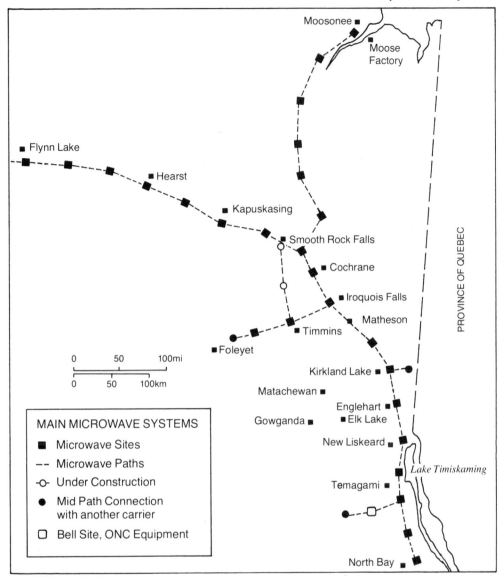

Ontario Northland Communications. ONC has developed into a sophisticated subsidiary of ONTC, providing a network of telecommunication throughout the northeast.

which originally was to open new country and develop its resources. Electronic communications presented opportunities to adapt and expand; private enterprise had to be accommodated rather than overwhelmed by a Commission backed with government legislation. At the same time, if the ONTC had given way to Northern Telephone, the result in the end would have been a monopoly by Bell Canada.

Agreements have been preferable – agreements which have left the government-controlled Commission a viable and solvent enterprise in its own right. The

185

capacity to adapt, to function as a competitive business under defined criteria of efficiency, to distinguish between policy and management, to plan for solvency and at the same time to respond to public inquiry as an agency responsible to the body politic – this capacity was illustrated again in the acquisition of freight and passenger facilities for water, air, and highway traffic.

Development of these services came also in the twenty years after World War II, but the possibilities were evident for a decade before 1940. In 1932, with asphalt highways being constructed to North Bay from Toronto and Ottawa, the Commission secured an exclusive franchise for all bus and truck service north of North Bay. Bus service began in the Timmins-Cochrane area in 1936. That same year legislation allowed the Commission to acquire trucks, trailers, buses, and aeroplanes, and to operate them as "a public carrier of passengers and freight." In 1937, the dominion government incorporated the Northern Canada Transportation Company under the control of the Commission, which then introduced bus service from Kirkland Lake to Rouyn.[19]

At the end of World War II, Drew and Reynolds envisioned an expansion in all these modes of transportation. Reynolds in 1945 wrote to the Air Transport Board in Ottawa, seeking assurance that Austin Airways, a small private company, would not be granted "exclusive rights to operate an air service in the region of Moosonee and James Bay."

At the same time, Reynolds succeeded in buying out both the Temagami and the Nipissing Navigation Companies. To serve the cottages and camps on Lake Temagami he acquired a number of landing barges used in World War II and ordered construction of a new passenger boat which was named the *Aubrey Cosens*, after a young former employee of the T&NO who had been awarded the Victoria Cross posthumously in 1945 during fighting in the Netherlands. For the service on Lake Nipissing from North Bay to the French River, another new boat was built and given the name *Chief Commanda*. Legislation in 1946 extended the Commission's authority to undertake services in these new areas by allowing it to "acquire, construct...and operate hotels, tourist resorts, restaurants, boats and vessels and lines of boats and vessels."[20]

It was typical of George Drew and of Colonel Reynolds that when they decided to expand into tourist traffic, they should appoint another colonel in charge of the new service. This time it was Colonel W.W. Johnson, DSO, MC and two bars, whom Reynolds recommended to Drew barely a month after his own appointment as chairman. Johnson at the time was Commanding Officer of the northern part of Military District No. 2 and on the lookout for post-war employment. In 1945 he became Assistant Manager, Navigation, at a salary of $4,800. With this appointment Drew had secured supplementary income and distinct if modest titles on the Commission for Reynolds, Williamson, and Johnson – all of them retired colonels on pension.[21]

As examples of patronage such appointments could be exaggerated. The three men together earned less than $15,000 in 1945 and their combined increased salaries from the Commission never totalled $23,000. They were also conscientious and often effective in public relations, being congenial to businesmen and Chambers of Commerce. But they were also amateurs, unable to contribute the specialized knowledge in finance and technology needed during a difficult period of expensive conversion. The navigation service on Lakes Nipissing and Temagami was a relatively small operation. Tourist income from these sources remained marginal; the equipment on Lake Temagami was sold to Shell Canada in 1966. While boat service helped to build the tourist industry on both lakes, it could not compare with the problems of diesel conversion, of purchasing a thousand new box cars, of sophisticated telecommunications; above all, with the prospect of meeting the growing competition from highway traffic.

The notion of an "exclusive franchise" on the highways, expressed in 1932, could not hold against the competitive pressure of bus and trucking companies. Nor did the will to resist such competition continue, either in the government or in the Commission itself. When McCallum Transport Limited of Oshawa, the company which specialized in the movement of new automobiles, applied in 1947 to the Ontario Municipal Board for a licence to ship automobiles north of North Bay, the ONTC could have objected. On request from McCallum, it withdrew its opposition on the grounds that "such shipments are permitted generally throughout the rest of the province." So, too, was the shipment of many other goods. Because trucks with their faster service were making inroads on freight traffic, and the ONTC neither could nor would defend any "exclusive franchise," the only alternative was to enter into competition. A trucking service from Toronto to Timmins had to be studied, and in 1948 the Commission applied for its own licence to the Ontario Municipal Board.

Since licence requirements of the Public Commercial Vehicles Act did not apply to the Commission, and companies acquired by the Commission enjoyed "all the powers, rights... and immunities conferred by law... upon the Commission," certain advantages could be expected to follow if a suitable trucking company were acquired. In addition, as an agency of government, the ONTC was assured of financial resources. The challenge was to protect its investment against increasing haulage of freight on the highways.[22]

In 1952 the Commission authorized a thorough economic study of Walter Little Transport Limited of Kirkland Lake, which was being offered to the Commission for $275,000. The final report by two economic consultants was a comprehensive document on the economy of the northeast. It recommended that the ONTC should enter into the business of trucking, but not through the acquisition of Walter Little Transport. Archie Freeman summarized the report for the Commission, giving reasons why the offer should be refused. Specifically, the margin of profit was too low, arising from heavy dependence on one-way traffic from Toronto and on one staple load, the food cartons of A & P Stores. This traffic might be expanded, but the company's equipment was worn, and it would require a large capital infusion just at a time when the Commission was committed to heavy expenditures.[23]

More generally, Freeman concluded that he was reluctant to add trucking to the rail services of the ONTC. The public could charge, he said, that the Commission was "forging the chains of a monopoly" with support from the provincial government. He was disturbed about the possible hostile reaction of railway labour unions, and "about the principle of public ownership versus private enterprise." For the same reasons, Freeman was also opposed to the acquisition of Star Transfer, a much larger and more successful trucking company in Timmins. But Star Transfer continued to grow and Freeman retired in 1958. By then, too, the Commission had completed its heavy investment in diesel conversion and new box cars.

In 1960, after two detailed technical studies, the Commission finally bought Star Transfer from the Passmore family in Timmins, keeping two members of the family in executive positions at reduced salaries. The purchase price was $670,000 for a total of 117 units of trucking equipment.[24] The figures and final arrangements all accorded with the careful recommendations of the management consultants Woods, Gordon and Company, and Clarkson, Gordon and Company.

Acquisition of Star Transfer gave to the ONTC a trucking service with facilities to store and carry freight from Toronto north as far as Hearst and Chapleau. With further investment in long forty-ton trailers and powerful trucks, the new company developed a profitable two-way traffic into the North, carrying commodities from Toronto and returning with bulk goods, such as the lumber and paper of northern mills, for clients wanting faster service than that of the train. The ONTC advertised northern highways as "The Route of the Yellow Giants." Earned income of Star Transfer increased by 40 per cent from 1960 to 1965, with a fourfold growth in profit, enabling the Commission to approve regular investment in new equipment. Movement into the field of trucking proved finally to be a profitable enterprise, indicating that the ONTC could adapt to the competition of freight traffic on the highways.

By the mid 1960s the ONTC was well on the way to becoming a complex transportation system, following the much larger Canadian models of the CPR and CNR, although smaller in scale and confined to a region. From its beginning as a railway powered by steam locomotives over a distance of little more than a hundred miles, it had become a rail network extending almost to the shore of James Bay, with branch and spur lines that tapped all of the major resource industries of the northeast. Its diesel engines now pulled long rows of cars loaded with ore and pulp to smelters and mills in the North, or to markets in the South.

Transportation of these staples encouraged in turn the search for new resources, attracting investment into extractive industries, and providing employment which gradually expanded the small urban communities between North Bay and Cochrane, Hearst and Moosonee. From its base in these small northern communities, surrounded by mines, forests, and scattered farms, the Commission has branched out carefully into other forms of transportation and communication – to buses and trucks on the highways; to transmission of the spoken and printed word by electronic signals.

More recently the Commission has added the ferry service on Lake Huron from Manitoulin Island to Tobermory at the tip of the Bruce Peninsula; and the small blue and yellow aircraft of its Norontair fleet have become familiar sights in northern skies, providing a faster form of travel by air. The efficiency and the integration of these new facilities confirm the well-founded and continuing capacity of the ONTC to respond to the regional needs of government and people in the north of Ontario.

Conclusion

Looking back on the history of the Ontario Northland Transportation Commission, the reader must be struck by what that history tells us about public ownership in the North American environment. Typically Canadian, it could not have been legislated into being in the United States, as it was in Ontario in 1902. Yet no one then or since ever referred to it as a socialist enterprise.

Though called a "Commission" because of its assigned tasks by government, the T&NO Railway (and its successor, the ONTC) from the beginning was not very different from a company owned and directed by the provincial government. The Commission constituted a board of directors over management, with authority derived from the crown.

Because of this ultimate sanction of the crown, through the form of the Lieutenant Governor in Council, the Commission enjoyed immunity from corporate and municipal taxes, although it became subject to the Municipal Tax Assistance Act in the 1950s.[1] In 1906 the T&NO was the cause of the first public debt of the province of Ontario, and its costs still constituted 47 per cent of the debt of Ontario at the time of World War I. When Premier Ferguson fixed the public debt of the Commission at just over $30,000,000 in 1924, he assumed that returns from the revenue of the railway would justify any burden on the taxpayers of the province; yet he made no attempt to establish a minimal rate of interest or a sinking fund to retire the principal over a period of years. Later, in the 1930s, after the furor over the Racine Report had died down, Mitchell Hepburn adopted a similar attitude. The debt of the Commission came to be viewed as a subsidy, a built-in cost of developing and maintaining a way of life in northeastern Ontario. Subsequent premiers have done the same, simply acknowledging the debt in the annual audited report of the Commission.

In return for this immunity from taxes and non-payment of a long-standing debt, certain obligations lay on the Commission, obligations which have entered into our ready acceptance of public ownership generally in Canada. Canadians have come to acquiesce in schemes of public enterprise, partly for reasons of geography, because of the difficulty of transporting products over the severe and unyielding terrain of the Precambrian Shield; partly for reasons of proximity to the United States, with its continually expanding sources of capital. For protection, Canadian investment has more readily accepted direct participation by government in public enterprise. The consequences for the ONTC have been twofold.

189

First, from its very beginning, the railway functioned as a public utility, not beginning as a private business which later had to be absorbed by government, like the Welland Canal in 1840, or the production plants of Ontario Hydro at Niagara. The public character of the Commission, however, was always defined by businessmen, lawyers and politicians who were all agreed on the ethic of competitive individualism and of capitalist methods. Public ownership never interfered with that ideology. The original members of the Commission, and particularly the chairmen, were all businessmen who had demonstrated their capacity to accumulate capital. Serving from a sense of loyalty and some degree of public service, they were not expected to make money directly from their membership. But there was never any question that their first duty was to enable entrepreneurs and corporations to exploit resources from the North for the benefit of southern markets.

Those markets were seldom open and competitive. They were generally dominated if not actually controlled by small groups of owners and executives. In time these groups of businessmen and politicians have related to one another in a tension between free business enterprise and government regulation, the two sides reconciled, brought together, made amicable, through a common attitude toward the extraction and the marketing of northern resources. This common interest helps to explain the success of the Commission, since it is founded on the premise that public ownership of transportation is simply one device among others for exploiting the ores and the forests of the northern part of the province.

The second consequence of this acquiescence in public ownership has been political. While viewed as an instrument of economic development, the Commission has also reflected the partisan character of Ontario politics. Before the end of World War II, the province was governed with one interruption by a two-party system divided not by ideology but by economic interest and political connection. With each change of party government, the membership of the Commission altered. Yet fundamental assumptions remained the same toward the twin goals of business efficiency and northern development, so long as they were carried out by appointees of the party in power.

Because the politics of Ontario have for a century been dominated by the power of the cabinet, and within the cabinet the premier has been pre-eminent in authority, the Commission has really been governed for most of its history by the premier of the province. It was he, and not the Legislative Assembly or even the cabinet, who decided to which department the Commission should report. Until the 1950s this power of the premier derived only occasional support from the civil service. In the days of a relatively weak bureaucracy, the premiers of Ontario relied on direct and sympathetic communication with businessmen of the province, and particularly of Toronto. Whitney, Ferguson and Hepburn all considered these connections as preferable sources of advice by comparison with the work of civil-service professionals.

With the election of George Drew in 1943 and the long tenure of the Conservative party, the partisan character of the Commission has been only slightly obscured. Continuity of membership has reflected the party in power. More significant in terms of change has been the attempt to clarify and delineate the line of responsibility between the Commission and the cabinet. George Drew, Leslie Frost, and John Robarts, when they were premiers, sensibly sought to delegate this reporting to a specific department of the provincial government. But the lines were never continuously defined. This uncertainty reflected a failure by politicians and their business associates to make a clear distinction between the form of the state and the form of successful business enterprise.

Though honestly concerned with community service and northern economic development, the publicly owned ONTC can still be conceived as a corporation over which the premier of the province functions as chairman of the board, while the cabinet and the party in power acquiesce as majority shareholders. As for the people of northern Ontario, they have for nearly three-quarters of a century developed a close affinity with the regional function of the ONTC. If it is sometimes seen from northern communities as a colonial vehicle of an "imperial" government in Toronto, the people of the North have also established a deep historical association between the ONTC and their own social, economic, and political life.

Notes

Abbreviations

A.R.   – Annual Report, Temiskaming and Northern Ontario Railway, and ONTC after 1946.

Minutes – Minutes of the Temiskaming and Northern Ontario Railway (now in PAO up to 1934).

ONR   – Ontario Northland Railway.

ONTC   – Ontario Northland Transportation Commission.

PAC   – Public Archives of Canada.

PAO   – Public Archives of Ontario.

R.S.O.   – Revised Statutes of Ontario.

T&NO   – Temiskaming and Northern Ontario Railway.

Chapter 1: The Idea of a Railway: Ontario First

1. For a lucid interpretation and a scholarly citation of sources on this exploitation of Ontario forests in the nineteenth century, see H. V. Nelles, *The Politics of Development* (Toronto 1974), pp. 10–18, 52–56.

2. M. Zaslow, "The Ontario Boundary Question," *Profiles of a Province* (Toronto 1967); Len Parker, "The Fight for Ontario's Tidewater," ONTC *Quarterly* (1960).

3. PAO, Wadsworth Papers (A-IV-5, W.R. Wadsworth, "A Retrospect"); C.C. Farr, *Lake Temiscamingue District* (Toronto 1894); S.A. Pain, *The Way North* (Toronto 1964), pp. 75–77.

4. Ontario. Legislative Assembly. *Report*, Director of Colonization, 1900 (Toronto 1901); and 1905 (Toronto 1906). Timiskaming District was surveyed into 24 townships in 1887. By 1900 only seven had been opened and it was estimated there were 350 people settled on 17,920 acres at the head of the lake.

5. *ibid.*, 1900. See also *Newspaper Hansard for Ontario*, 6 and 8 March 1900. Interview, Donald McKelvie, New Liskeard, May 1974. In October 1899 a meeting of settlers was held in the Presbyterian Church at New Liskeard, attended by the Commissioner of Crown Lands, the Director of Mines, the Inspector of Colonization Roads, and the Director of Colonization. When the settlers pressed the urgent need of a railway to end their isolation, the Commissioner of Crown Lands "promised to act at the earliest possible moment."

6. PAO, Pamphlet Collection, W.A. Charlton and C.G. Harvey, *Hudson's Bay Railway Route* (Toronto 1898); Col. Josiah Harris, *The Chartered Hudson's Bay and Pacific Railway Route* (1897).

7. Information on these railway proposals is in PAO, Pamphlet Collection; and in Toronto Central Library, Baldwin Room, Pamphlet Collection. See also G.H. Stanford, *To Serve the Community: The Story of the Toronto Board of Trade* (Toronto 1974), pp. 91–92.

8. *Canadian Annual Review*, 1901. O.S. Nock, *Algoma Central Railway* (London 1975), pp. 32–35.

9. PAO, Pamphlet Collection (1902).

10. *Newspaper Hansard for Ontario*, Feb. 21, 1900; G.W. Ross, *Getting Into Parliament and After* (Toronto 1913), pp. 208–11; Morris Zaslow, *The Opening of the Canadian North 1870–1914* (Toronto 1971), p. 147.

11. Nelles, *Politics of Development*, pp. 228–29.

12. Margaret Ross, *Sir George W. Ross* (Toronto 1923), pp. 103–106; *Canadian Annual Review*, 1901, 1902.

13. *Newspaper Hansard for Ontario*, Apr. 24, 1900.

14. Report of the Survey and Exploration of Northern Ontario, under the authority of E.J. Davis, Commissioner of Crown Lands (Toronto 1901).

15. *Newspaper Hansard for Ontario*, May 1, 1900.

16. PAC. Latchford Papers, vol. 6 and 7; *Statutes of Ontario*, 2 Edw. VII. c. 9.

17. *Newspaper Hansard for Ontario*, Feb. 28, 1902; Toronto *Globe*, Feb. 28, 1902; Toronto *Mail and Empire*, Feb. 28, 1902; *Canadian Annual Review*, 1901, 1902; M. Zaslow, *Opening of the Canadian North*, p. 180.

18. Toronto *Mail and Empire*, Feb. 28, 1902; *Globe*, Feb. 28, 1902.

19. *Journals of the Legislative Assembly of Ontario*, 1902, pp. 229, 234; *Statutes of Ontario*, 2 Edw. VII, 1902, c. 9.

20. PAC, Latchford Papers, vol. 6; *Minutes*, May 10, 1902.

21. *The North – Past, Present, and Future* (North Bay, ONTC, undated).

22. Toronto *Globe*, March 19, 1902.

23. H.J. Morgan, *Canadian Men and Women of the Time* (Toronto 1912).

24. *ibid.*; *Canadian Trade Index* (Toronto 1906); *A.R.*, 1902; PAC, Latchford Papers, vol. 6; Scott and Astrid Young, *O'Brien* (Toronto 1967), p. 40. Each of the five members of the Commission, including the chairman, received an honorarium of $1,000 a year. The salary of the chairman was changed to $5,000 by the Conservative government in 1906.

Chapter 2: The Miracle of Cobalt

1. *A.R.*, 1902, pp. 5–7; PAC, Latchford Papers, vol. 6 and 7.

2. *A.R.*, 1902, p. 16. The wealthy Ottawa lumbering family of J.R. Booth owned and operated the Canada Atlantic Railway until 1904, when they sold it to the Grand Trunk.

3. *Minutes*, Sept. 2, Oct. 1, Nov. 8, Dec. 3, 1902.

4. *A.R.*, 1903, pp. 38–39.

5. The best account of the Cobalt silver boom is D.M. LeBourdais, *Metals and Men* (Toronto 1957), ch. 7. See also L.C. Brown, *Cobalt, the Town With a Silver Lining* (Toronto, Department of Mines and Northern Affairs 1970), pp. 2–6; T.W. Gibson, *Mining in Ontario* (Toronto, 1937), pp. 51–53; Nelles, *Politics of Development*, pp. 150–79; S.A. Pain, *The Way North*, pp. 101–27; J.A. McRae, *Call Me Tomorrow* (Toronto 1960), ch. 10; and various materials in the Cobalt Mining Museum.

6. Gibson, *Mining in Ontario*, p. 52.

7. It was not unusual for discoveries to be made by labourers and prospectors who sold out for a few thousand dollars to local entrepreneurs. The men who bought their claims all ended as millionaires. LeBourdais, *Metals and Men*, pp. 129–31. S. and A. Young, *O'Brien*, pp. 42–52.

8. Gibson, *Mining in Ontario*, p. 55.

9. "So We'll Sing a Little Song of Cobalt," ONTC *Quarterly* (1948). Caldbick was in fact Chief Constable of the Northern Police District, appointed by the Conservative government of James Whitney as the result of a political recommendation. See Douglas Baldwin, "Cobalt as an Urban Frontier Town," (paper presented at the annual meeting of the Canadian Historical Association, 1978). Interview with Constable Caldbick's son, Mr. Samuel Caldbick, a crown attorney in Timmins, May 1974.

10. See H.A. Innis, *Settlement and the Mining Frontier* (Toronto 1936), chs. 7 and 8.

11. *Statutes of Ontario*, 4 Edw. VII, 1904, c. 7.

12. Nelles, *Politics of Development*, pp. 132, 168; *A.R.*, 1913. Much of the ore transported south went to the United States, or to small refineries at Deloro, Thorold, and Welland. The refinery at Deloro was owned by M.J. O'Brien, initially to process ore from his silver mine.

13. The synopsis of this dispute is in PAO, ONTC files.

14. Royal Commission on the Mineral Resources of Ontario, *Report* (Toronto 1890), xvi–xvii; D.M. Watson, *Frontier Movement and Economic Development in Northeastern Ontario, 1850–1914*, unpublished M.A. Thesis, Department of Geography, University of British Columbia, 1966, ch. 6.

Chapter 3: Made in Ontario: Financed in Toronto

1. *A.R.*, 1904, 1905. In 1904 the Empire Lumber Company bought title from the T&NO

Commission to 47 lots at Latchford for $50 each. PAO, Whitney Papers, Cobalt Town Lots.

2. *Minutes*, I, Oct. 25, 1902 to Jan. 16, 1905.

3. *A.R.*, 1902, p. 45, for the words of Premier Ross. Over 18,000 tons of rail were ordered from Charles Cammell & Company of Sheffield through James Cooper of Montréal, for a total price of over $500,000. The Chief Engineer and the Commission expressed "a strong objection to placing the order in the United States." In 1905 the federal government placed a duty of $7.00 a ton on imported steel rails, but Algoma Steel Company still had trouble meeting the specifications of the T&NO Commission. See also *Minutes*, Oct. 25, 1902; Jan. 20, June 25 and Nov. 12, 1904; Jan. 16 and Apr. 12, 1904. On the Steel Company of Canada, see William Kilbourn, *The Elements Combined* (Toronto 1960), pp. 54-6.

4. Interview, A. James Foster, Mimico, May 1974.

5. *A.R.*, 1905, pp. 25, 90-1.

6. Morgan, *Men and Women of the Time.*

7. In addition to Cox, the Board of the James Bay Railway consisted of William Mackenzie who controlled the Toronto Street Railway Company, Frederic Nicholls of the Toronto Electric Light Company, Hugh Lumsden who owned the boat service on Lake Timiskaming, and Donald Mann. These five obtained subsidies totalling more than $1,000,000 to build from Toronto to Sudbury, incorporated this line into the east-west Canadian Northern Railway, and abandoned any obligation in their charter to build north to James Bay. See *Statutes of Canada*, 58-9 Vic. 1895, c. 50; and 60-1 Vic. 1897, c. 47. G. R. Stevens, *Canadian National Railways*, 2 vols. (Toronto 1952), II, pp. 30-81; H. V. Nelles, *Politics of Development*, pp. 117-19, 230-1; and T.D. Regehr, *The Canadian Northern Railway* (Toronto 1976), pp. 255-8.

8. The relevant legislation is in *Statutes of Ontario*, 2 Edw. VII, 1902, c. 9; 3 Edw. VII, 1903, c. 4; 4 Edw. VII, 1904, c. 71. The amending Act of 1903 fixed the rate of interest at 4 per cent, and stipulated that lands granted to the Commission "shall not include timber or mineral." See also Special Report of Assistant Commissioner of Public Works, Jan. 13, 1905, in *A.R.*, 1904, pp. 92-4.

9. Toronto *Globe*, Jan. 8, 1904, p. 10.

10. The amending Act of 1904 gave authority to the Commission to estimate costs at $30,000 per mile, a figure essential for public borrowing of the necessary funds. *Statutes*, 4 Edw. VII, 1904, c. 8. See *Newspaper Hansard for Ontario*, Feb. 6, 1904, quoting figures by Premier Ross on the costs per mile of other railways in Canada, and showing those for constructing the T&NO as the lowest in the country.

11. Ames resigned primarily because of serious financial problems in his brokerage firm. See Toronto *Globe*, Jan. 18, 1904, p. 10.

12. The correspondence from Ames, Wood, and Ryan to Premier Ross is dated Sept. 1903 to Jan. 1904, and is in PAO, RG3, Ross Papers. See also *Minutes* for those months, and *A.R.*, 1903, 1904.

13. *Globe*, Jan. 25, 1904, p. 10; and *Weekly Globe*, Jan. 27, 1904; Morgan, *Men and Women of the Time.*

14. PAO, Ross Papers; *Minutes*, Oct. 20, 1903, May 14, and Dec. 1, 1904; *A.R.*, 1905.

Chapter 4: A Change of Government

1. Ontario, *Sessional Papers*, Return from the Records of the General Election...in 1905; C.W. Humphries, "The Sources of Ontario 'Progressive' Conservatism, 1900–1914," *Canadian Historical Association, Historical Papers* (1967), pp. 119–29; *Canadian Annual Review*, 1905; Alexander Fraser, *History of Ontario*, 2 vols. (Toronto 1907), I, pp. 473–5.

2. Toronto *Globe*, Feb. 22, 1905, p. 8.

3. Scott and Astrid Young, *Silent Frank Cochrane* (Toronto 1973), pp. 11–21.

4. Morgan, *Men and Women of the Time.*

5. *ibid.*, John S. Ewing, "The History of Imperial Oil Limited," unpublished MSS, Harvard Business History Foundation (Boston 1951) ch. II, pp. 59–69, ch. V, p. 17 (Copy in possession of Imperial Oil Head Office, Toronto); J.T. Saywell, "The Early History of Canadian Oil Companies," *Ontario History*, LIII (1961), pp. 67–72; Charles Whipp and Edward Phelps, *Petrolia 1866–1966* (Petrolia 1966). For a lighter treatment of Englehart, see Ian Sclanders, "The Amazing Jake Englehart," *Imperial Oil Review*, XXXIX (Sept. 1955); and a small pamphlet by Michael Barnes, *Jake Englehart* (Cobalt 1974).

6. PAO, RG8, Provincial Secretary's Department, Box 10. The letters in these files are a better guide to Englehart's character and ideas than anything so far written about him. On Hanna and Imperial Oil, see *Imperial Oil Review*, I (Sept. 1917), p. 2. In order to place such men as Englehart and Hanna in context with the successful Canadian business élite at the turn of the century, see the essay by T.W. Acheson, "Changing Social Origins of the Canadian Industrial Elite 1880–1910," *Business History Review*, XLVII (1973), reprinted in Glenn Porter and Robert Cuff, eds., *Enterprise and National Development* (Toronto 1973), pp. 51–79.

7. PAO, RG8, Boxes 9 and 10. Englehart to Hanna, June 22, 1908, Oct. 15, 1914.

8. *A.R.*, 1907, pp. 29, 38; *A.R.*, 1908, p. 12. An excellent study of the mix of British and European immigrants in this period is Desmond Glynn, *Immigration and the Canadian Trade Unions 1900–1914*, M.A. Research Paper, History Department, York University, 1973. On similar attitudes to immigrants arriving at Toronto from southern and eastern Europe, see R. Harney and H. Troper, *Immigrants* (Toronto 1975).

9. *A.R.*, 1906, p. 22.

10. PAO, RG3, Whitney Papers, T&NO; Canada, *House of Commons Debates*, LXVI, June 4, 1913, pp. 12170–12202; and S. and A. Young, *Silent Frank Cochrane*, pp. 149–51. The subsidy made a significant difference to the Ontario budget for 1913. See Stewart Bates, *Financial History of Canadian Governments* (Ottawa 1939), p. 179.

11. PAO, RG8, Provincial Secretary's Department. Englehart to Whitney, June 7, 1906; Toronto *Globe*, June 7, 1906, Nov. 21, 1907; Toronto *News*, June 1906.

12. *A.R.*, 1907, 1908. From this base in his general store, John McChesney went on to establish a substantial lumber business in the North.

13. PAO, Whitney Papers, correspondence between Matheson and Whitney for October 1905. Matheson was responsible for consolidating this and subsequent debts. *Newspaper Hansard for Ontario*, March 16, 1906 and April 12, 1907.

14. *Statutes of Ontario*, 5 Edw. VII, 1905, c. 10; and 7 Edw. VII, 1907, c. 18.

Chapter 5: The People's Railway

1. *A.R.*, 1910. Taped interview with Mr. and Mrs. Frank Herron, New Liskeard; Mrs. George

Booth, Matheson; and Mr. A.J. Foster, Mimico, May 1974; Cobalt *Daily Nugget*, Dec. 9, 1909.

2. *A.R.*, 1906, p. 42; *A.R.*, 1909, p. 164; R.D. Tennant, *Ontario's Government Railway* (Halifax 1973), p. 82.

3. *Sunshine Sketches of a Little Town* (Toronto 1948), p. 8.

4. Interview, Donald McKelvie, May 1974; PAC, Latchford Papers, vol. 2. Years later, Russel would write: "Whitney's first act upon assuming power was to wipe out the Commission and appoint another, and they in turn froze out the Chief Engineer...along with others of my staff of engineers." W.B. Russel to Senator W.H. McGuire, July 16, 1934, PAO, Hepburn Papers, General, 1934, T&NO; Nelles, *Politics of Development*, pp. 150-1; Pain, *The Way North*, p. 109.

5. Anson Gard, *North Bay: Gateway to Silverland* (Toronto 1909); S. John Mason, *Haileybury* Cobalt 1974).

6. *Statutes of Ontario*, 4. Edw. VII, 1904, c. 7.

7. *A.R.*, 1906, 1908.

8. *Newspaper Hansard for Ontario*, Feb. 20, 1908. Similar criticism of the T&NO Commission for its sale and handling of town lots was voiced by the Cochrane *Northland Post*, July 1, 1910, Aug. 5, 1910, Jan. 13, 1911, July 14, 1911.

9. Cobalt *Daily Nugget*, Oct. 13, 1909.

10. *Newspaper Hansard for Ontario*, March 16, 1906, April 12, 1907.

11. See C.W. Humphries, "The Sources of Ontario 'Progressive' Conservatism, 1900-1914," *Canadian Historical Association, Historical Papers* (1967), pp. 118-29.

12. Cobalt *Daily Nugget*, Oct. 19, 1910; *A.R.*, 1911, 1912, 1913; Len Parker "The Story of the N.C.R.," ONTC *Quarterly* (1956 and 1957); R.D. Tennant, *Ontario's Government Railway*, ch. 2; J.E. Due, *The Intercity Electric Railway Industry in Canada* (Toronto 1966), pp. 94-5.

Chapter 6: Gold and Fire

1. LeBourdais, *Metals and Men*, ch. 8; Gibson, *Mining in Ontario*, pp. 11-13.

2. Pain, *The Way North*, pp. 155-7; McRae, *Call Me Tomorrow*, ch. 11; A.A. Cole, *The Mining Industry in that part of Northern Ontario served by the Temiskaming and Northern Ontario Railway* (Toronto 1922), p. 9; and Ontario Department of Mines Bulletin No. 83, *Twenty-Five Years of Ontario's Mining History* (Toronto 1932), p. 22.

3. Cochrane *Northland Post*, Oct. 21, 1910, Jan. 20, 1911. See also the advertisement for this stage service by the Porcupine Transport Syndicate in the Cobalt *Daily Nugget*, Jan. 25, 1910.

4. Cochrane *Northland Post*, Dec. 2, 1910, Dec. 21, 1910.

5. Details on construction of this line are in *A.R.*, 1911, pp. 15-17. On the use of prisoners see New Liskeard, *Temiskaming Herald*, June 16, 1910, and Cochrane *Northland Post*, March 3, 1911.

6. *A.R.*, 1911, 1912.

7. Cochrane *Northland Post*, July 21, 1911; Toronto *Globe*, July 14 and 17, 1911; *A.R.*, 1911, pp. 187-8; Interviews, John Campsell, Porcupine, and Eva DeRosa, South Porcupine, May 1974; Department of Lands and Forests, *A History of Cochrane Forest Dis-*

trict (1964), pp. 33–5; Frank Rasky, *Great Canadian Disasters* (Don Mills 1961), pp. 189–96.

8. *Northland Post*, July 14 and 21, 1911. On July 14 the Toronto *Mail & Empire* estimated that a hundred people had perished in the Porcupine district alone, most of whom were from Toronto, or England, or the United States. Two of the Americans were listed as "dark" or "coloured." Three days later the same paper stated on its front page that "sixty-three bodies have been recovered, and the death toll will not exceed 70 or 75."

Chapter 7: Toward a Northern Community

1. PAO, RG8, Periodic Reports of J.L. Englehart to Provincial Secretary, 1914–1918; *A.R.*, 1916, p. 13; *A.R.*, 1917, p. 16; *A.R.*, 1918, p. 16; North Bay *Nugget*, Centennial Edition, 30 June 1967, p. 11.

2. Interview, Mr. And Mrs. Will Gard, North Bay, May 1974. The depression of 1912 is discussed in R.C. Brown and R. Cook, *Canada 1896–1921* (Toronto 1974), pp. 198–200.

3. *A.R.*, 1912, pp. 2021; *A.R.*, 1913, p. 21; ONTC Archives, "File Under Review," covering all correspondence re: Gowganda extension, Oct. 1912 to Dec. 1919.

4. Interviews, Bill Ross Jr., North Bay; and Jim Fletcher, Corbeil, May 1974.

5. *A.R.*, 1908, p. 12.

6. *ibid.*, 1911, p. 199.

7. *ibid.*, 1913; pp. 9–10; Brown and Cook, *Canada 1896–1921*, p. 160.

8. PAO, RG8, Box 9, Hanna, by A.A. Cole, "Cobalt and Porcupine," (1915), sent to Englehart and Hanna for approval.

9. *ibid.*, Englehart to General Freight and Purchasing Agent of the T&NO, Jan. 3, 1916, copy to Premier Hearst.

10. *ibid.*, Dr. C.C. James to Englehart, Feb. 10, 1916.

11. *ibid.*, Englehart to C.C. James, Feb. 15, 1916.

12. *ibid.*, Roadmaster to Supervisor of Maintenance, Dec. 14, 1915. Logs unacceptable as ties were readily sold by farmers to pulp and paper companies.

13. PAO, RG3, Hearst Papers, J.F. Whitson to Premier Hearst, Jan. 24, 1916. For a more general discussion of settlement in northern Ontario, see R.C. Lambert and Paul Pross, *Renewing Nature's Wealth* (Toronto 1967), ch. 15.

14. *A.R.*, 1916, p. 27.

15. Toronto *Mail and Empire*, Aug. 2, 1916.

16. Interview, Cobalt, May 1974.

17. PAO, Northern Ontario Fire Relief Committee, *Report*, Sept. 24, 1917.

18. *ibid.*

19. *ibid.*; Interview, Samuel Caldbick, Timmins, May 1974.

Chapter 8: Private Decisions and Public Policy

1. Haileybury *Haileyburian*, Oct. 13, 1905.

2. Peter Oliver, "Sir William Hearst and the Collapse of the Ontario Conservative Party,"

Canadian Historical Review, LIII (March 1972), pp. 21–50; reprinted in his *Public and Private Persons* (Toronto 1975); W.R. Young, "Conscription, Rural Depopulation, and the Farmers of Ontario," *C.H.R.*, LIII (Sept. 1972), pp. 289–320.

3. Ontario, Sessional Papers, Return from the Records of the General Election...in 1919.

4. E.C. Drury, *Farmer Premier* (Toronto 1966), passim.

5. PAO, RG8, Provincial Secretary's Department, W.J. Hanna, Box 9.

6. PAO, RG3, Hearst Papers, T&NO, March–Sept. 1919.

7. *ibid.*

8. From 1905 to 1919 the Commission paid $5,000,000 into the Consolidated Revenue Fund. The $2,000,000 subsidy from the federal government in 1913 was additional. By 1919 the funded debt owing to the province was $22,335,000. See Appendix C; and D.E. MacDougall, Executive Director, Financial and Purchasing Services, ONTC, *Statement on Capital Financing* (1973).

9. PAO, RG3, Hearst Papers.

10. PAO, RG3, Drury Papers, General, 1919, T&NO; see also E.C. Drury, *Farmer Premier*, p. 101.

11. PAO, Drury Papers.

12. Drury, *Farmer Premier*, p. 146.

13. Toronto *Mail and Empire*, Oct. 5, 1922; R.S. Lambert and P. Pross, *Renewing Nature's Wealth*, Ontario Department of Lands and Forests (Toronto 1967); PAO, Northern Ontario Fire Relief Committee, 1922.

14. *Memories of the Great Fire of 1922* (Cobalt 1973); Leslie McFarlane, *Haileybury Fire* (Cobalt 1972), containing excerpts from the Sudbury *Star*, Oct. 7 and 11, 1922.

15. Interview, Bill Ross Jr., May 1974.

16. PAO, Northern Ontario Fire Relief Committee, *Report* (Nov. 25, 1922).

17. *ibid.*

18. *A.R.*, 1917, pp. 29–30; L. Carson Brown, *Kirkland Lake – 50 Golden Years*, Department of Mines and Northern Affairs (Toronto 1970), pp. 4–11; Pain, *The Way North*, ch. 21; LeBourdais, *Metals and Men*, ch. 9.

19. PAO, RG8, Provincial Secretary's Department, W.J. Hanna, Box 9.

20. Ontario Department of Lands and Forests, District History Series No. 15, *A History of Swastika Forest District* (Toronto 1964), p. 14; *A.R.*, 1919, pp. 17–18.

21. PAO, Drury Papers, General, Larder Lake, 1920.

22. *ibid.*

23. *ibid.*

24. *ibid.*, Lee to Drury, July 29, 1920; T.F. Sutherland to Drury, Aug. 14, 1920.

25. ONTC Archives, Cole to Lee, Nov. 28, 1922.

26. *ibid.*, George Lee, "Official Statement re: Kirkland Lake Branch," Apr. 13, 1923.

27. July 12, 1924. The *Northern Miner* was just one of the Ontario papers which dwelled on this new northern interest of the two financial capitals of eastern Canada. See Ottawa *Journal*, Nov. 2, 1925, and Sept. 5, 1926; North Bay *Nugget*, Apr. 13, 1926; and Toronto *Star*, Nov. 29, 1927.

28. Taschereau wanted delay in the courts, while he pressed the CNR to build to Rouyn.

According to George Lee, the CNR preferred to stay out of the project, but felt unable to oppose the wishes of the Québec premier. The tensions between Taschereau and Ferguson could have been arbitrated by the federal government, but Mackenzie King refused to intervene. As a result, the issue had to go before the Supreme Court and the Judicial Committee. For Taschereau the delay worked in his favour: by the time of the final decision, the CNR had almost completed its own line, and in 1928 Rouyn had two railway outlets. See PAO, Ferguson Papers; and PAC, Mackenzie King Papers, both of which are used by Peter Oliver, G. Howard Ferguson: Ontario Tory (Toronto 1977), pp. 197–8.

29. Until 1942 the Nipissing Central continued to function as a separate company with members of the Commission sitting as its Board of Directors. In 1942 the Board of Transport Commissioners in Ottawa approved an application to lease the NCR to the T&NO Commission. Thereafter the earnings of the NCR were shown as $1.00 a year rental, with all other profits, expenses, and losses merged with those of the Commission.

Chapter 9: The Illusion of Moosonee

1. *A.R.*, 1905, p. 59.

2. *ibid.*, 1911, pp. 22–3, 106, 115.

3. PAO, RG8, Hanna, Box 9, Englehart to Hearst, May 29, 1914.

4. Oscar Skelton, "A Seaport for Ontario," *Queen's Quarterly*, XVI (1909), p. 375.

5. Sept. 27, 1918.

6. The plant of the Abitibi Company came into production in the years 1914 and 1915, with forest reserves to support it of well over 4,000 acres. Support for the company received strong approval from G. Howard Ferguson, appointed Minister of Lands, Forests, and Mines in 1914.

7. *A.R.*, 1919, p. 18; *Newspaper Hansard for Ontario*, May 5, 1920.

8. ONTC Archives, Resolution passed by Cochrane Board of Trade, April 12, 1920.

9. M.B. Baker, "Iron and Lignite in the Mattagami Basin," *Annual Report of the Ontario Department of Mines*, No. 20 (1911), pp. 234–8.

10. Canada, Senate, *Report of the Special Committee to Report on the Navigability and Fishery Resources of Hudson Bay and Strait* (Ottawa 1920).

11. *A.R.*, 1922, p. 10; ONTC Archives, Lee to McLaren and Martin, Jan. 17, 1923.

12. Ferguson's statement was issued Sept. 28, 1923. For reports and interpretation see the following northern newspapers: Haileybury *Haileyburian*, Oct. 4, 1923; *Cochrane Northland Post*, Oct. 12, 1923; Nov. 2, 1923; North Bay *Nugget*, Nov. 20, 1923, Feb. 15, 1924.

13. Cochrane *Northland Post*, March 14, 1924; *Financial Post*, May 23, 1924. For Ferguson's speech in the Legislative Assembly, see Toronto *Globe*, March 11, 1924; Toronto *Mail and Empire*, March 11, 1924; and Ottawa *Journal*, March 11, 1924.

14. PAO, RG3, Ferguson Papers, Box 12, Hydro.

15. S.B. Clement, "Report on the Hudson Bay Region, Relative to Extension of the T&NO Railway from Coral Rapids to Moose Harbour," ONTC Archives, May 1929.

16. J.L. Englehart, "A Bill to Authorize Extension of the T&NO Railway to James Bay," ONTC Archives, 1920.

17. Copy of letter, W. Tees Curran to Premier Taschereau, Nov. 21, 1923, ONTC Archives.

18. This letter was introduced as evidence into the Proceedings of the Racine Inquiry, PAO, RG.18, B–87, p. 694.

19. Ferguson and McLean met through McLean's interest in the Grenville Crushed Rock Company. Its first quarry was located in Ferguson's constituency, not far from his home town of Kemptville. I am indebted for this information on H. F. McLean to Mr. Charles Hyson of Etobicoke, a former engineer with H. F. McLean Limited.

20. S. B. Clement, "Construction of the T&NO Railway extension to James Bay," *Canadian Engineer*, 66 (May 1934), pp. 5–6.

21. Interview, North Bay, May 1974.

22. Clement, "Construction...," *Canadian Engineer* (May 1934).

23. J. G. Kerry, "Proposed T&NO Terminal on James Bay," *Canadian Engineer* (May 1914), p. 690.

24. PAO, Miscellaneous Collection (1931); George Lee to Premier G. S. Henry, Nov. 18, 1931.

25. ONTC Archives, "Programme for the Official Opening of the James Bay Extension," July 15, 1932.

Chapter 10: Chaos and Charisma

1. *A.R.*, 1928, pp. 5–7.

2. *ibid.*

3. *A.R.*, 1931, p. 5.

4. Michiel Horn, ed., *The Dirty Thirties* (Toronto 1972), pp. 1–30.

5. *ibid.*; G. R. Stevens, *History of the Canadian National Railways* (N.Y. 1973), p. 362.

6. *A.R.*, 1933, p. 5; *Minutes*, March 2, 1934; PAO, RG.18, B–87, T&NO Railway Inquiry, Proceedings (1934), pp. 303–12. Employees organized in the federated trades were retained on condition that their work-week dropped to 35 hours at reduced pay. The Commission took this step as a member of the Railway Association of Canada.

7. Interviews, Tom Sykes and Bill Ross Jr., North Bay, May 1974. Bill Ross' description of hoboes probably came from Jack London's book, *The Road* (reprinted London 1967). See also Irving Abella and David Miller (Editors), *The Workingman in the Twentieth Century* (Toronto 1978).

8. *Newspaper Hansard for Ontario*, March 30, 1933; Lambert and Pross, *Renewing Nature's Wealth*, pp. 306–8. On the Kapuskasing Soldier's Settlement of 1917, see Peter Oliver, *G. Howard Ferguson*, pp. 70–1.

9. PAO, *Return from the...General Election...in 1934*; Toronto *Globe*, Aug. 7, 1934; Neil McKenty, "Mitchell Hepburn and the Ontario Election of 1934," *Canadian Historical Review*, XLV (1964), pp. 302–10; McKenty, *Mitch Hepburn* (Toronto 1967), pp. 47–60.

10. PAO, RG3, Hepburn Papers, Private (1934), *Abitibi...Inquiry*; Toronto *Globe*, July 18, 1934; Nelles, *Politics of Development*, pp. 473–9; Oliver, *Howard Ferguson*, pp. 105–14, 157–8.

11. PAO, Hepburn Papers, *Abitibi...Inquiry*; Merrill Denison, *The People's Power* (Toronto 1960), chs. 21, 22.

12. PAO, *Return from the...General Election...in 1934*; McKenty, *Mitch Hepburn*, p. 60.

13. North Bay *Nugget*, Aug. 3, 1934.

Chapter 11: Under Attack

1. The difference in scale was considerable. While Ontario Hydro was capitalized in 1934 at nearly $360,000,000, assets of the T&NO were valued at less than $45,000,000. Denison, *The People's Power*, p. 190; and *A.R.*, 1934.

2. Toronto *Globe*, Aug. 9, 1934.

3. North Bay *Nugget*, Aug. 8, 1934.

4. *ibid.*, Aug. 13, 1934.

5. *Temiskaming and Northern Ontario Inquiry*, Report of Armand Racine, Oct. 4, 1934 (Toronto 1935). This report of twenty-five printed pages is based on three volumes of typewritten evidence in PAO, RG.18, B–87, *Proceedings*.

6. See Appendix A.

7. Racine Inquiry, *Report*, p. 16.

8. PAO, Racine Inquiry, *Proceedings*, pp. 60–2.

9. *ibid.*, pp. 494, 541.

10. North Bay *Nugget*, Aug. 29, 1934.

11. *ibid.*, Sept. 12, 1934.

12. *ibid.*, Aug. 29, 1934.

13. F.B. Beemer to Premier Hepburn, July 26, 1934; D.G. Grant to Hepburn, Aug. 14, 1934, PAO, Hepburn Papers, Private (1934), T&NO.

14. *ibid.*

15. Roy Thomson to Premier Hepburn, Oct. 13, 1934, Hepburn Papers, Public (1934), T&NO. Thomson had obtained the licence to operate his North Bay radio station (CFCH) after election of the federal Conservative government of R.B. Bennett in 1930. While his efforts to obtain advertising revenue from the T&NO Commission were unsuccessful, he remained on good terms with George Lee. *Minutes*, April 21 and Nov. 30, 1931.

16. Lee's pension actually came to $4,680, but Lang and Hepburn personally cut it back to $3,000. It was restored to $4,680 after George Drew became Conservative premier in 1943. *Minutes*, Dec. 10, 1934, July 5, 1935, Dec. 16, 1943; PAO, Hepburn Papers (1937), T&NO; North Bay *Nugget*, Oct. 15, 1934.

17. *ibid.*, Oct. 19 and 26, 1934.

18. Ian H. MacKenzie to Premier Hepburn, Sept. 27, 1934; L.P. Burns to Hepburn, Oct. 9, 1934, PAO, Hepburn Papers, Private (1934), T&NO.

19. W.G. Nixon to Hepburn, July 26, 1934, Oct. 19, 1934, PAO, Hepburn Papers (1934), W.G. Nixon file.

20. Interview, A.H. Cavanagh, North Bay, Nov. 4, 1975.

Chapter 12: Continuity in a Political Frame

1. See *Minutes*, Dec. 10, 1934, when Racine moved that further dismissals be made in line

with his report, only to find that no other member of the Commission supported him. Slaght, the most prestigious member, never really attended. He was elected MP for Parry Sound in the federal election of 1935, but kept the legal business of the T&NO.

2. PAO, Racine Inquiry, *Proceedings*, 199.

3. H.N. Baird to Hepburn, Feb. 21, 1935, PAO, Hepburn Papers, Public, (1935), T&NO *Canadian Transportation* (July 1937); *A.R.*, 1937, pp. 6-7.

4. Lang to Hepburn, Dec. 17, 1936, PAO, Hepburn Papers (1936), T&NO.

5. PAO, Racine Inquiry, *Proceedings*, 108.

6. PAO, Hepburn Papers, Private (1936, 1937), T&NO.

7. *ibid.*, Mosher to Hepburn, April 24, 1937. The contract with the Brotherhood of Railway and Steamship Clerks was signed May 1, 1937. See *Official Register of Agreements*, No. 2315, ONTC Archives.

8. Hepburn to Cavanagh, Oct. 7, 1936, PAO, Hepburn Papers, Private (1936), T&NO.

9. *A.R.*, 1938, p. 7; 1939, p. 7. The Inn was destroyed by fire in 1939.

10. Hepburn also "requested" from Cavanagh that the T&NO give some advertising business to the London *Advertiser*. Similarly, three years later he instructed Cavanagh to "make certain that no advertising from your railway goes to the Toronto *Saturday Night*, which is owned and operated by the Consolidated Press Limited." Hepburn Papers, Hepburn to Cavanagh, Dec. 20, 1934 and Dec. 17, 1937; McKenty, *Mitch Hepburn*, pp. 181-2.

11. C.H. Black to Hepburn, Nov. 1, 1937, PAO, Hepburn Papers, Private (1937), T&NO.

12. Interview, North Bay, May 1974.

13. PAO, Hepburn Papers, Fleming to Hepburn, Oct. 20, 1934. Fleming was a good friend of G.B. Alford, Purchasing Agent of the T&NO, with whom he negotiated business for his firm, Richardson, Bond & Wright in Owen Sound. Interview, Stanley Gowan, North Bay, Sept. 1975.

14. PAO, Hepburn Papers, Private (1935), T&NO, Cavanagh to Hepburn, Jan. 24, 1935; Hepburn to Cavanagh, Feb. 1, 1935.

15. *A.R.*, 1937, p. 9.

Chapter 13: Adaptation and Experiment

1. *A.R.*, 1939, pp. 18-19.

2. *ibid.*, 1938, p. 6.

3. PAO, Hepburn Papers, Private (1935), T&NO, Lang to Hepburn, Feb. 19, 1935.

4. "Highway Services," ONTC *Quarterly* (1960).

5. PAO, Hepburn Papers, Private (1936, 1938), T&NO; *Minutes*, June 8, 1939, May 16, 1940; *A.R.*, 1936-1940; Interview, A.H. Cavanagh, Nov. 4, 1975.

6. *A.R.*, 1940, p. 6.

7. *Historical Tables of the Mineral Production of Canada* (Ottawa, Bureau of Statistics 1945), p. 51.

8. S.A. Pain, *Three Miles of Gold* (Toronto 1960, pp. 79-81).

9. See above. Chap. 9, Note 9.

10. Ontario Research Foundation, "A Technical and Economic Investigation of Northern

Ontario Lignite," *Annual Report*, Ontario Department of Mines, 42 (1933), part 3, pp. 18–24.

11. PAO, Hepburn Papers, Private (1936, 1938), T&NO.

12. *ibid.*, (1941, 1942), Lignite.

13. Hamilton *Spectator*, Aug. 12, 1942.

14. *Northland Post*, Aug. 13, 1942; Toronto *Globe*, Aug. 17, 1946; PAO, Drew Papers, 211-G, Frost to Wills, May 31, 1946, Cavanagh to Department of Mines, Feb. 1, 1944.

Chapter 14: The Premier versus the Chairman

1. *A.R.*, 1946, p. 13.

2. PAO, RG3, ONTC, Box 2. The figures are selected and quoted in an economic study by Edward Kriz and Lewis Sorrell, to recommend whether the ONTC should expand into highway transportation, *Kriz Report* (1952), Part B, pp. 55–83. Statistics on population are taken from Canadian census returns for 1941 and 1951. For a statement of concern that the figures continued to represent a population growth "below the provincial average," see *Design for Development: Northeastern Ontario Development Region*, Analysis, Phase I (Department of Treasury and Economics, Regional Development Branch, Jan. 23, 1971), pp. 1-3.

3. Toronto *Star*, Jan. 19, 1940.

4. North Bay *Nugget*, Jan. 19 and 22, 1940.

5. *ibid.*, March 27, 1940.

6. The correspondence and the press release are in PAO, Hepburn Papers, Private (1940), T&NO. Lang's reply is not included but it was printed in the North Bay *Nugget* and Toronto *Globe & Mail*, April 1, 1940. Lang died in February 1941 and Cavanagh arranged to pay his widow $5,000 on the premise that, if Lang had been in good health, "he would have received an appointment carrying a salary of not less than 50 per cent of his rate as chairman." *Minutes*, Nov. 7, 1941.

7. Interview, A.H. Cavanagh, North Bay, May 1974.

8. PAO, Hepburn Papers, Private (1938), T&NO.

9. *ibid.*, (1940).

10. *ibid.*, (1941), Cavanagh to Hepburn, April 1, 1941. Lang's statement on the scheduled rights of employees, "regardless of trade union affiliation," is in *Minutes*, May 18, 1938.

11. Both letters are in Hepburn Papers (1940), T&NO.

12. North Bay *Nugget*, April 1, 1940.

Chapter 15: Toward a New Commission

1. Hepburn Papers (1940), T&NO. A copy of the Order-in-Council appointing Nixon at $5,000 above his salary as MPP is in *Minutes*, June 23, 1941.

2. PAO, Hepburn Papers, Private (1940), T&NO; Conant Papers (1942), T&NO.

3. North Bay *Nugget*, Aug. 3 and 5, 1943; Ontario, *Sessional Papers*, Return from the records of the General Election...in 1943.

4. PAO, Drew Papers, 211-G. ONTC Recommendations.

5. North Bay *Nugget*, Aug. 2, 1944. Interview, Donald C. MacDonald, Queen's Park, January 1976.

6. PAO, Drew Papers, 211-G. The notes calculated that the Executive represented over 1,700 unionized employees.

7. Lee was also intent on restoring his pension. Cavanagh raised it shortly after to $4,680, from the $3,000 settled by Lang and Hepburn. The average pension for 131 former employees in 1943 was much less than $600 a year. See *A.R.*, 1943; *Minutes*, Dec. 10, 1934, Oct. 23, 1937, Dec. 16, 1943. The size of the average pension is in PAO, RG3, ONTC, Box 5.

8. PAO, RG3, Drew Papers, File 159-G; North Bay *Nugget*, March 20, 1940; Toronto *Globe and Mail*, Sept. 18, 1944. Officials advising Frost clearly had in mind the growth in numbers of French Canadian settlers and the success of the Québec government at promoting group settlement on similar northern lands.

9. Interview, H. A. Wills, Toronto, January 1976. Mr. Wills was publisher and editor of the Cochrane *Northland Post* from 1940 to 1970.

10. Interview, the late Judge Harry J. Reynolds, North Bay, January 1976.

11. *Who's Who in Canada* (1947-1948).

12. Williamson established good relations among businessmen in the North, and he wrote well, but he was appointed as a good friend of Drew and Reynolds. His starting salary was $3,600, for the purpose of writing a history of the railway and the North, "and to perform such duties as may be assigned to him...from time to time." *Minutes*, July 3, 1945.

13. North Bay *Nugget*, July 30, 1943, Aug. 15, 1944; Interview, Judge Harry J. Reynolds, North Bay, January 1976.

14. For the whole of northern Ontario, the total number of seats was eleven. In 1943 they went overwhelmingly CCF. Though the Conservatives swept the province with sixty-six seats in 1945, they carried only one in the North. The CCF in the 1945 election were reduced to eight seats provincially, but seven of these were in the North. The party was the effective opposition in northern Ontario even after the election of 1948, yet it had a negligible influence on the ONTC, and little apparent concern with its affairs. But many of the CCF members were new and inexperienced men who accepted the historically partisan control of the Commission. Interviews, C. H. Taylor, North Bay, and D. C. MacDonald, Queen's Park, January 1976.

15. Aug. 17, 1944.

16. PAO, RG3, ONTC, Box 6.

17. *ibid.*, Drew Papers, 211-G.

18. *ibid.*, ONTC, Box 6, Drew to Reynolds, Aug. 23, 1944.

Chapter 16: Efficiency of the Colonels

1. North Bay *Nugget*, Aug. 17, 1944; Timmins *Daily Press*, Aug. 26, 1944.

2. *Minutes*, Nov. 7, 1944.

3. *ibid.*, Dec. 2, 1944, Feb. 21, April 6, May 21, 1945.

4. PAO, Drew Papers, 211-G, file: ONR Policy, Aug. 18, 1945.

5. PAO, Conant Papers (1942).

6. PAO, Drew Papers, 211-G. Col. E.J. Young to Col. G.C. Blackstock, and Blackstock to Col. Reynolds, July 13, 1945.

7. *ibid.*, Toronto *Globe and Mail*, March 23, 1964; Statutes of Ontario, 10 Geo. VI, 1946, c. 67.

8. R.S.O., 1950, c. 264.

9. PAO, RG3, ONTC, Box 2, March 5, 1949; and Drew Papers, 211-G, file: ONR air service.

10. *Minutes*, Sept. 17, 1949, R.S.O., 1937, c. 55, s. 17 and 21(3).

11. *Minutes*, Sept. 2 and Nov. 8, 1902. See above, chapter 2.

12. *Statutes of Ontario*, 11 Geo. VI, 1947, c. 74; R.S.O., 1950, c. 264, s. 7(g).

13. *Minutes*, Nov. 18, 1946, July 22, 1949. Similar requests for smaller amounts had been made periodically by other northern towns. The tensions were finally removed by passage of the Municipal Tax Assistance Act in 1952, which enabled towns and cities to receive payment from crown agencies assessed annually through the Department of Municipal Affairs. See *Statutes of Ontario*, 1952, c. 66; R.S.O., 1960, c. 258; R.S.O., 1970, c. 292.

14. Interview, the Hon. Roland Michener, Toronto, Dec. 1975.

15. PAO, ONTC, Box 6, April 10, 1946.

Chapter 17. Transition in a Post-War World

1. *Minutes*, Jan. 28, Feb. 12, 1947.

2. PAO, ONTC, Box 1.

3. Interviews, the Hon. Roland Michener, Toronto, Dec. 1975; A.H. Cavanagh, North Bay, Nov. 1975; Judge Harry J. Reynolds, North Bay, Jan. 1976.

4. Statements prepared by the T&NO Commission for the Racine Inquiry (1934), ONTC Archives.

5. PAO, Drew Papers, 211-G, Young to Drew, March 28, 1947.

6. Interview, A.H. Cavanagh, North Bay, Nov. 1975. The issue of Cavanagh's salary may have been a grievance within the Commission. Reynold's salary was raised from $6,000 to $9,000 by Order-in-Council in 1948; Freeman earned less than $10,000 when he became general manager in 1947, and in 1953 that figure was raised to $11,100. *Minutes*, Dec. 23, 1941, Feb. 12, 1947, July 4, 1947, April 24, 1948, Jan. 15, 1953; PAO, RG3, ONTC, Box 4.

7. PAO, Drew Papers, 211-G.

8. For an organization chart in 1946, see *ibid.*

9. PAO, RG3, ONTC, Box 1.

10. *Statements...for the Racine Inquiry* (1934), ONTC Archives; *Minutes*, April 16, 1934.

11. *Minutes*, Dec. 10, 1934, Jan. 21, 1935, Jan. 8, 1937; *A.R.*, 1938.

12. PAO, Hepburn Papers, Private (1938), T&NO, Lang to Hepburn, Dec. 1, 1938.

13. PAO, RG3, ONTC, Box 5.

14. *A.R.*, 1943, p. 9.

15. *Minutes*, May 19, 1944.

16. PAO, RG3, ONTC, Box 5.

17. *ibid.*, Reynolds to Drew, April 9, 1946.

18. *ibid.*, Trowhill to Reynolds, Nov. 12, 1946.

19. *ibid.*, Box 6.

20. *ibid.*

21. *ibid.*, Box 5.

22. Figures taken from *Statements...for Racine Inquiry* (1934), ONTC Archives.

23. Interview, Corbeil, May 1974.

24. PAO, RG3, ONTC, Box 5.

25. *ibid.*

26. *A.R.*, 1961-65, *Statement on Capital Financing*, prepared by D.E. McDougall, Executive Director Financial Services, ONTC (1973).

Chapter 18. A Modern Transportation System

1. The report is in PAO, RG3, ONTC, Box 2; Interview, Jim Fletcher, Corbeil, May 3, 1974.

2. *A.R.*, 1933; PAO, RG3, ONTC, Box 2, Freeman to Michener, Feb. 15, 1947.

3. *Statutes of Ontario*, 2 Edw. VII, 1902, c. 9, s. 9; *R.S.O.*, 1937, c. 55, s. 23.

4. The report of this committee is in *Minutes*, Feb. 24, 1950. See also ONTC *Quarterly* (1952, 1953).

5. *A.R.*, 1947, 1948; *Minutes*, Dec. 15, 1947, June 13, 1949, Aug. 7, 1952, Nov. 16, 1953.

6. PAO, RG3, ONTC, Box 4, Jan. 5, 1950.

7. *Minutes*, Nov. 5, 1947.

8. PAO, RG3, ONTC, Box 1.

9. *Minutes*, Feb. 24, July 15, 1950; R.D. Tennant, *Ontario's Government Railway*, p. 93.

10. North Bay *Nugget*, Oct. 28, 1953.

11. PAO, Ferguson Papers, Box 12, Hydro, Premier Ferguson to Mr. Drummond-Hay, President, Macdonald-Cartier Club, Winnipeg, May 16, 1929; cf. Nelles, *Politics of Development*, pp. 157-66.

12. *Minutes*, Jan. 18, Sept. 14, 1935.

13. *R.S.O.*, c. 53, s. 6(c).

14. *Minutes*, Nov. 18, 1929.

15. *ibid.*, Jan. 28, 1930.

16. *ibid.*, Aug. 16, 1932, June 10 and 22, 1935.

17. *ibid.*, June 25, 1946; Interview, Hon. Roland Michener, Toronto, Dec. 1975.

18. *A Description of Ontario Northland Communications* (ONTC, North Bay 1975); R.D. Tennant, *Ontario's Government Railway*, ch. 4.

19. *Minutes*, Jan. 6, April 7, 1932; *R.S.O.*, 1937, c. 55, s. 6(d).

20. PAO, Drew Papers, 211-G, file ONTC, 11 Dec. 1945; *A.R.*, 1945, 1946; ONTC *Quarterly* (1946); *R.S.O.*, 1950, c. 264, s. 7(e).

21. PAO, RG3, ONTC, Box 1, Reynolds to Drew, Sept. 30, 1944.

22. *Minutes*, July 4, 1947; PAO, RG3, ONTC, Box 4; *R.S.O.*, 1950, c. 264, s. 10.

23. PAO, RG3, ONTC, Box 2, "Kriz Report." Walter Little Transport was subsequently sold to Dominion Freightways Company.

24. *A.R.*, 1960, 1965; ONTC *Quarterly* (1961, 1964). The reports from Woods, Gordon, and Clarkson, Gordon, are in ONTC Archives.

Conclusion

1. See above, Chap. 16, note 13.

Appendix A

A LIST OF SIGNIFICANT DATES

F.R. Latchford, Minister of Public Works, introduced first T&NO Bill into Legislative Assembly of Ontario. January 15, 1902

T&NO Bill passed and becomes Statute. March 17, 1902

First sod turned at North Bay. May 10, 1902

First Commission appointed. July 24, 1902

First section (North Bay to New Liskeard) begins normal operation. January 16, 1905

Second section (New Liskeard to Cochrane) begins normal operation. November 30, 1908

Head Office moved from Toronto to North Bay. March, 1921

Contract let for first extension north of Cochrane. January 9, 1922

Formal ceremony marking completion of line to Moosonee. July 15, 1932

Racine Inquiry. August-September, 1934

First acquisition of buses, beginning of a transportation system. March, 1936

Change of name to Ontario Northland Transportation Commission. April 5, 1946

Change from steam to diesel locomotives. 1947-1957

Acquisition of Star Transfer (trucking). 1960

Appendix B

TEMISKAMING AND NORTHERN ONTARIO RAILWAY COMMISSION (1902 to April 9, 1946), and ONTARIO NORTHLAND TRANSPORTATION COMMISSION (subsequent to April 9, 1946)

1902: A.E. Ames, Toronto, Chairman; E. Gurney, Toronto, Commissioner; M.J. O'Brien, Renfrew, Commissioner; B.W. Folger, Kingston, Commissioner; F.E. Leonard, London, Commissioner; P.E. Ryan, Toronto, Secretary-Treasurer.

1904: Robert Jaffray, Toronto, Chairman; E. Gurney, Toronto, Commissioner; M.J. O'Brien, Renfrew, Commissioner; F.E. Leonard, London, Commissioner; B.W. Folger, Kingston, Commissioner; H.W. Pearson, Toronto, Secretary-Treasurer.

1905: Cecil B. Smith, Toronto, Chairman; J.L. Englehart, Petrolia, Commissioner; Denis Murphy, Ottawa, Commissioner; H.W. Pearson, Toronto, Secretary-Treasurer.

1906: J.L. Englehart, Petrolia, Chairman; Denis Murphy, Ottawa, Commissioner; F. Dane, Toronto, Commissioner; A.J. McGee, Toronto, Secretary-Treasurer.

1914: J.L. Englehart, Petrolia, Chairman; Denis Murphy, Ottawa, Commissioner; George W. Lee, North Bay, Commissioner; A.J. McGee, Toronto, Secretary-Treasurer.

1915: J.L. Englehart, Petrolia, Chairman; Denis Murphy, Ottawa, Commissioner; George W. Lee, North Bay, Commissioner; W.H. Maund, Toronto, Secretary-Treasurer.

1918: J.L. Englehart, Petrolia, Chairman; George W. Lee, North Bay, Commissioner; Hon. Dr. R.F. Preston, Carleton Place, Commissioner; W.H. Maund, Toronto, Secretary-Treasurer.

1920: George W. Lee, North Bay, Acting Chairman; Hon. Dr. R.F. Preston, Carleton Place, Commissioner; W.H. Maund, North Bay, Secretary-Treasurer.

1921: George W. Lee, North Bay, Chairman; Lt. Col. L.T. Martin, Ottawa, Vice-Chairman; Col. John I. McLaren, Hamilton, Commissioner; W.H. Maund, North Bay, Secretary-Treasurer.

~~1934: Premier Mitchell Hepburn, St. Thomas, Chairman; Arthur Slaght, Toronto, Commissioner; Armand Racine, Windsor, Commissioner; Malcolm Lang, Haileybury, Commissioner; C.V. Gallagher, Timmins, Commissioner.~~

1934: Malcolm Lang, Haileybury, Chairman; Premier Mitchell Hepburn, St. Thomas, Commissioner; Arthur Slaght, Toronto, Commissioner; Armand Racine, Windsor, Commissioner; C.V. Gallagher, Timmins, Commissioner; A.H. Cavanagh, North Bay, General Manager; W.H. Maund, North Bay, Secretary.

1935: Malcolm Lang, Haileybury, Chairman; A.H. Cavanagh, North Bay, General Manager; W.H. Maund, North Bay, Secretary.

1937: Malcolm Lang, Haileybury, Chairman; A.H. Cavanagh, North Bay, Vice-Chairman and General Manager; W.H. Maund, North Bay, Secretary.

1940: A.H. Cavanagh, North Bay, Chairman and General Manager; W.H. Maund, North Bay, Secretary.

1941: A.H. Cavanagh, North Bay, Chairman and General Manager; A. Freeman, North Bay, Secretary-Treasurer.

1944: Col. C.E. Reynolds, North Bay, Chairman; R.S. Potter, Matheson, Commissioner; R.A. Aubert, Englehart, Commissioner; A.H. Cavanagh, North Bay, General Manager; A. Freeman, North Bay, Secretary-Treasurer.

1946: Col. C.E. Reynolds, North Bay, Chairman; Col. Hon. G.A. Welsh, Toronto, Vice-Chairman; R.S. Potter, Matheson, Commissioner; R.A. Aubert, Englehart, Commissioner; A. Freeman, North Bay, Secretary-Treasurer; A.H. Cavanagh, North Bay, General Manager.

1947: Col. C.E. Reynolds, North Bay, Chairman; Col. Hon. G.A. Welsh, Toronto, Vice-Chairman; R.S. Potter, Matheson, Commissioner; R.A. Aubert, Englehart, Commissioner; A. Freeman, North Bay, General Manager; S.W. Gowan, North Bay, Secretary.

1949: Col. C.E. Reynolds, North Bay, Chairman; W.B. Harvey, North Bay, Vice-Chairman and Industrial Commissioner; Col. Hon. Wm. Griesinger, Toronto, Commissioner and Minister (Planning and Development); R.S. Potter, Matheson, Commissioner; R.A. Aubert, Englehart, Commissioner; A. Freeman, North Bay, General Manager; S.W. Gowan, North Bay, Secretary

1955: Col. C.E. Reynolds, North Bay, Chairman; A.R. Herbert, M.P.P., Cobalt, Vice-Chairman; Col. Hon. Wm. Griesinger, Toronto, Commissioner and Minister (Planning and Development); R.S. Potter, Matheson, Commissioner; R.A. Aubert, Englehart, Commissioner; A. Freeman, North Bay, General Manager; S.W. Gowan, North Bay, Secretary.

1958: Col. C.E. Reynolds, North Bay, Chairman; A.R. Herbert, M.P.P., Cobalt, Vice-Chairman; W.A. Johnston, M.P.P., South River, Commissioner; R.S. Potter, Matheson, Commissioner; R.A. Aubert, Englehart, Commissioner; A. Jardine, North Bay, General Manager; S.W. Gowan, North Bay, Secretary.

1960: Col. C.E. Reynolds, North Bay, Chairman; W.A. Johnston, M.P.P., South River, Vice-Chairman; J.A. Fullerton, M.P.P., Thessalon, Commissioner; R.S. Potter, Matheson, Commissioner; R.A. Aubert, Englehart, Commissioner; A. Jardine, North Bay, General Manager; S.W. Gowan, North Bay, Secretary.

1962: W.A. Johnston, M.P.P., South River, Acting Chairman; J.A. Fullerton, M.P.P., Thessalon, Commissioner; R. Brunelle, M.P.P., Moonbeam, Commissioner; R.S. Potter, Matheson, Commissioner; R.A. Aubert, Englehart, Commissioner; J.A. Kennedy, North Bay, Commissioner; W. Roy Thompson, Swastika, Industrial Commissioner; A. Jardine, North Bay, General Manager; S.W. Gowan, North Bay, Secretary.

Appendix C[1]

Financial Statement, 1904-1971, with explanations

Date	Evaluation of Assets – Property (road and equipment only)	Provincial Loan Account, funded debt, demand loans and debentures	Paid to Treasurer of Ontario
1904		$ 6,000,000	
1905	$ 7,400,000	7,500,000[2]	$ 100,000
1906	9,650,000	9,250,000	158,000
1907	11,300,000	11,700,000	235,000

Date	Evaluation of Assets – Property (road and equipment only)	Provincial Loan Account, funded debt, demand loans and debentures		Paid to Treasurer of Ontario
1908				$ 350,000
1909	$14,700,000	$15,300,000		550,000
1910	15,900,000	16,100,000		420,000
1911	17,200,000	17,500,000		515,000
1912	18,500,000	18,700,000		510,000
1913	19,300,000	19,700,000		250,000
1914	20,000,000	20,240,000		225,000
1915	20,100,000	20,480,000		225,000
1916	20,700,000	21,183,000		1,000,000
1917	21,300,000	21,600,000		250,000
1918	21,845,000	21,820,000		300,000
1919	22,400,000	22,335,000		—
1920	22,600,000	22,700,000		100,000
1921	23,700,000	23,600,000		200,000
1922	25,100,000	25,650,000		600,000
1923	27,700,000	28,000,000		750,000
1924	30,750,000	30,207,934[3]		750,000
1925	32,600,000	''	+ 2,200,000	750,000
1926	33,300,000	''	''	1,000,000
1927	36,200,000	''	+ 4,000,000	1,300,000
1928	37,200,000	''	+ 6,000,000	1,300,000
1929	37,500,000	''	+ 6,350,000	1,100,000
1930	39,400,000	''	+ 8,000,000	850,000
1931	42,800,000	''	+ 11,000,000	850,000
1932	44,200,000	''	+ 12,600,000	400,000
1933	44,200,000	''	+ 13,000,000	50,000
1934	44,200,000	''	+ 6,000,000	—
1935	44,200,000	''	+ 13,000,000	245,600[4]
1936	43,000,000	''	+ 12,200,000	—
1937	44,000,000	''	+ 11,100,000	—
				Retained as surplus – balance accumulated
1938	44,400,000	30,207,934 +	10,425,000	2,630,000
1939	44,560,000	''	+ 9,718,000	3,470,000
1940	44,900,000	''	+ 9,082,000	4,620,000
1941	44,900,000	''	+ 8,066,000	5,940,000
1942	45,200,000	''	+ 6,946,000	7,250,000
1943	45,400,000	''	+ 5,821,000	8,430,000
1944	45,450,000	''	+ 5,291,000	9,480,000
1945	45,690,000	''	+ 5,155,000	10,165,000
1946	47,270,000	''	+ 5,014,000	11,550,000[5]
1947	48,700,000	''	+ 4,868,000	12,850,000[6]
1948	49,589,000	''	+ 6,216,000	13,083,000
1949	50,340,000	''	+ 9,526,000	13,800,000
1950	51,100,000	''	+ 8,861,000	15,350,000
1951	54,270,000	''	+ 8,190,000	17,350,000
1952	58,195,000	''	+ 12,512,000	19,050,000
1953	61,364,000	''	+ 10,827,000	19,745,000
1954	61,900,000	''	+ 15,634,000	20,714,000
1955	62,200,000	''	+ 14,434,000	22,220,000
1956	63,794,000	''	+ 13,226,000	24,237,000
1957	66,063,000	''	+ 11,784,000	24,570,000
1958	66,480,000	''	+ 10,047,000	25,480,000
1959	66,549,000	''	+ 8,803,000	26,061,000
1960	66,875,000	''	+ 8,048,000	26,256,000
1961	66,355,000	''	+ 7,280,000	26,280,000
1962	69,425,000	''	+ 14,106,000	26,642,000
1963	71,878,000	''	+ 17,621,000	25,917,000[7]
1964	71,900,000	''	+ 17,458,000	25,065,000
1965	71,148,000	''	+ 17,458,000	24,737,000
1966	76,457,000	''	+ 16,649,000	25,109,000
1967	80,000,000	''	+ 25,700,000	26,486,000

Date	Evaluation of Assets – Property (road and equipment only)	Provincial Loan Account, funded debt, demand loans and debentures		Retained as surplus – balance accumulated
1968	$79,785,000	$30,207,934	+ 23,300,000	$27,077,000
1969	80,035,000	''	+ 23,500,000	27,709,000
1970	80,017,000	''	+ 23,000,000	27,988,000
1971	81,075,000	''	+ 24,000,000	28,954,000

NOTES TO APPENDIX C

1. Based on the Annual Reports of the Commission. Figures are given to the nearest thousand.

2. After the election of the Whitney government in 1905 an Amendment Act (5 Edw. VII, ch. 10) established for the first time a separate account in the Treasury Department for receipts and expenditures on T&NO construction. The proceeds to that date of the total bank loan of $7,000,000 were credited to this account and from 1905 to 1924 the provincial government could advance to this account "such monies as may be required for the construction of the said railway..." These "advances" steadily accumulated without bearing interest, as investment by the government in the capital cost of the railway. Annual payments to the Provincial Treasurer by the T&NO Commission were the financial returns on this accumulated investment.

3. The investment as a non-interest bearing loan from the provincial government became fixed in 1924, one year after the election of Howard Ferguson as premier. Thereafter, new loans and debentures – to finance, for example, extension of the line to Moosonee and to Kirkland Lake and Rouyn – had to be made with chartered banks at specific terms of interest and repayment. The Commission generally arranged its loans with the Bank of Nova Scotia.

4. Though early legislation referred to the establishment of a sinking fund, such a fund was never established. Annual payments were made to the Consolidated Revenue Fund after 1905, and the last payment to the Treasurer of Ontario was made in 1935. Between 1905 and 1935 a total of $15,233,892.41 was paid into the Consolidated Revenue Fund – an average annual payment of $766,000, or just over two per cent a year on the provincial loan account. Sixty per cent of this $15,000,000 was paid in the decade from 1922-31. After 1935 all net earnings were retained by the Commission and incorporated as surplus in the retained income account.

5. The Annual Report for 1946 contained the auditor's statement that from 1942-46, taking the annual increase of the surplus (net profit) as earnings on the $30,200,000 debt, the average annual interest would have been 3.67 per cent.

6. From 1904 to 1934 the financial year of the Commission ended on October 31; between 1934 and 1947 on March 31. With the transfer of the audit to the Provincial Auditor in 1947, the fiscal year coincided with the calendar year, ending on December 31. In his first audit of 1947, and for a few years after, the Provincial Auditor noted: "while the operating accounts of the Commission show a Net Income of (more than) $1,138,000...it should be observed that no interest has been required from the Commission on the loan of $30,207,934.92 owing to the Province of Ontario."

7. In each of the financial years 1963-66, the Commission operated at a net loss. The losses for each of these years, totalling over $3,260,000, were compensated by the provincial government and stated in the Annual Reports for 1965-68. These, however, were the only years in the history of the ONTC when such losses occurred and had to be recovered from the provincial government.

Index

PHOTO CREDITS

We would like to acknowledge the help and co-operation of the directors and staff of a number of public institutions, private firms and individuals who made photographs available and gave us permission to reproduce them.

Abitibi Paper Company Limited, 53
Alice Browne, New Liskeard, 1, 58
Lemuel Carr, Timmins, 8, 12, 20, 21, 43
Margaret Clemens, Thunder Bay, 17
Cobalt Mining Museum, 27
Eva De Rosa, Timmins, 25, 26
Helen Smith Dixon, Stratford, 7, 9, 14, 15
Paul Hermiston Mining Museum, Cobalt, 13, 44
Hollinger Mines Limited, 65, 66
Mrs. A.C. Kilgour, North Bay, 59, 60
Ministry of Natural Resources, Province of Ontario, 33, 45
Noranda Mines Limited, 57
Ontario Northland Transportation Commission, 10, 16, 24, 28, 32, 51, 55, 64, 67, 68, 69, 70, 71, 72, 73, 74, 75, 76, 77, 78, 79, 80, 81, 82, 83
Public Archives of Ontario, 3, 5, 6, 11, 18, 19, 22, 23, 29, 30, 31, 34, 35, 36, 37, 38, 39, 40, 41, 42, 46, 47, 48, 49, 50, 52, 54, 56, 61, 62, 63